Infographics

FOR

DUMMIES

by Justin Beegel, MBA

Founder & President, Infographic World, Inc.
and the Infographic World Design Team

FOR
DUMMIES
A Wiley Brand

Infographics For Dummies®

Published by: **John Wiley & Sons, Inc.,** 111 River Street, Hoboken, NJ 07030-5774, www.wiley.com

Copyright © 2014 by John Wiley & Sons, Inc., Hoboken, New Jersey

Published simultaneously in Canada

For general information on our other products and services, please contact our Customer Care Department within the U.S. at 877-762-2974, outside the U.S. at 317-572-3993, or fax 317-572-4002. For technical support, please visit www.wiley.com/techsupport.

Wiley publishes in a variety of print and electronic formats and by print-on-demand. Some material included with standard print versions of this book may not be included in e-books or in print-on-demand. If this book refers to media such as a CD or DVD that is not included in the version you purchased, you may download this material at http://booksupport.wiley.com. For more information about Wiley products, visit www.wiley.com.

Library of Congress Control Number: 2013954217

ISBN 978-1-118-79238-4 (pbk); ISBN 978-1-118-79227-8 (ebk); ISBN 978-1-118-79239-1 (ebk)

Manufactured in the United States of America

10 9 8 7 6 5 4 3 2 1

Contents at a Glance

Table of Contents

Introduction

*R*ight at the intersection of art and journalism, technology and storytelling, lies the infographic. Ranging in size and scope from a three-inch pie chart to a multipage, full-color spread, infographics add visual appeal and detail to virtually any story. This is an interesting time for infographics. On one hand, print media that routinely featured charts, graphs, diagrams, and graphic illustrations has diminished. On the other hand, we humans are connected to media all day, every day, through our computers, tablets, and phones. We crave information and entertainment, and in a world that's crowded with data, an attractive visual presentation can help your story stand out. When print media was king, most graphics were *static* — designed only for reading and impossible to change after publication. In the Internet age, though, graphics are going live, with interactive features that reel in readers and make information incredibly relevant, fun, and personal.

So, as you decide what data you want to illustrate with an infographic — your *story* — we'll help you figure that out, along with our advice for combining smart research, design, and technical skills to turn your story into a great infographic. We'll also teach you how to find the biggest and best audience for your work.

About This Book

This book is a collaborative, collective effort from the folks of Infographic World. We're a visual communications agency focused on (you guessed it!) infographics, designing for corporations, sports leagues, television networks, media outlets, universities, and nonprofit entities (like hospitals and charities). These diverse clients all have one thing in common: the need to share their stories and messages in a compelling manner. We help them do that by telling their stories visually.

On our staff, we have a wide range of complimentary talents that mesh and help us achieve our goals. We have fantastic designers, strategists, writers, and managers. Even if you're not working in a firm as fully developed as ours — you might be working solo, wearing many hats — these skillsets give you a broad feel for the steps to designing and deploying infographics.

Our goal here is to lead you through every stage of infographic design and development. We begin by showing you the power of visual images, and how you can and should use them to make your message stand out. We show you how to develop your own style, while still working within guidelines of potential clients. We show you some of the best ways to use design software to add visual interest to your work.

And finally, because an infographic isn't much use if it doesn't have an audience, we show you how to attract readers and perhaps even how to get your graphic to go viral.

Foolish Assumptions

Yeah, it's wrong to assume, but we had to make a few guesses about you, anyway:

- You want to or need to create infographics, whether for your job or a personal interest, like blogging.

- You have a computer (Mac or PC) and know how to use word-processing functions, navigate the Internet, and maybe even have some simple design program experience.

- You pay attention to the news and have some ideas of what topics interest today's readers.

- You're savvy enough with social media that we don't need to tell you what Facebook is.

Conventions and Icons Used in This Book

The whole point of an infographic is to communicate clearly. So, to avoid any misunderstandings, here are a few things you should know:

- We use the words "infographic" and "graphic" interchangeably.

- Although many infographic designers prefer to work on Mac computers, PCs are acceptable. So in cases where a keyboard command or a menu path is different for a Mac than on a PC, we specify what to do for each (Mac is always first) like this: ⌘+V/Ctrl+V.

- Web addresses and Photoshop layer names appear in monofont `like this` so they stand out from regular text.

- When we want you to follow a menu path, it looks like this: Choose Window➪New.

Like all *Dummies* books, this one uses a few simple icons to help highlight some important information. (Graphic symbols in a book about infographics? Nice synergy, huh?)

The Tip symbol calls attention to some important tips, tricks, and shortcuts. Some of these are of a technical nature, while others focus on the content of your infographic or ways to work efficiently.

The Remember icon highlights information that you may come back to time and again as you're working with infographics. We may also use this symbol to remind you of information mentioned earlier in the book.

Don't worry, we use this icon sparingly. The Warning icon points out some potential pitfalls as you work with your graphics. Some of the warnings may seem intuitive, like when we remind you to save your work, but they're all worth noting.

Beyond the Book

We've provided additional information about infographics online to help you on your way:

- **Cheat Sheet:** Check out www.dummies.com/cheatsheet/infographics.

- **Online articles:** On several of the pages that open each of this book's parts, you'll find links to what the folks at *For Dummies* call Web Extras, which expand on some concept we've discussed in that particular section. You'll find them at www.dummies.com/extras/infographics.

Where to Go from Here

Okay, it's time to design. Take a look at the Table of Contents to determine where you'd like to begin. If you want a little theory behind your work, start at the beginning. If you're wondering where to go to get the statistics that drive many an infographic, skip to Part II, where we talk about gathering data. Or, if you've been designing simple infographics already and are ready to apply some technical flourishes, you may want to head straight to Part III. Remember, the way you use this book is entirely up to you.

We'd love you to hang on our every word, of course, but *Infographics For Dummies* is organized so you can quickly find the information you need and bypass what you don't. Perhaps you're very proficient in Photoshop, but you've never worked in Adobe Illustrator. There's an app — um, "chap" — for that.

Or maybe you're wondering how to market your work to social media. You can skip to Chapter 13, which details how and when to share your infographics. You can always backtrack to the earlier chapters for some deeper reading when you have time.

And, if you want to seek inspiration from some of the amazing work that our staff designers have done, feel free to check out our website, `http://infographicworld.com`. You'll be amazed at what infographics can really do.

Part I
Getting Started with Infographics

In this part . . .

- You'll learn how visual information excites and informs readers.

- We'll help you marshal your resources for creating infographics.

- You'll learn the differences between infographics for editorial and advertising purposes, as well as the differences between static and interactive infographics.

- Find out how to establish your own approach to infographics, setting your own artistic style and learning how to make your work shine while still working within guidelines from supervisors.

1

Unlocking the Power
of Infographics

*H*umans are incredibly visual creatures. Thousands of years ago, cave-dwellers used visual images to track time, to depict their prey, and to record their celebrations. Later, civilizations created hieroglyphics and visual symbols for letters and numbers, providing a code to organize their communication. Visual communication can bridge cultures — travelers on any continent can find a pharmacy, a hospital, and the correct restroom thanks to the power of simple graphic images.

Flash back to the 1970s for a moment. Most Americans read a newspaper or two. *The New York Times* was so heavy with text that it was dubbed "The Old Gray Lady." Most households had a TV. News was broadcast three times a day, on the three major networks. Corporate reports were very dense, with pages full of text and little more than the occasional headline to break them up. The Internet as we know it today was but a dream.

Also in the 70s, newspapers and magazines began to use *infographics* — charts, maps, and diagrams — to illustrate and illuminate news stories and break up columns of gray text. Infographics have been with us for a long time, but they've matured and become more and more dynamic, especially with the advent of the Internet. Nowadays, infographics can be quite sophisticated, showing condensed ways of looking at data and figures and information. You can pack quite a lot of valuable information in a small, attractive, and entertaining piece of content.

Recognizing the Value of Visuals

Speaking of the advent of the Internet. . . . No news flash here, but we live in an ever-increasing electronic and digital age. Most folks are barraged all day by some sort of media clamoring for attention. Most people have Internet access at their fingertips via smartphone, tablet, or computer. All that "Hey, look at me!" can make a person weary, and the overload of messaging and devices has taken a toll on the human attention span.

Those folks who deliver content — be it via television news, print journalism, a corporate report, website — realize that they have a short window of opportunity to grab a viewer's attention. And with only about eight seconds to do that, enter the increasing use of infographics, which are meaty morsels of lots and lots of content in attractive, digestible, informative chunks, whether online or in print.

An increasingly multimedia and online technology climate shift has fostered an explosion of infographics within all forms of communication. The old way of communicating messages in a text-heavy manner is simply not effective anymore. There is simply too much research and science behind the power of visual storytelling to ignore. Companies and organizations cannot afford to be out of date. It's time to embrace the power of visualization, and find a way to incorporate it into what you and your company do every day.

If we haven't convinced you by now, plenty of research backs up this idea that visual communication can provide quicker, clearer comprehension of complex topics. Here are a few statistics:

✔ More than 80 percent of the learning we do takes place visually.

> www.hp.com/large/ipg/assets/bus-solutions/power-of-visual-communication.pdf

✔ The average person retains only 20 percent of what's read when it's delivered in text-only format.

> www.hp.com/large/ipg/assets/bus-solutions/power-of-visual-communication.pdf

Print isn't dead

The New York Times produces some of the best, smartest infographics in the world. Corporate reports feature charts, graphs, and illustrations to highlight information. Nonprofit organizations rely on infographics to spur potential donors and volunteers to action. Magazines like *National Geographic* create infographics that rival the excellence of their photography. Although an ever-growing number of websites and blogs compete to take the place of print vehicles, infographics still are widely used and very valuable to content providers.

✔ Images are liked on Facebook 200 percent more than text.

```
www.jeffbullas.com/2012/08/27/the-facts-and-figures-about-the-
            power-of-visual-content-infographic
```

✔ On average, websites register a 12-percent increase in traffic after publishing an infographic.

```
www.wpvirtuoso.com/a-guide-to-content-management-marketing
```

✔ The Wharton School of Business determined that when listening to presentations, 67 percent of the audience were persuaded by the verbal presentations that had accompanying visuals compared with 50 percent of the audience when it was verbal only.

```
www.macrovu.com/VTVCInterEffectiveness.html
```

The same Wharton study found that visual language shortens meeting time by 24 percent. That's some serious added productivity.

A great infographic leads readers on a visual journey, telling them a story along the way. Powerful infographics are able to capture people's attention in the first few seconds with a strong title and visual image, and then reel them in to digest the entire message. Infographics have become an effective way to speak for the creator, conveying information and image simultaneously.

Here's a hypothetical example to demonstrate this idea. You just completed detailed and accurate market research for your company, looking into all sorts of pinpointed information about your target demographic. The purpose of this market research is to help your sales and marketing teams better understand your customer. The results — hundreds (or thousands) of stats compiled in an Excel document — are then written up and presented in a PDF document using nothing but words.

Seeing is believing

In 2011, molecular biologist John Medina published *Brain Rules,* a fascinating account of how the brain processes information. It's a great book all around, but two rules are particularly interesting.

Rule #4: We don't pay attention to boring things.

Returning to *The New York Times* and the corporate reports examples, we know today that readers simply do not stick with material that is too dense. Medina's book suggests that humans need a spark every ten minutes or so to entice us to pay attention. Infographics can provide that spark.

Rule #10: Vision trumps all other senses.

Medina's research led him to determine that a person who hears information will remember ten percent of that information three days later. If pictures are added to that information, the subject remembers 65 percent of the information three days later.

This opens the door for great graphic presentations of information. Media outlets, corporations, nonprofit groups, sports leagues, and more now know that telling their stories with pictures as well as with words helps attract and retain readers.

This shouldn't be a problem, right? The results are so compelling that people will be willing to read 50 pages of findings, right? Sorry. They won't. You can have the greatest data in the world, but if you don't have the proper way to communicate this data effectively, you won't get anywhere.

The solution? Create a visual to showcase the market research findings in a way that people will actually digest. For the average Joe, choosing between wading through a 50-page text-heavy PDF or perusing a visual like the infographic presented in Figure 1-1 is an obvious choice.

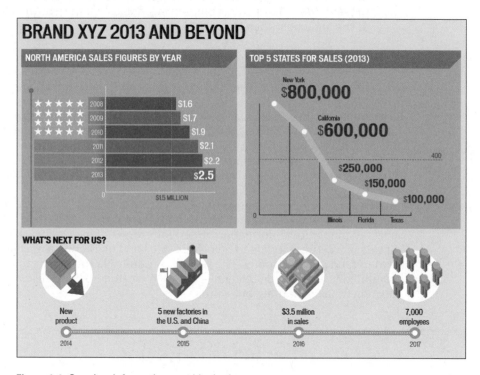

Figure 1-1: Concise, informative graphic that's easy to consume.

The power of infographics is that it keeps things short and sweet. Instead of some 50-page tome, you could present three or four pages of infographics, with a few pointed sentences, to communicate your key data points.

The concise, pointed nature of an infographic works well with the fact that people's attention span is decreasing significantly. This is especially the case online, where every website on the planet is competing for your reader's attention at any given moment. It's far too easy for someone to come to your website, lose interest and be gone all within a few seconds. It's often said that you have four to six seconds to grab someone's attention when they come to your website. Are you going to accomplish this by having a lot of text and a couple of charts or by having a stunning visualization front and center?

So You Want to Be an Infographic Designer

When you were a kid, and some well-meaning adult asked you what you wanted to be when you grew up, what did you say? A professional athlete? A doctor? Dancer? Firefighter?

We've never met a soul who set out to be an infographic designer — but we certainly know some great ones. A few followed logical paths toward infographic design, and a few more wound crazily through other careers and professional skills before coming to infographic design. Many professional infographic designers are artists or writers. Some are graphic designers, whose primary work responsibilities involve page layout and creation of art elements.

But this is a DIY world, and you can indeed teach yourself the art of the infographic. Stick with us as we talk about everything you'll need to do so, from research skills to technical tools.

Filling Your Toolbox

We spend a lot of time discussing specific creation (software) tools and techniques later in the book, particularly in Chapter 3 (designing your approach to infographics), Chapter 9 (Adobe Illustrator), and Chapter 10 (Adobe Photoshop).

Assuming you're just starting out with infographics, though, start with a good foundation. Our first recommendation is to be a voracious reader. Whether you prefer print or an online version, take a look at a few newspapers every day. Read something national in scope (*The New York Times, The Wall Street Journal*) and a local newspaper, too. Because infographics distill data — sometimes, lots of data — consider yourself as a journalist who not only reports (without bias) but does research as well. Sure, graphics play a major role (go figure) in infographics, but so does the data underlying your presentation.

As an infographic designer, you're not just an artist. The best infographics designers are really considered "data journalists." The more infographics you take time to really examine, you'll start to get a sense of what type of material can be turned into a graphic.

As for more tangible tools you'll need, make sure that your computer is in good working order and can support the design software you'll need. It's a designer's worst nightmare to have repeated computer crashes as deadline looms. You'll obviously need an online connection as well as basic office productivity apps, Adobe Acrobat, some sort of photo management app, and Adobe Creative Suite. Can't forget about the behind-the-scenes code creation if you're going to post online (and you should). Some folks like to create animated or interactive infographics (or add sound or movie files) program in Flash, but that can cause problems (we talk about that later). Probably the safest bet is to use HTML5 and CSS3 and JavaScript.

We're pretty proud of the information we present later in the book, but if you'd like some face-to-face tutorials, keep an eye out for classes in programs like Illustrator and Photoshop. Continuing education programs at local colleges and high schools often provide excellent ways to learn the basics of new computer software.

Good planning before your project gets rolling can save you from a lot of stress later.

Assembling Your Team

In this section, we assume that you're not working alone. Perhaps you work for a company looking to expand its marketing efforts by placing infographics on social media. Maybe you're a writer for an online news site, and you're hoping to generate more infographics. Or maybe you're a university researcher, and it's dawned on you that your research could use some graphic presentation to make sure people are reading and understanding your work.

Bottom line: You need to assemble some internal resources and work closely with the people who will make your plans come to fruition.

Using internal resources

When a company decides to use its own employees to create infographics, they are choosing to work with people who know the brand and the messaging and feel of the company better than anyone outside the company ever will. Gut-checks like this are definitely very important when an infographic needs to align with a company's brand.

Using in-house staffers also helps the assigning staffer confer with the artists more easily than if using external freelancers. Granted, with the rise of telecommuting and people working remotely, this benefit is definitely lessened a bit.

If you're going to build your infographic in-house, you'll need to make sure you have people dedicated to the following tasks/roles:

- ✔ **Brainstorming the idea for the infographic.**
- ✔ **Researching data to support the infographic and help tell the story.**
- ✔ **Fact-checking the data.**

  Fact-checking should definitely be done by someone other than the person who did the research.

- ✔ **Writing the copy.**
- ✔ **Editing the copy.**

  Again, have this done by someone other than the copy writer.

- ✔ **Coming up with the infographic concept and design ideas.**
- ✔ **Designing the infographic.**
- ✔ **Reviewing the entire infographic.**
- ✔ **Implementing any changes requested by supervisors.**

This is not to say you need a different person for each task, but whoever you put in charge of the infographic should be mindful of all those duties. Depending upon the size and scope of your project, anywhere from one person to a team of three or four or more could take it on.

Having a tech person or two in the loop and on your side is a good idea. In today's digital world, you want to make sure that all your work is compatible with the website, blog, or document that will eventually showcase your work.

In a larger company, the person you have in mind to work on infographics may have many other responsibilities as well. Your graphic may or may not take precedence. Depending upon your project's priority level, you may have to wait before a request is handled. If your deadline is going to be tight, we recommend making sure that the artist can complete your work in the time-line that *you* set. Sometimes you can help an artist clear a little time in his schedule by asking various department heads to be mindful of your project.

Working with your online team

Your online team is the group of people who handle all the content that goes onto a website. At this point, virtually every company has one although it might be outsourced. The online team is likely to include coders, web designers, and any number of technical support staffers.

The online team knows the technical requirements of your particular website better than anyone. One important element that you'll have to be mindful of as an infographic designer is the size limitations for content on a website. This is more important than it may seem.

Space on websites is measured in pixels. When you're preparing to place your infographic, there may be other permanent items on the page, like advertisements, or links to other areas of your website. This being the case, you need to know how many pixels your infographic should be to fit on the page properly and co-exist with other permanent content on the page.

The online team will also coordinate with you about the file formats you need to deliver to them, how long it will take to get the infographic onto the site (as with other teams at your company, they will likely be getting pulled in many different directions with requests), and other important tasks to launch the infographic.

Getting your social media team ready

The social media team will need to be prepared in advance of you launching the infographic. Given the importance of social media in the marketing and promotion of the infographic, everyone needs to be on the same page.

Your company's social media experts (which may include marketing staffers, the webmaster, social media strategists, among others) will help you determine the best day and time to release your infographic and begin marketing and promoting it. (More on this is discussed in Chapter 13.) Bear in mind that the social media team will be balancing other requests to have material tweeted or posted to the company's Facebook page. So again, collaboration is key: The more notice you give people about your project, the more smoothly things will go.

Speaking of professionals . . .

The obvious pro to hiring an infographic agency is very simple: They do nothing but create infographics, every single day. Some obvious bias here. Justin is, after all, the CEO of Infographic World. Here is a brief list of projects that Fortune 500 companies have hired us (at Infographic World), to do:

- Help build more engaging PowerPoint presentations that don't leave audiences with glazed eyes.

- Create website content to help establish a client as a thought leader within its industry and drive more traffic to its website.

- Improve SEO ranks by creating and placing infographics online, with the goal of getting other websites to link to them.

- Create a visually stunning annual report or investor report.

- Communicate market research.

- Release content on social media channels to entice readers and encourage readers to share that content.

- Create brochures and other documents for conferences.

Working with the social media team can also help you set the tone for your project. Depending on the content of the infographic and the target audience, you can set a tone that's serious or snarky, news-oriented or feature-focused. This can help guarantee that you get the readers you want.

Working with a marketing team

These days, one of the primary goals for creators of infographics is to have them go viral. This generates traffic and links back to your website, which will help promote your work, your blog, or the company you're working for.

If you're creating a graphic for a company with a marketing team, taking advantage of the marketing team's insight and expertise early on will pay dividends in the end. The staff members most likely to handle these duties may fall under the labels "marketing," "public relations," or "communications." These folks

- Prepare campaigns to get exposure for the infographic by building lists of websites to place the infographic, finding the best contact people, and determining how and when to pitch your infographic.

- Know what sorts of topics, statistics, and angles will be most effective in getting the infographic out to the masses and how content appeals to various audiences.

- Put more pairs of eyes on the infographic, finding things in the approach that might be misguided or a poor fit for your target audience, and share their take on how content appeals to various audiences.

Going with the professionals

The alternative to building an infographic in-house is to hire an infographic agency to build it for you. Like with the internal route, there are pros and cons for either path. You first need to determine whether you have the budget. Depending upon the company, the cost to get an infographic built by someone skilled can range from $700 to $6,000, depending on the size of the graphic and the scope of the content you want displayed, not to mention the quality of the infographic agency you want to hire.

Most agencies focused on infographics have systems in place to create projects efficiently and at a high quality. You may flinch at some quotes, but using an outside agency may actually be less expensive in the long run when you factor in the number of internal staffers and the cost of diverting them from their ordinary responsibilities.

Working with Decision Makers

Whether you're working solo or as part of a team, the first and most important thing to do is keep the decision makers within your company or organization in the loop the entire time. Unless you're the owner of the company (and even then, there might be investors who could qualify), you'll have someone (or several "someones") who needs to approve the infographic before it's put onto your client's website or into company marketing and sales materials. Here are a couple real-world examples you might encounter:

- If you're working for a corporate client — say, designing charts and graphs for an annual report — you will probably work with everyone from the company's art director to the CEO before getting sign off on your work.

- If you're working with a team of journalists on a big event — say, covering the Olympics for Associated Press — your infographics will have to pass muster with sports editors, news editors, top managers, and ultimately newspaper editors all around the world.

Real-world disclaimer: Our firm has had instances where all the work took place before the decision makers entered the process — *never a good idea.* The last thing you want is to go through the entire process of building an infographic — whether done internally or by hiring an infographic agency — only to have the decision makers see it after it's fully complete. You're just tempting fate that the decision makers will want major changes or disagree entirely with how the vision of the infographic was brought to life.

You should work *with* decision makers — not around them or against them — to make sure the final infographic project meets everyone's needs. Here's how things can go awry and how they could have been avoided.

1. **You get a great assignment to create an infographic for a large corporate client. Congratulations!**

2. **Your contact person is a midlevel marketing manager.**

    Wrong: You assume that she is the only person who will approve your work.

    Right: You immediately find out whether anyone else will be signing off on your project.

3. **You begin creating and revising your infographic. This stage can take weeks or months, depending on your client's needs and deadlines.**

    Wrong: You continue to work exclusively with your initial contact person. You're incorporating her suggestions, unaware that other decision makers haven't seen your work.

    Right: You make sure that your contact person is fully informing her boss as well as anyone else who will ultimately sign off on your infographic.

4. You start to look for buy-in and approval.

> *Wrong:* The marketing manager signs off on your work. Trouble is, his boss hates it — and only now do you realize that the marketing manager wasn't the top decision maker. So, you begin revising your work. Then you find out that the boss's boss loved your original product. The decision makers begin revising their vision of your work. Your previous weeks of work are down the drain. After another couple of weeks of revisions, the company signs off on your project. The job is finally done, but it wasn't the wisest use of time and resources.

> *Right:* You make corrections and changes according to the whole team's specifications. Your infographic gets final approval and is published. Well done!

If you're not the final decision maker at your company, do yourself a favor and make sure to identify all decision makers upfront and then keep them in the loop as you work on your infographics. There's just too much time and money to be lost and wasted by waiting until the end of the process to get their input.

2

Exploring Infographics

*I*nfographics may seem to be a modern means of communication, but their roots go way back to the eighteenth century. In 1786, the marvelously named William Playfair published *The Commercial and Political Atlas,* which used graphics to illustrate facts about the English economy. Playfair is generally accepted to be the inventor of the line graph, the bar chart, and the pie chart.

Infographics have come a long way since then. Today, the applications of infographics for information and marketing purposes are virtually limitless. Before you jump into the process of creating your own infographics, take the time to nail down the ultimate purpose of your work. Whether your goal is to inform, entertain, or convince, that goal will determine how you research, plan, design, and publish your information graphic.

Establishing Your Voice

Infographics generally fall into one of two categories: promotional or informational. And although you can certainly have a bit of both elements within one infographic, you almost always will have one or the other as your primary focus.

Over time, you will be able to establish a tone — "voice" — for your infographics. Some designers' work appears highly authoritative. Other artists bring a more whimsical touch. A critical first step in finding that voice is knowing your purpose.

Your infographic voice doesn't always have to stay the same and certainly should change over time. As you develop and gain practice at creating infographics, you may find your original way of doing things doesn't work. Never stop growing and learning.

Promoting with brand infographics

Most infographics are marketing materials in one way or another; some advertising messages are just hidden better than others. Brand infographics can be appropriate for

- ✔ Promoting or explaining services and products
- ✔ Explaining sales or internal survey data
- ✔ Establishing your company as a thought leader

Most brand infographics will use corporate or campaign branding to help viewers identify them as part of a particular brand. At a minimum, brand infographics should carry a corporate logo.

The most unobtrusive location for a logo is toward the bottom of the infographic, as shown in Figure 2-1. We recommend resisting the urge to place your logo at the top of your infographic, as readers may be immediately turned off by what they view as a clear advertisement.

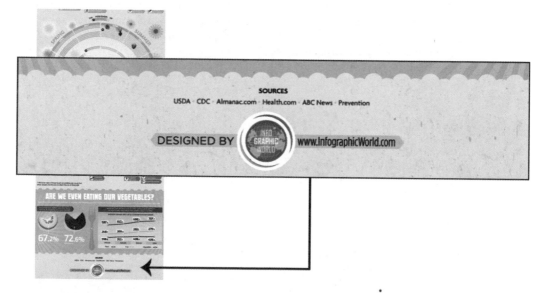

Figure 2-1: Place a simple, unobtrusive logo at the bottom of your graphic.

In certain cases, a blatant advertising message is okay. (See Figure 2-2.) If you're creating an infographic to be viewed by people within your own company or those you're hoping will become clients, there's very little need to be shy or coy about promoting your products or services. In these cases, your audience knows that they're seeing an advertising or a marketing message, and they're fine with it. So take advantage of the opportunity to promote your service or product in a clever, inventive way.

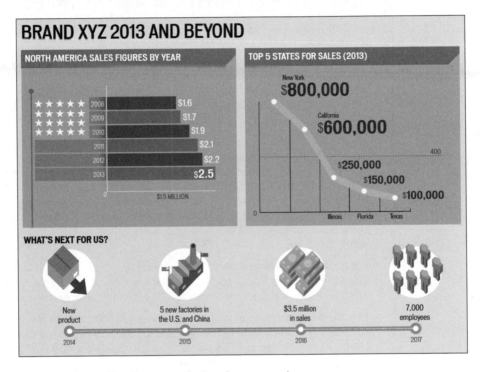

Figure 2-2: Clearly identify your marketing pieces as such.

Infographics like this can be appropriate for

- Trade shows
- Sales department leave-behinds
- Brochures
- Posters
- Product instructions

This type of graphic will most likely have an authoritative tone, but the desired tone varies depending upon the company. For example, an infographic for a snowboard manufacturer may incorporate the loose, fun vibe that has become associated with the sport.

Educating with informational editorial infographics

Editorial graphics are akin to news articles in that their primary purpose is to transmit information. Under the umbrella of editorial graphics, there are several different types, with different balances of bias versus objectivity. Here is a look at a few:

- ✔ A blizzard hit your town. The local newspaper creates a graphic that shows snowfall over the past 20 years, maps out the weather front that brought the blizzard, and shows which roads are designated as snow emergency routes. The graphic is purely informational, without any obvious bias.

- ✔ You come upon a graphic called "50 Incredible Facts About Skin." The graphic is nicely researched, beautifully designed, and appears to be a simple collection of interesting tidbits about skin. But, wait! At the bottom of the graphic, you discover that it was created by a company that sells and delivers beauty products. Infographics like this straddle the line between informing and promoting. It's up to the reader to discern the difference.

- ✔ It's flu season, and in a parenting magazine, you see a cool infographic showing how the flu spreads. Sources are doctors. There's no mention of any particular company or product. It's probably pure editorial content.

    In a different magazine, you see a similar graphic on the flu. However, the copy recommends disinfecting your house with SuperClean wipes. Hmm. At the bottom of the page, in small type, you find that the content was sponsored by SuperClean Corp. This infographic is an ad although it is informational as well.

- ✔ You read a lively, engaging infographic on beers of the world. The tone might vary considerably depending upon who created it. If a journalist created it for a men's magazine, it probably has some attitude, with language targeted to appeal to a young male demographic. If a brewery created the infographic, it's probably designed to inform and may have a more serious tone.

One of the biggest benefits of skewing your work toward editorial infographics is they are more likely to be shared organically by web users than infographics that carry heavy branding and are obvious advertisements. Totally unbranded infographics are ideal, but that's not always possible because infographics can be expensive to produce.

Editorial infographics can have myriad purposes, including:

- ✔ Stating facts or explaining processes
- ✔ Exploring the history of a person or topic
- ✔ Comparing companies, countries, educational institutions, teams, and so on
- ✔ Supporting a political ideology

These educational approaches will typically follow a somewhat standard flow:

1. Establish a problem/topic/proposal.

   What is the issue you're going to be discussing or addressing in the infographic? Think of this like a lede in a newspaper or a thesis statement of a term paper. You need to clearly state what the infographic is about. For instance, imagine that you're going to create an infographic exploring the ways how everyday Internet users put their personal information at risk.

   A *lede* is the introduction to a story or graphic. It's a journalistic term that may have gotten its funky spelling to differentiate it from *lead,* as in the metal type that was formerly used to print newspapers and books.

2. Offer statistics as evidence.

   This is where the bulk of your research (read more about that in Chapter 5) comes in. Here, you offer data, facts, and analysis about the topic you just introduced. For example, you might offer statistics about identity theft, hacking, malware, passwords, and mobile security.

3. Conclude with a "So what?" statement.

   The most effective infographics will take some sort of stand even if it seems obvious. Readers will expect a destination at the end of the road; they won't be happy if the pavement just stops. Continuing our example, your conclusion could offer some analysis on which anti-malware programs are the best, or what readers can expect to spend for the best protection.

Working with Infographics

Most infographics today are *static*: that is, without interactivity or animation. They are generally the least expensive to produce and post online (in terms of bandwidth), and the easiest for viewers to see/download, which makes them the go-to option for companies that want to communicate an idea through infographics.

Learn to walk before you run — that is, learn to create static infographics before other types of infographics.

Identifying what makes an infographic

You might not realize this, but you've been encountering infographics for most of your life. Have you ever seen a transit map? Then you've seen an infographic. Sure, you could read the list of the public transit lines in your city, but you'd only get a partial understanding of the scope of options. You wouldn't see how the various lines intersect. The map takes the basic information and translates it into a better venue for your brain to process.

At its most basic, an infographic translates information into an image. This could mean taking U.S. unemployment data for the past ten years and creating a line chart to help people visualize the instability of the economy. Or it could mean taking that same data and creating a map so viewers can see which areas of the United States are struggling the most.

Every infographic should have the same basic components:

- Accurate, compelling data
- Clever, well-crafted (and limited) writing
- Creative data visualizations
- Consistent visual style

In a well-made infographic, those parts will feel seamless and organic — everything will seem as though it was meant to go together.

Sticking with what works

Most infographics are now optimized for use on the Internet. There's a big benefit here in terms of content. Given that the Internet is a repository for, well, everything, there's almost certainly an audience out there for what you have to say.

Technically speaking, working with an online format means that after you get the hang of designing infographics, you can use the same basic approach and format over and over again, provided you can come up with fresh content.

The typical static infographic is tall and vertical, allowing users to scroll to read all the information. This lends itself very easily to storytelling because readers are compelled to scroll to see the next bit of information. The flow is quite natural. Sticking with that format is a good idea.

Become a subject matter expert

We recommend becoming as well-versed as possible in one or more general topics so you can learn to speak with authority and become knowledgeable about the data related to that topic. If you want to create infographics about business, learn to read annual SEC reports or stock information. If you want to develop infographics about professional sports, read box scores and learn about the teams and players. And after you become an expert, exploit those topics. Create infographics that are variations on a theme. For example, say you want to specialize in infographics related to social media: You could explore topics like these:

- General social media use
- Social media and relationships
- Workplace limitations on social media
- The technology of social media
- Social media evolution
- Social media and sports
- TV and social media

The point is to get really good at infographics in a few areas by exploring as many subtopics within those areas as you can. That not only gives you experience at creating different kinds of infographics, but it also allows you to position yourself as an expert and thought leader in the space.

Considering possibilities beyond the static infographic

Static infographics may be the most commonly produced type of infographic today, but they are far from the only kind. And for some topics, static storytelling may have limitations that would damage a reader's understanding of the topic.

In later sections, we'll explore in more detail other types of infographics. Interactive and animated infographics are a growing field in infographic design and development. They take far longer to produce and are more expensive to produce, but an effective interactive or animated design can do things static infographics simply cannot.

Interactive graphics also tap into readers' desire to share content. As we write this book, *The New York Times'* graphic on regional dialects is sweeping the country. Based on Harvard research, the graphic asks readers to answer 25 questions on various regional sayings, and then generates a guess on where the reader is from. It's pretty brilliant, and it's probably the future of infographics.

Predicting the Lifecycle of Infographics

Some infographics will see a huge amount of traffic right after they're launched; others take more time to spread around the Internet. Which pattern is best is debatable and depends largely on the topic at hand, but in general, an infographic should fall into one of three categories:

- **Timely:** Timely infographics are related to topics that take place only once and have a relatively brief window in the public consciousness. Major news events such celebrity deaths, corporate bankruptcies, and elections fall into this category. Holidays, anniversaries of major events, and other notable dates also fall into this category. An infographic about the career timeline of Michael Jackson, for instance, would apply.

- **Related:** Related infographics are inspired by news events, holidays, or notable dates but don't deal directly with the event. Continuing our example, a graphic related to Michael Jackson could show the top-selling albums of all time (which includes Jackson's iconic *Thriller*). It's not a direct tie, but a related one.

- **Evergreen:** Evergreen infographics aren't related to any event or person in the news. They have no seasonal component, and they're not tied to anything timely. Sticking with our music theme, an infographic about how CDs are made would apply because it's music-related but not specific to any artist or genre.

The follow sections explore the three general areas in more depth.

Timely: Sharing breaking news

Although your infographic is unlikely to be the sole source of breaking news, it can help readers' understanding of a breaking news event. For instance, many people learned on Twitter in October, 2011 that Apple co-founder Steve Jobs had died. An infographic wasn't going to be the first anybody heard of it.

But at Infographic World, we created an infographic looking back on his life and his accomplishments (we called it *Farewell to a Genius*), in a way to showcase a visual story that had not been told yet. (See Figure 2-3.) So in that sense, the infographic was breaking news. This graphic ended up being a viral sensation, getting featured on Mashable for several weeks, and then getting picked up by tens of thousands of other websites across the world over time.

Another way your infographic can be seen as "breaking news" is by illuminating an issue or piece of data in a way people hadn't considered before. Data by itself is interesting enough, but without context, understanding of it can be shallow. A good goal for your infographic should be to surprise people with your data. Tell them something they didn't already know.

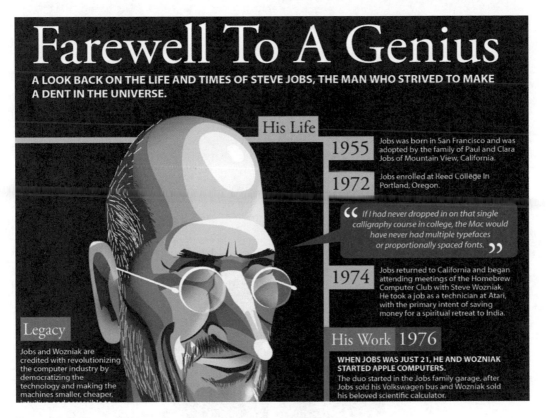

Farewell To A Genius

A LOOK BACK ON THE LIFE AND TIMES OF STEVE JOBS, THE MAN WHO STRIVED TO MAKE A DENT IN THE UNIVERSE.

His Life

1955 — Jobs was born in San Francisco and was adopted by the family of Paul and Clara Jobs of Mountain View, California.

1972 — Jobs enrolled at Reed College in Portland, Oregon.

❝ *If I had never dropped in on that single calligraphy course in college, the Mac would have never had multiple typefaces or proportionally spaced fonts.* ❞

1974 — Jobs returned to California and began attending meetings of the Homebrew Computer Club with Steve Wozniak. He took a job as a technician at Atari, with the primary intent of saving money for a spiritual retreat to India.

Legacy

Jobs and Wozniak are credited with revolutionizing the computer industry by democratizing the technology and making the machines smaller, cheaper,

His Work 1976

WHEN JOBS WAS JUST 21, HE AND WOZNIAK STARTED APPLE COMPUTERS.
The duo started in the Jobs family garage, after Jobs sold his Volkswagen bus and Wozniak sold his beloved scientific calculator.

Figure 2-3: Telling a visual story can illuminate breaking news.

For instance, did you know that more Americans are in prison than are active-duty members of the military? After some research, you learn that in 2011, there were more than two million incarcerated offenders in the United States. In 2013, there were slightly less than 1.5 million active-duty members of the military.

By comparing the figures graphically, you're taking existing data and looking at it and presenting it in a new way to tell an original story. Figure 2-4 shows how you could compare the two numbers in an infographic.

Timely infographics can be immensely successful, but be warned: Their popularity will wane as public interest in the news cools. We kept this in mind as we built the Steve Jobs graphic because we knew that as a story fades from the front pages, reader interest in our infographic wouldn't last forever. For this reason, we created the infographic from beginning to end in less than 30 hours following his death.

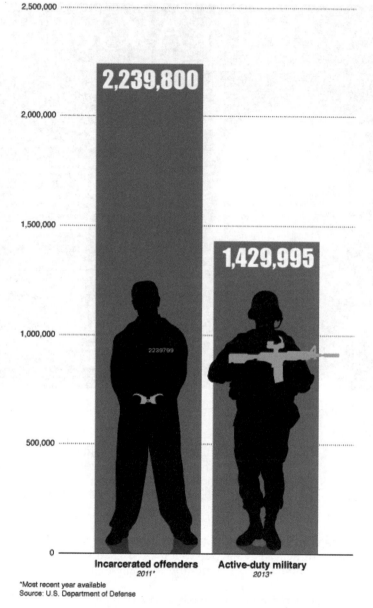

2,500,000

2,239,800

2,000,000

1,500,000

1,429,995

1,000,000

2239799

500,000

0

Incarcerated offenders
2011*

Active-duty military
2013*

*Most recent year available
Source: U.S. Department of Defense

Figure 2-4: Using data to tell a surprising element of a story.

Related: Telling a relevant tale

You may not wish to rush into production with an extremely timely infographic. After all, that's a major commitment of resources. Instead, maybe you want to take a news event, find a somewhat related topic, and develop an infographic inspired by the news event.

When choosing these tangentially related topics, explore potentially unseen or previously unconsidered aspects of an event. Use the news event as a point of departure, allowing your topic to have a life of its own while still retaining a sense of timeliness.

In other words, don't take on the news event directly. Take a different view of it. Broad ideas in this vein include

- The business of *<fill in the blank>*
- *<fill in the blank>* around the world
- The evolution of *<fill in the blank>*
  - By state
  - And kids
  - And elderly people
- The future of *<fill in the blank>*

Approaches like this allow you to take advantage of the built-in popularity of current events while expanding the overall lifespan of your infographic. You'll get the best of both worlds, giving your infographic a ready-made audience in the short term and allowing the audience to continue building even after the immediate interest fades.

You don't have to even mention the news event in your infographic in many cases. Otherwise, you run the risk of the piece immediately becoming out-dated in the case of rapidly developing news. The ideal approach is to make the infographic appear as though it were planned all along and is simply ben-efitting from fortuitous timing.

Evergreen: Letting things build

The final approach to infographics is to completely ignore current events and explore ideas at your own pace. These evergreen pieces will have a virtu-ally limitless shelf life (depending on the topic), so it's wise to have a mix of timely and evergreen pieces.

Infographics of this type may not have a huge audience at first, but they can build viewers over time if the topic has interest year-round. These pieces often are the most appealing because they allow the data to take you wher-ever it goes and craft a design that's completely organic and springs totally from the content.

When you aren't going for the immediate impact of a timely infographic, make sure your topic is interesting all on its own. The best way to do that is to explore the techniques we talk about earlier, including becoming an expert in a given field. This strategy gives you the best chance of knowing what will interest the audience. If you have some knowledge and expertise in science, for example, you could craft an infographic on the lifecycle of the frog. If you're an Internet expert, you could design an infographic showing how a search engine works.

Engaging Viewers with Animation and Motion

Traditional static infographics are powerful and certainly have their place, but some stories can't be told through static imagery and charts alone. Some demand more bells and whistles, including motion, sound, and interactivity.

Although these techniques are relatively new, they are becoming extremely popular with readers who have come to crave constant entertainment and engagement. As you build your skills as an infographic designer, you'll definitely want to add some of these design skills to your roster.

Bringing infographics to life with motion and sound

Animated and video-based infographics (we are using those terms interchangeably) give you the opportunity to present stories in ways that provide more depth and perspective than static infographics. Such stories can include highly complex processes, mechanical illustrations, or long stories.

How do you know when opting for an animated infographic is the best idea? That will most likely depend on the amount of information you have or the complexity of the story you need to tell. But mostly, the question you need to answer is deciding the best format to explain the information at hand.

As we discuss throughout the book, people are visual, and motion speaks to people in a way that static imagery simply can't. To be sure, a static infographic can have a similar effect, but it's not nearly as powerful.

For example, infographics that include motion can help explain how the gears of a watch work by truly showing the viewer.

Motion infographics also allow you to tell the story in the exact order you want and be sure that viewers are consuming it as you intended. After all, with a static infographic, you can never really be sure whether viewers read the piece as you intended. If you've created the piece effectively, you have a good idea that they have, but you can never be totally sure. With a motion infographic, though, that concern isn't present. After all, nobody is going to start a video in the middle.

Most animated or video infographics also will include a sound element, which could be a piece of music, sound effects, or voice narration — usually a combination of all three. Sound gives you just another tool to help clearly, cleverly, and effectively explain the topic at hand. Sound is important in motion graphics for

- ✓ Establishing a mood
- ✓ Creating a sense of authority
- ✓ Connecting viewers
- ✓ Providing emotional depth

We've seen a narrated infographic on discovering celestial objects that used an outer-space backdrop, spinning asteroids, and mystical music to accomplish all of these effects.

Motion infographics are much more complex and expensive to produce than static infographics, but they give you such a unique method for storytelling that it's critical not to overlook them as important tools.

Creating an interactive infographic experience

Much like motion graphics, interactive infographics provide you with another powerful way to involve your viewers in the topic. *Interactive* infographics include features that allow the readers to explore the infographic in their own ways. This customized view can come about in a number of different ways — whether by clicking on a part of the graphic to view data or by moving components of the graphic to access more information. Like motion graphics, interactive graphics have their own unique benefits and reasons why you might choose them. A few include

- ✓ An abundance of data
- ✓ Overly complex processes or explanations
- ✓ Large, detailed maps
- ✓ Lengthy text
- ✓ Data that will affect different readers in different ways

Perhaps the most compelling reason to explore using an interactive solution to your topic is when you have a huge amount of data. Say you have data comparing every single state in the United States in a variety of categories. You could do this with a static approach, but you'd be asking your readers to stay tuned for a very long infographic. It's difficult to hold interest that long.

Instead of expecting viewers to stick with you for a long time, you could instead provide them with an interactive experience that would allow them to explore the data on their own time and at their own pace.

One of our earlier interactive projects features a state-by-state comparison of a number of lifestyle factors, such as education, church attendance, obesity rates, crime rates, and more. We compiled the data for all 50 states and then created an interactive format allowing readers to see data for whatever states they want, in whichever categories they choose.

We then color-coded the states red or blue to show whether each state's voters had chosen John McCain or Barack Obama in the 2008 presidential election. (See Figure 2-5.) We drew very few explicit conclusions about the data and the states' political character. By letting the readers use the data in their own manner, we really left it up to them.

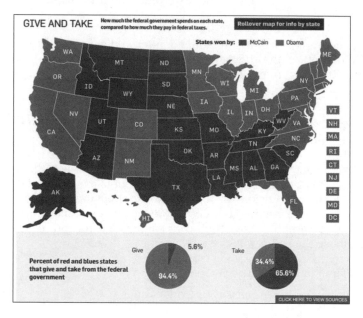

Figure 2-5: Using interactive features to let readers explore data.

A few elements that all effective interactives should have include

- Intuitive experience
- Clear organization
- Wise user control (let them do what they want, within reason)
- Multiple pages (rather than long scrolling)

Knowing when an interactive infographic is too much

Just because you have a ton of data doesn't mean you should create an interactive info-graphic. If you're in the midst of coming up with the story and flow of your interactive, and it feels rather sparse and superfluous, that's a good sign that you may not need to create an interactive after all. A static or even an animated infographic may work better for your purposes.

Consider paring down the information to only the most critical. What are the five pieces of data people need to know to understand the story you're trying to tell? Trim what you've gathered only to that information.

And if you really believe the data you have gathered is interesting enough and you want people to be able to absorb it all, you could create a series of infographics rather than jamming too much content into one single product.

Choosing to create an interactive infographic isn't the end of the discussion. In addition to the research, writing, and design aspects of interactives, you must decide which coding language to use to build your interactive.

You have two main options: Flash and HTML5. Using Flash allows you to create a, well, "flashier" experience in a shorter timeframe because you need to create less code on your own. The biggest drawback to using Flash is that it can't be viewed on iOS devices and older Internet browsers with compatibility issues. HTML5's biggest drawback is that it takes a great deal of time because the coding process is long and complex. You'd be wise to develop talent in both options; you may encounter projects that call for either one.

3

Designing Your Approach to Infographics

As you're setting your course as an infographic designer, you'll want to spend some time thinking about your philosophy. You'll find many different philosophical approaches to conceptualizing, building, and refining infographics. There is no one-size-fits-all approach, and your path will undoubtedly be influenced by your own taste and creative leanings.

For example, you may prefer simple infographics focused on charts and graphs. Or you may prefer to take charts and graphs and reinterpret them into a more complex visual scheme. Maybe you prefer visuals that are icon-based, or you want more elevated artwork.

The good news is that a market and audience exist for virtually any idea you can come up with as long you have the building blocks of good information and good design. In this chapter, we show you why it's so important to develop a process for gathering information, deciding on a visual game plan, creating a design, refining the design, getting a project approved, and then releasing your completed infographic to your target audience.

Establishing a Work Process

As you begin your work as an infographic designer, we recommend establishing systems for how you'll work and the methods you'll use to create your graphics. Of course, no two graphics are identical, so your process won't be the same *every* time. Still, you'll find that developing an assembly line–like approach that you repeat with every single project will mean that you can focus on the important things. Why do you think basketball players practice shooting for hours? When it's time to launch their shot, they don't have to think about how they make their hands and legs do what they need to do. It's muscle memory.

Your process may look something like Figure 3-1.

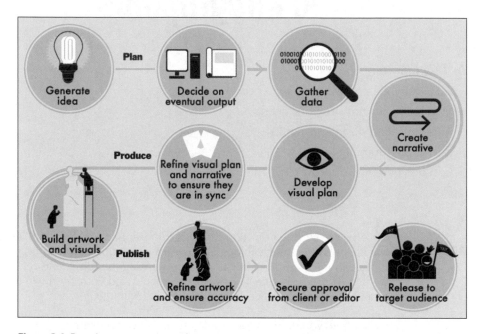

Figure 3-1: Develop your own creative process.

Process: Not one-size-fits-all

Although there is no single answer for every infographic producer when it comes to how the work gets done, what's important is that you find a process that works for you — and stick to it. Also, don't fear making changes to that process when something clearly isn't working. Maybe getting approvals from your internal editors is taking too long. If so, address the issue, put a new policy in place, and move on.

Remember: Creating a standard approach for creating your infographics isn't meant to make your job boring. Rather, it's meant to free you, to allow you to focus on bigger picture issues — and those bigger picture issues will help build your skills and reputation as an infographics producer.

Deciding on your eventual output

In Chapters 1 and 2, we discuss a myriad of ways in which infographics can bring a story to life. So now, assume that you received your assignment from a client or editor, or you came up with your own brilliant idea that you will pitch to an editor or create for your own website or blog.

Your next big decision is the eventual output for your work: namely, whether your infographic will be static or interactive, and whether it will be published in print or online. Will you be creating a traditional web-based infographic that's tall and thin? Or is it a magazine graphic, where you'll have to choose whether to lay it out horizontally or vertically? Is the piece interactive or animated? How much physical space or virtual bandwidth will your client give you? Knowing the answers to those questions is crucial to help you determine how much time and technical skill you'll need for your project.

- **Print**
  - *Size:* Single-column, two- or three-column, or full page
  - *Orientation:* Vertical or horizontal
  - *Color:* Black-and-white or color
  - *Print finishes:* Whether the graphic will be used in a newspaper, magazine, or marketing brochure

- **Static online**
  - *Size:* Usually width in pixels

    Check the specifications of any site or host that will be publishing your infographic.
  - *Orientation:* Usually vertical, but can be horizontal

- **Interactive online**
  - *Size:* Pixels are the standard measurement

    Specific requirements will vary by website.
  - *Coding language:* Flash versus HTML and CSS

    Flash may be on its way out because of technical difficulties for iOS devices.

- **Animated**
  - *Size*

    Don't pile on too many features in an animated infographic because big files load slowly and perform poorly.
  - *File type:* QuickTime, GIF, and so on

File size matters

Most infographics you create will be JPEG files, which can be easily shared via social media and e-mail. An optimal file size for easy sharing is about 1MB. This size allows the artwork and text to be crisp and clear without making the website hosting the infographic load too slowly.

If you expect your graphic to be widely viewed on mobile devices, aim for smaller than 1MB. Remember that mobile users pay for their bandwidth and often don't have optimal download speeds. That being said, you must still make sure that your graphic is legible, so you may want to explore alternatives to using one large graphic — perhaps you can tell your story in three smaller ones.

Social media concerns

With Facebook's relatively frequent redesigns, you need to keep current on any changes made to its image specifications. You may want to create a preview image for posting to Facebook so the infographic appears more easily in followers' feeds. The same holds true for other social media channels, such as Twitter and Pinterest.

Gathering data

With a plan in hand for your project, you'll begin to map out your story by gathering data. At the core of every infographic is data — that's the "info(rmation)" part of "info-graphic" — so gathering that information must be a crucial part of your process. Even if it isn't the very first step (after all, you might think of an idea before you know what information is out there), information-gathering is always one of the first steps.

Good data serves as the foundation for everything to come after. If your data isn't accurate, your infographic won't be successful.

Just as there's no one way to approach infographics, there's no single way to gather data. You could

- **Explore databases.**

   Many government agencies and universities have publicly accessible databases.

- **Examine tax records.**

   Call or visit a township assessor's office.

- **Search historical records.**

   Try a university library or county historical society.

✔ **Conduct in-person research or interviews.**

   Get out of the office and meet people.

✔ **Read books, maps, and almanacs.**

   Online or paper versions are great.

✔ **Browse the Internet.**

We discuss information-gathering in more depth in Chapter 5.

Also on your docket are the ways to keep track of your data: old-school notebook, Microsoft Word file, spreadsheet program? All are viable options, depending on your work style and the type of research involved. For example, data tracked over several years works well in a spreadsheet. If you're interviewing someone to get your data, take a practice run to see whether you prefer typing notes into a Word file or jotting them down in a notebook.

While you're researching, keep close track of the sources you use. Any facts that make it into your final infographic should be attributed, most likely in a footnote at the base of your graphic. As long as you properly attribute, you won't need to seek specific permission to use publicly available information.

Create narrative and flow

Remember that infographics tell a story. We talk about visual storytelling in Chapter 1, and you'll see more evidence of the power of a cohesive story throughout the book. For now, as we help you establish your process, run through an example of how your graphic will flow, both textually and artistically.

Say it's Olympics season. A young figure skater just captured the gold medal on the strength of her triple-axel jumps. You design an infographic that explains a triple axel.

A logical narrative would deconstruct the jump, from the skater's first moment to the last. You would design art that shows each step, making sure the story and the visuals are in sync. Perhaps your graphic begins with some introductory text about the skater, but after that, stick closely to the narrative of this graphic — that gold-medal jump.

Develop and refine your visual plan

Starting with a blank canvas can prove intimidating. Hopefully, you won't really have to do that. You've probably been mulling over some visual ideas in your mind as you compiled your data. Having an idea and translating it into a completed piece of work are, of course, very different prospects.

Various methods can help you along the way to ensure that the vision you have in your mind is carried through to the final product, whether you yourself are creating the design or you're working with someone else to complete it. We rely on wireframes and mood boards.

Working with wireframes

Regardless of whether you or someone else will physically create the design, it's still vital to produce a *wireframe,* which is a rough sketch that shows the layout and general design of your infographic. Depending on whether you're creating the infographic for yourself or a client, it may also be part of a formal approval process. (Read about wireframes in more detail in Chapter 7.)

Wireframes help people imagine what the finished product will look like — which helps you as well as your client. For instance, you might have a grand visual idea, but after you start creating your wireframe, you realize that you have too much content (or not enough) to make it work.

Depending upon your client and/or your individual process, your wireframe may be quite simple and general. Say you're creating a timeline of advances in medicine. Your wireframe could be basic, like Figure 3-2, without artwork, colors, or particular fonts.

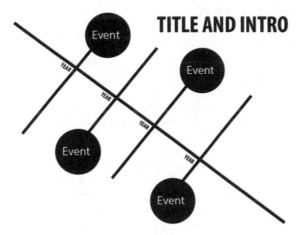

Figure 3-2: Creating a simple wireframe for an infographic.

Or, your wireframe could be more developed, involving some of the specific elements you intend to use in the finished product, such as the colors you're proposing to use. See Figure 3-3.

You can further develop your wireframe by including imagery in the style of what you intend to use in the finished product — something like Figure 3-4.

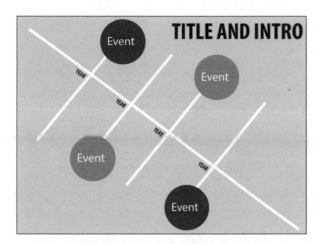

Figure 3-3: Providing more details in a wireframe.

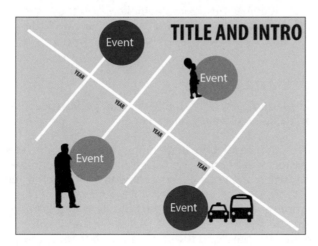

Figure 3-4: Adding simple artwork to a wireframe.

Each more-developed wireframe example gives a good idea of the visual approach. The level of detail you use in a wireframe should match your client's specifications and skill. A client (or boss) who has experience in visualizing artistic concepts may want only the most basic wireframe. Those who are not as adept at visualizing concepts may require a more detailed wireframe.

If your client doesn't specify how detailed the wireframe should be, we recommend taking a middle-of-the road approach, so as to provide enough details to proceed but not lock into an official design.

Working with mood boards

Think of a mood board for an infographic like a Pinterest board. Say you're redecorating your living room. You might pin images of furniture, paint swatches, lamps, rugs, and accessories. The images would provide inspiration while you shop for the room. A mood board for an infographic can have the very same effect, providing inspiration and answers for you as you ask yourself the basics:

> *What colors should I use? What visual style should I use? What fonts would be appropriate? What sort of finishing touches could I use?*

Inspiration can come from anywhere — other infographics, print design, TV commercials, fine art — so never close yourself off to inspiration. Keep an open mind.

Whether you share your mood board with your clients is up to you and will most likely be decided by the same measures you use to determine what type of wireframe to provide: Are they creative thinkers? Do they even want a high level of involvement? If not, a mood board can be your own little source of inspiration.

Build artwork and visuals

The most difficult — and most important — part of your process is crafting the visuals. Good design looks easy but never is.

The design process should take the lion's share of the time allocated to the project. If you spend a week coming up with the content, spend two weeks on the design. A poor translation of solid content won't get much traction.

We spend a *lot* more time discussing design, both later in this chapter and in all of Part III of this book. For the moment, just know that it will be the biggest expenditure of your time, and it will ultimately become your professional signature, so it's got to be good.

Refine artwork and ensure accuracy

When your research and design work is done, you'll combine them into an infographic that should roughly mirror the plan you made when you built your wireframe. Remember, though, that a wireframe is really just a draft. Now is the time to take a critical look at your work. If your artwork needs changes, go ahead and make them. If your data has any gaps or mistakes, fix them. You may alter your infographic dozens of times before handing it in for approval, and that's fine — it's all part of the process.

Leave yourself enough time to make any edits, both large and small. Most people aren't very good at self-editing, and that goes for designers, too. Get as many pairs of eyes on the work as possible, and never take any edits personally.

Getting your project approved

Securing approval for your work is an important step that we visit several times in the course of this book. In this step, you can expect to work with a variety of people, including art directors, marketing directors, publications managers, and sometimes even the top executive at the company you're working for.

Ask your contacts to explain the process you will have to follow. Chances are that it will vary from one client to the next. Some clients make changes in many incremental steps; others may ask for one extensive round of changes.

The changes you may have to make could include content, design, or both. Keep an open mind and be prepared to talk through all requests. No matter what processes you set up for yourself, you'll need to remain flexible enough to work with any and all clients.

Sharing your creation with your audience

After you perfect the design (that's possible, right?), it's time to release your work to your audience. This could be as simple as tweeting it or sharing it on your Facebook page, or as complex as having a large-format poster printed at a professional shop.

In the case of interactive or animated infographics, you also often must contend with unforeseen technical issues — errors hidden in code or incompatibility with Internet browsers.

In today's fast-paced, web-dominated media landscape, a goal of almost every infographic producer is for the piece to become viral. In other words, you want it to be shared around the Internet. We discuss this in greater detail in Chapter 13. A dream scenario could go something like Figure 3-5.

We'll come back to this idea throughout the book. For now, start thinking about the ways in which you want to transmit your graphic to the world.

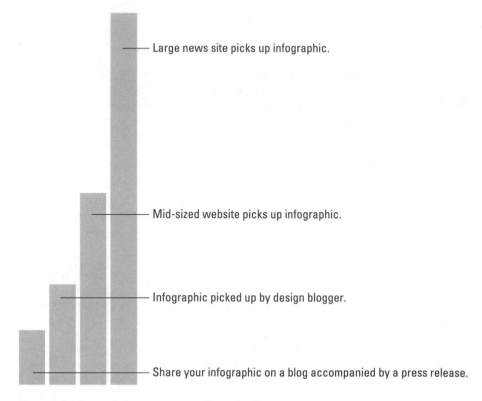

Large news site picks up infographic.

Mid-sized website picks up infographic.

Infographic picked up by design blogger.

Share your infographic on a blog accompanied by a press release.

Figure 3-5: Likes and shares can grow dramatically.

Assembling the Tools of the Trade

All the smart processes in the world won't help much if you don't have the proper tools in place to take advantage of them. Here's what you should consider as you make sure your technology, staff, and business relationships are in good working order.

Lining up your technology tools

The most important aspects of technology for infographic designers are design programs and tools. Think of it this way: You never want a picture in your head to be something you can't re-create because you don't have the digital tools you need to make it happen. This is a digital world, and you can't rely on analog art tools like pens and sketchpads if you want to be successful in that digital landscape.

Here are some examples of the tools that you may want to gather. You don't need all of these to get started as an infographic designer, but if you'll be working with infographics on a regular basis, start accumulating the following:

- **A really good computer**
- **Reliable Internet access**

  There's nothing worse than completing a project, and then having technical trouble transmitting it to a client or editor. Chances are that you'll be relying heavily on the Internet for everything from research to sharing work with colleagues to publishing your infographic, so make sure your connection is solid.

- **A good-quality monitor**

  Make sure your monitor is big enough to allow you to see your work in detail. Screen sizes tend to range from 15" to 30" inches (measured diagonally). Aim for 24" or bigger. Check out resolution numbers as well; these are improving all the time, and some monitors are as clear as high-definition TV.

- **Up-to-date graphic design software,** such as Adobe Illustrator and Photoshop.
- **Digital illustrating tools**

  Illustrator and Photoshop dominate the category, but less-expensive options such as Corel's Painter and Intaglio for the Mac are good ways to start dabbling.

- **Interactive coding programs**

  You don't need to become a full-time coder to develop infographics. As more and more infographics showcase interactive features, though, it's a terrific idea to develop some basic skills in HTML and CSS. One cool way to do so is through Code Avengers, a free tutorial (www.codeavengers.com).

Mac or PC?

Macintosh computers, in their early days, were a clear favorite with graphic designers, who loved their reliability, ease of use, and attractive display. The differences between Macs and PCs have narrowed considerably, though.

Many infographic designers will take a strong stance in favor of a Mac or PC. We won't. It really comes down to personal preference and accessibility. Macs are more expensive. The programs you run are probably more important than the computer you use.

Design tools aren't the only technology considerations to keep in mind. If enough work comes your way, you'll need a system for keeping track of documents and files both internally and for your clients. Whether you use a free tool like Google or paid software like Basecamp (`https://basecamp.com`, a project management system) for managing content, creating a workflow is vital.

Gathering a work force

Nobody can do everything alone. Many hands touch an infographic during the process, including

- Researchers
- Writers
- Editors
- Designers
- Illustrators
- Interactive developers
- Publicists

Many websites and media concerns have their own publicists, who work to draw attention to certain stories. Some may not be familiar with infographics, but as the genre becomes more and more popular, they could start capturing more attention from publicists.

Each person plays a different role — and a person may play more than one — but infographic development is truly a team sport. If you know you have a weakness in one of these areas, it may benefit you to hire someone to handle those aspects of infographic design. You can allot a certain percentage of your fee to the others that help you.

Assembling a team can pay big dividends over time because a strong team can help you avoid costly revisions and polish your reputation as a professional.

Building professional relationships

A huge part of creating viral content is establishing and developing relationships with bloggers, thought leaders, business peers, reporters, and content editors. Targeting your infographics to blogs and news sites that specialize in the information you're showcasing can help you build relationships and can also help you get your work published and shared.

If, say, you want to develop a relationship with tech bloggers, work to become an expert in one or two areas of technology and create infographics on those topics. This allows you to promote yourself as an expert in the area and encourage the blog to begin to see you as a partner in creating visual content.

Again, we'll look more closely at how to get your work published later in the book. (See Part IV.) For now, just start thinking about where you'd like to see your work featured. Become a diligent reader of those websites or publications so you can see what they've published — and start polishing your ideas for future content.

Developing Design Principles

Good design is good design. This applies to graphic design, newspapers, and even interior design. There are several principles that you should know (and know when to bend).

Balance

Adequate balance gives your infographic visual stability, preventing one element from dominating the visual and inappropriately pulling readers' focus. It keeps the design from being top- or bottom-heavy or skewing to one side or the other.

A terrific rule of thumb for creating a balanced infographic is to divide your page into thirds, using a grid, as shown in Figure 3-6. The thirds can go from left to right, or from top to bottom. Either way, your *dominant* element — the part of the graphic that illustrates your main idea — should occupy about two-thirds of your design.

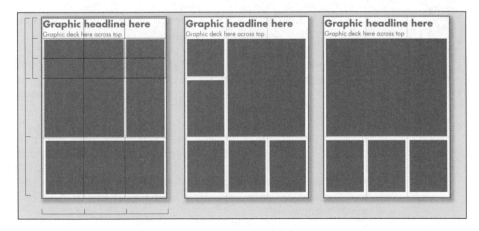

Figure 3-6: Balancing visual elements improves the look of your infographic.

Experimenting with balance

There's more than one way to create a visually appealing infographic. Refer again to the three examples in Figure 3-6. The first features only three distinct art elements: one dominant chart at the top left, a smaller art element at the top right, and a fairly large element anchoring the bottom.

The second has six parts, so it is a bit more complex, but still nicely balanced and quite clear. Again, it has one visually dominant element. To unite the rest of the design, use spacing, subheads (generally a word or two that leads into a new section) or decks (a sentence or two that adds information), and color to guide the viewer through the narrative.

The third layout allows the dominant element to take up the entire top of the graphic. This might be a good choice if the artwork is very appealing, or if the story is really compelling. Supporting information takes a back seat, at the bottom of the infographic.

Any of these three layouts would work really well. The nature of the data and the character of the illustrations will determine which layout works best for *your* infographic.

Making the most of white space

"White space" is a really important element of design that can help you achieve balance in your infographics. First off, white space isn't always white — it's just the name for the open space between art and text elements.

White space allows the eye to take a break between one part of your infographic and the next. It ensures that your graphic is clear and legible. You should build some white space into your design.

Don't just slam together your artistic elements and let the gaps serve as your white space.

Figure 3-7 shows how random white space can actually damage the balance of an infographic. This graphic would be improved by bringing the smaller art elements into proportion with each other, and creating more equal amounts of white space between them all.

Consider the number and type of illustrations and charts you're showing, and think about their content as well. You probably don't want all your supporting elements to be line charts because that would be boring. You don't want to create a hodgepodge of data visualization, either, because that can dilute your message. Experiment with forms that will support your dominant element without distracting from it.

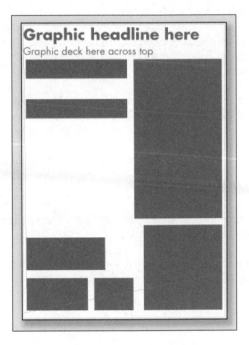

Figure 3-7: Not a good use of white space.

Hierarchy

Creating hierarchy in visual elements helps readers know where to look for the most important information. This means establishing size and treatment for various elements:

- ✓ **Main titles**

    These will be the largest font size you use.

- ✓ **Subtitles**

    These will probably be the same font, or sometimes a different treatment of the same font; for example, Times New Roman in bold for the headline and without bold for the subtitles. They will be in a smaller font size.

- ✓ **Instructions**

    These aren't always in the form of text; some infographics show direction with arrows or other visual elements. Sometimes, though, you may guide a reader to the next section of your infographic with a text cue or transition, such as, "Then" or "As a result." You may want to give this the same font as a subtitle, or you may opt for something subtly different.

✔ **Body text**

This will often differ from the text used in the main title and subtitle. It will be smaller, but make sure it's not too small to be legible.

✔ **Interactive text**

Check with your art director or your client contact. Many publications use a slightly different font for interactive text, such as URLs.

✔ **Chart labels**

These may be the same size as body text, but they are often a different font.

✔ **Notes/sources**

Notes and sources are probably your smallest typeface. Create unity by making them the same as another element.

Viewers should never have to guess at what to look at next. And in the case of interactive infographics, they should have clear instructions about where to click and what to do.

Unity

Bringing the visual elements together creates a sense of unity. When all the pieces fall into place, the design will feel as if everything was meant to be where it is. This is easier to achieve when one person creates every visual element, but depending on the particular visual treatment, one person may create the artwork, and another person complete the design.

With different collaborators, the artists must communicate effectively about the style of the artwork as well as the colors and fonts being used so that elements don't clash with each other.

Proportion

Visual hierarchy is important to the design principles of your infographic, but information integrity is also important. Be sure to consider the importance of various pieces of data to avoid creating misleading impressions in viewers' minds. For example, if you're doing an infographic on leading home run hitters in Major League Baseball, your charts on hits and slugging percentage ought to be more dominant than stats on those players' errors.

Avoid placing unrelated charts too close together. Not only could readers be confused as to why the charts are next to each other, but they could assume they are on the same scale — which they may not be.

Color

Each topic is different. A piece about politics may require more subdued colors, while something related to entertainment could call for a bright scheme. You may also wish to create a preferred color palette for your infographics (so long as your client doesn't have other ideas) that create an identity for your pieces. This is fun and easy to do with a mood board, as we discuss earlier.

Regardless of your approach to color, there's no doubt that color is possibly the most powerful way to set a mood.

Fonts

Include too few typefaces, and your infographic could feel boring. Include too many, and you run the risk of making it look like a ransom note. A general guideline is to use no more than three typefaces in your design.

We talk more about fonts in Chapter 7. For now, here are some basic things to keep in mind.

First of all, make sure the font you choose is readable. This sounds like an obvious rule, but as you experiment with different typefaces, you will discover that some fonts are most legible in large sizes, but become muddled or crowded in smaller point sizes. Check your fonts both on the computer screen and on paper because sometimes what looks great onscreen doesn't translate as well to print documents.

Make the most of the fonts that come with your computer and the software you've already purchased. For example, the latest version of Adobe Illustrator comes with about 90 fonts. Adobe also sells add-on sets that could add dozens more fonts to your toolbox. Even Microsoft Word has dozens of fonts to choose from.

After you own these programs, you can use the fonts in any way you like — for personal projects, or for work that you intend to sell, like your infographic.

But if you actually read your End User License Agreement, you'll discover that what you *can't* do is give that font away to anyone else. As an infographic designer, a good way to prevent anyone from copying your font is to embed it in your work. We talk some about the technical aspect of embedding in Chapter 4. For now, just know that it's a way to transmit and publish your file without leaving the font accessible to others who might snatch it up for their own use.

And, a word on cost. The fonts that come with your software program certainly aren't free, but when you bought the program, you bought those fonts. If you want to add to your collection by purchasing fonts individually from font designers or various design websites, you may pay $25 to $100 per font. Is it really worth getting your heart set on one of these? It's also possible that the designer hasn't cleared the font for commercial use, which could land you in legal trouble.

Certainly, if your client wants an exclusive font, you must use it, but you may be able to include it in your bill for the project. Ask about this when you're negotiating your pay.

Respecting Brand Guidelines

Working with clients will inevitably mean interpreting and following their brand guidelines and, occasionally, trying to stretch those guidelines. Keep your own branding guidelines in mind as well.

Consult brand guidelines to give you a sense of the overall corporate look and feel. Some companies will want to create a sense of elegance; others will be most comfortable with a sense of whimsy. Exploring brand guidelines can help determine which type of client you are working with.

Because your client will almost certainly want your work to fit in with their corporate identity, here is some of the terminology you're likely to encounter. Any or all of these characteristics may be addressed in brand guidelines:

- **Equity:** The power a company derives from having a well-known name
- **Experience:** Whether your company is an established powerhouse, or a cool new kid
- **Values:** Whether your company has an affiliation with a particular social issue, such as the environment
- **Personality:** Young and fun, or serious and buttoned-down
- **Positioning:** Market dominance
- **Vision:** Focused on the future
- **Tone of voice:** Serious, humorous, snarky
- **Strategy:** Growth potential

Several areas of design should be covered in branding guidelines. Here's a look at what you can expect in terms of fonts, colors, and logos.

Using recommended fonts

If your client has brand guidelines, font usage will be one of the most important. Remember that your clients are used to seeing documents and communication with particular fonts. Seeing things outside that font can be off-putting.

Pay attention not only to the font families preferred but to the specific styles of font preferred. You may want to see publications the client has approved in the past to help guide you in usage of the client's preferred typefaces.

In the event you don't have access to the client's preferred fonts, you may ask the client to send the fonts for your usage or to reimburse you for purchasing them.

Working with logos

Your client also should provide you with logos to use in the infographic. You will need high-resolution files of about 300 dpi (dots per inch) to ensure that the logo reproduces well in various sizes and in various formats. Vector-based files are preferred.

Some clients will allow creative usage of their logos, but this is a risky prospect because most companies are protective of their logos, and copyright rules may forbid altering the logo. Given that logos are the most identifiable visual element for most companies, it's not hard to understand why companies generally want to maintain their integrity.

Working with colors

Many clients will allow a great deal of leeway in the colors used in an infographic. This can allow you to set your work apart from other artists your client may have hired. If much of a client's previous graphic material sticks to a monotonous color palette, maybe you could try something different. Pushing the limits could set you apart, especially if you can come up with a color scheme that really appeals to the client.

However, you may not want to stray too far from the guidelines they set forth. Just like with fonts, your client is probably accustomed to seeing certain colors, and seeing those familiar colors in your work may make the piece feel more comfortable for the client. Others simply stick to very specific choices to build up their brand identity, and we as designers must always respect that.

Using copy guidelines

Many companies will expect certain copy usage guidelines. Common copy stylebooks you'll encounter include Associated Press, APA, *The Chicago Manual of Style,* and MLA. When in doubt, check a Merriam-Webster dictionary or its online incarnation, `www.merriam-webster.com`.

Outlining the Approval Process

An integral part of working with clients is having your work approved. If you've followed the basic steps we outline here, the process should be smooth. Still, it's critical that you give your clients adequate time and opportunities to make their wishes and opinions known.

The approval process may look something like Figure 3-8.

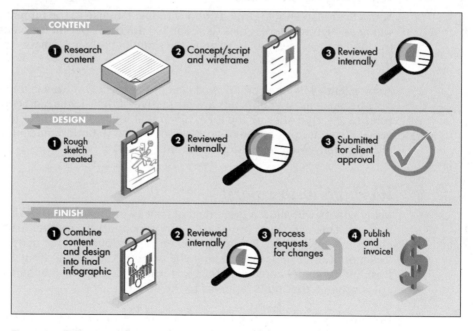

Figure 3-8: Following an infographic through the approval process.

Content

Concept/script and wireframe created

Reviewed internally

Submitted for client for approval

Design

Rough sketch created

Reviewed internally

First design draft created

Reviewed internally

At this point, you will most likely be asked to make several rounds of changes. Depending on how many people you're reporting to, and how well your infographic meets their needs, this process can be quick and painless or painstakingly slow.

Be polite, and communicate clearly.

After you secure full client approval, it's time to publish!

Whatever your specific process, make sure that you follow it each time and that you communicate the steps to everyone involved — writers, designers, clients. There should be no guesswork involved on either side.

We recommend sending your client a schedule at the beginning of the process. It could look something like this, depending on your client's deadline and your own scheduling needs:

Deliverable	*Date*
Concept/script and wireframe	1/1
Client feedback	1/3
Rough sketch	1/10
Client feedback	1/12
First draft	1/22
Client feedback	1/24
Second draft	1/27
Client feedback	1/29
Final draft	1/30

Although you might be tempted to give clients a chance to impose their own schedule, this inevitably leads clients to ask for shorter timeframes. We recommend resisting this temptation unless you have a very good reason to do otherwise. You need to give yourself every opportunity to make the work as creative and powerful as possible, and cutting time at any stage of the process can endanger that.

Part II
Starting with Data

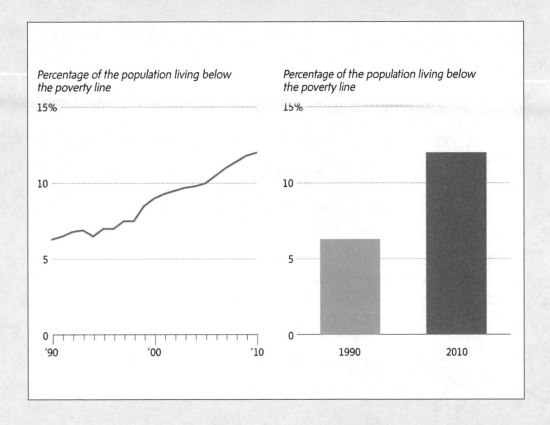

Percentage of the population living below the poverty line

Percentage of the population living below the poverty line

In this part . . .

- ✔ You'll learn how to seek out exactly the information you need to create smart infographics for your target audience.

- ✔ You'll learn how to sift through sources and find the most reputable ones.

- ✔ We'll talk about how to work through a sea of data to find and distill the perfect message for your infographic.

- ✔ We'll show you how to find trends and patterns and turn them into great infographics.

4

Informing Yourself

*B*efore you fire up Adobe Creative Suite — the package of graphic design and web development apps that you'll probably use as you design infographics — you need to know what your graphic is about and who your audience is. Those factors largely determine what information you include as well as how you present it. The goal, of course, is to make your infographic as effective as possible. After all, with all the blood, sweat, and tears we know you put into each piece — whether it's a graphic on school lunches in Albuquerque or mating habits of the buffy tufted-ear marmoset — you want it to have maximum impact. You want your audience, be it ten or ten million, to stare rapt and wide-eyed as they suddenly understand New Mexico school lunches or the buffy tufted-ear marmoset as they never have before.

Knowing what you want to say with your infographic and how to say it clearly and succinctly requires no mystical ability. It's mostly a matter of taking a moment to actually think it through. Consider looking at a map to find the shortest, most direct route from point A to point B. Even if you know generally which direction you're headed, you can save a lot of time and effort if you determine where you're going *before* you start your trip.

This chapter delves into what you need to consider as you plan the route to your goal of an amazing and effective infographic. Specifically, we discuss how to precisely define and focus your infographic as well as what it means to target your intended audience, and then we cover the technical details of printing specs and web dimensions.

Determining Your Infographic's Thesis

Every infographic needs a *thesis,* which is the point you're trying to make with your infographic. It's what your graphic, at its core, is about.

Generally speaking, infographics fall into the following camps:

- **Show how to do something or how something works:** Visuals can be invaluable when demonstrating the steps of a process, whether it's making a Caesar salad or showing how a combustion engine works. These graphics use images to help the reader understand complicated multistep processes. You can think of every instruction manual as an infographic.

  The point of the how-to type of infographic is fairly straightforward: to demonstrate a process. This type of infographic involves more questions and often more creative thinking, which is why this chapter focuses on how-to infographics.

- **Illustrate a point:** Information and statistics form the foundation of these infographics. Their purpose is essentially to illustrate a point with facts.

- **Motivate you to act:** A *call to action* urges the reader or viewer to do something.

Think of the thesis of your infographic as the argument it's trying to make. For your infographic to argue effectively, it has to stay focused, or it won't make an impact on the reader. To maintain focus, pin down your thesis as concretely as possible: You should be able to state it in a single sentence. Anything longer is likely overly complicated, which can quickly lead to an unfocused infographic.

Ideally, you know what your thesis is right from the start. But if you're not sure, two simple tips can help you formulate your thesis:

- **Ask yourself the five W's: who, what, when, where, why.** Answering how each relates to the point you're trying to make can help you work out what's important and what you need your infographic to convey.

- **Put your infographic's purpose into words.** Just because you're working in a visual medium doesn't mean you shouldn't write things out. Try writing a headline or a one-sentence summary of your infographic. Doing so will force you to put your thoughts into concrete terms and define the relationships between the elements in your graphic.

The underlying assumption here is that you might truly *not* know exactly what your infographic is about — and that can happen more often than you might think, particularly if you're creating a graphic for a client who has only a vague idea of what he wants.

Why spend so much time hammering out a thesis? Without one, your graphic may become convoluted and fail at its job of helping the reader understand — perhaps filling space with data that's interesting but not directly relevant.

Here's an example. Say you're working on a graphic with this thesis:

> Health issues caused by hospital mistakes are rising.

Say you find some interesting data showing that hospitals are closing in record numbers across the country. So, should you include that factoid? Well, unless you can also find a clear, proven link between hospital mistakes and hospital closures, the latter doesn't belong in your infographic. Our point: Add too much unnecessary information, and your point becomes unclear.

After you define your thesis, the next step is to figure out how to put your data, visuals, and text together into an actual infographic that's as informative and compelling as possible.

Thinking of the infographic's main points

Your thesis is the argument you're making. The data in your graphic is the evidence you present in support of that argument. You can also use data that provides the reader with context and a deeper understanding of your thesis to enrich your argument.

To achieve that goal, all the data you present has to relate to your thesis in a concrete way. Data that loosely centers on a theme isn't quite enough. A reader will recognize it for what it is: disjointed and unfocused information with no ultimate goal in mind.

As you think of the data you want to present, consider the points we describe in this section. The first is essential. The rest are elements to think about if you have remaining space to work in and want to elaborate on your thesis with data that adds depth and richness to your argument.

Using data to illustrate your thesis

Figure out what data directly proves your argument, which (after all) is the cornerstone of your infographic. For example, an infographic on the rising popularity of tofu in Europe should include stats showing that sales or consumption of tofu have gone up. Or, an infographic exploring the obscure subcultures that exist around online games might be composed entirely of examples and explanations of these subcultures.

Adding details to flesh out the main point

Other data you will likely want to include comprises anything that explains your thesis. This data provides your readers with context and enriches their understanding of the topic. Is tofu booming in Europe because vegetarianism is becoming more popular? Has a bumper year for soy beans made the crop suddenly inexpensive? As a journalist, it's always good to ask, "Why?"

Make sure there's a solid link between the data and your thesis. Avoid coincidence.

Looking for implications of your thesis

If your thesis has significant consequences, showing what they are helps illustrate why the point you're making is important. Say your graphic centers on a city's new subway system, and as a result of that system, people are driving less, and carbon emissions have fallen 20 percent. If it's relevant to your overall thesis, that information can demonstrate why the issue is worth the attention.

You should have already answered the "Why?" Answering the remaining W's — who, what, when, and where — can provide valuable context to your reader. Not every graphic needs to answer all these questions, but knowing the answers in your mind can help you clearly present your information and can also add another layer of interest to your infographic.

Correlation and causation

A well-known saying in the fields of science and statistics goes like this: *Correlation does not imply causation.* In other words, just because two events or trends occur together doesn't mean that one is the cause of the other.

Keep this in mind as you determine what to include in your infographic. Say you have two sets of data that seem linked. For example, one set shows that obesity is on the rise in a particular city, and another shows that healthcare costs are also going up in that city. The obvious conclusion one might draw is that the increase in obesity is pushing up the cost of healthcare, but the real reason may be more complicated than that. Perhaps healthcare costs have been rising in that area for years, and obesity is but one relatively insignificant factor in the trend. Being clear and accurate with your data in a situation like this is of the utmost importance.

So how do you verify a link between two data sets? Your own research may be enough, but if it isn't or if you have questions, get directly in touch with the persons or group that compiled the statistics. Ask them whether they have any idea what the cause is for the trend. They may have a very clear idea, or they may have only educated guesses. Talking with an expert should help you determine whether you can say outright that something is a cause or effect, or if you should put it forward your premise as only a suggested possibility.

The best way to make these distinctions clear is through your language. A text box and a few words can be enough to clarify something that might otherwise be misleading to a reader. And if your source tells you they only *think* there's a link — but really aren't certain — you can say that. Use language such as "experts believe" or "evidence suggests" that fits the situation. And don't worry that you're being noncommittal or wishy-washy; it's being accurate.

Using extra information wisely

Sometimes the most interesting information doesn't explain your thesis at all but acts as an engrossing subtopic or tangent. An infographic on how a disease works might delve into the latest treatment options, for instance. You might also find some obscure bit of data that isn't necessarily of great consequence but is still just plain fun or fascinating. Maybe the disease got its name from some bizarre reason that merits a small space in your graphic. There's nothing wrong with including that sort of information, especially if you know it will delight your readers. Just use your judgment and consider whether it will make your infographic better or detract from your point.

As you construct your graphic, periodically ask yourself whether each element relates to your thesis in a concrete way and also whether it adds value. If you find the answer is "no" with any element, cut it.

Organizing your information

The goal of your graphic is to convey information. To do that effectively, you need to plan your structure accordingly. Information works best in a hierarchy. The structure guides the reader, letting him know the main points as well as what information is supplementary. Think of this from a reader's viewpoint. If everything on the page is given equal treatment (see Figure 4-1), where should the reader start? A lot of data in your graphic can come across as information overload — and that feeling is more likely to alienate readers than draw them.

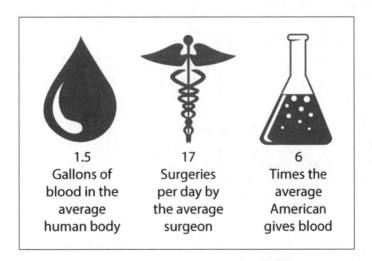

Figure 4-1: A graphic with no distinction among icons, statistics, and text.

An infographic, like a story, should have a beginning, a middle, and an end. The beginning is where your readers' eyes go when they first look at the page. If you're doing your infographic as a single page, with a chart that's larger than all the rest and contains an assortment of bright colors, that's where the readers' eyes are headed. That spot — the focal point of your graphic — should contain the most critical information.

From there, decide where you want your readers' eyes go next. Steer them to the next most important piece of information. Figure 4-2 actually guides the reader from a clear starting point to the conclusion with the help of subheadings and visuals along the way.

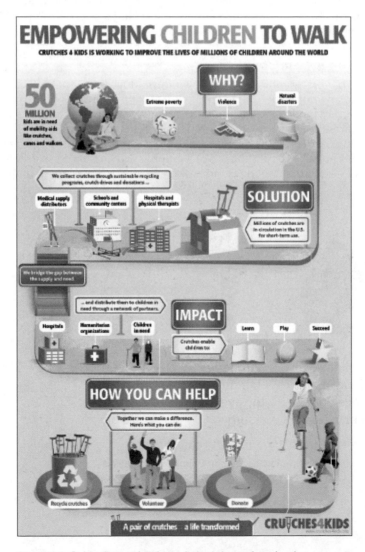

Figure 4-2: Guide the reader through the information clearly.

On that note, here are a few points to consider as you determine how you want to structure your information:

- **Real estate:** How much space you devote to a graphic element should match its importance. The data proving your thesis should get a relatively large amount of space. On the other hand, relatively insignificant data that requires a large map to display might be best reworked into a smaller element or even omitted.

- **Location:** People generally read from top to bottom, so elements at the top of the page tend to attract eyes first. This is true whether you're reading in print or online; however, online reading habits hew to an even tighter visual frame. Researchers have found what they call a *Google golden triangle,* which describes how users read all the way through the search result at the top of the page but then read a bit less of every search result below it, resulting in a rough triangle of material that is thoroughly read. The Google golden triangle is something to keep in mind as you're designing.

    Think about where to put your focal point, and how you want the graphic to flow into the other data you're including.

    That said, size can still trump location, meaning that an exceptionally large element at the bottom of the page might be where the reader's gaze goes first.

- **Colors:** Bright colors draw attention, as do graphical elements that employ several colors instead of being monochromatic. We don't recommend that your main chart should be a neon collage visible from space, but consider where your readers' eyes will go first — and where you want them to go from there.

The best infographics build a narrative in much the same way a story does, starting with a premise and then revealing something new at each turn. To a large degree, you can decide how your story unfolds by directing the readers' eyes to where you want them to go next.

At the end of this chapter, we discuss printing or publishing your graphics according to size specifications. The size of your graphic affects the ease of publishing it, so keep size in mind as you map out your visual story.

Calling out a call-to-action

The call-to-action infographic is another type of graphic that partially illustrates a point, but also has a larger job: to incite readers to action. A visual representation of a problem can make the problem feel more understandable and immediate than words alone, which is why nonprofit agencies and charities use these types of graphics frequently to solicit donations or get people involved in their cause.

Because the underlying goal of a call-to-action infographic is to get people to act, the information you select and how you organize it needs to be tailored to that purpose. That makes the call-to-action graphic slightly different than graphics created, say, to go with a newspaper article. Where the thesis of a news graphic might be implied but not stated outright, the thesis of a call-to-action infographic will usually be spelled out prominently. A strong call-to-action infographic also tends to dispense with nuance in favor of a blunt, direct approach.

In this section, we give you a few guidelines for creating an effective call-to-action infographic.

Your call-to-action is your focal point

Earlier in this chapter, we state that your thesis should be the focus of your infographic. Forget that for a minute. In a call-to-action infographic, you'll likely want the appeal to the reader to be the center of attention. The first place your readers' eyes should go is to the call that directs them to act. Think of it this way: If you have your readers' eyes for only a second, you want the message they walk away with to be, "Go! Act!"

The data you present now falls into more of a supporting role: It helps convince the reader to act. The design elements we mention earlier — real estate, location, and colors — are very important as you design your call-to-action and any charts you're including.

Maximize your impact with minimum information

A call-to-action infographic needs to convey its message as quickly and briefly as possible.

The point, again, isn't to provide a nuanced view of a complex topic, but to prompt the reader to act.

As an example, say you have a client combatting poverty in a particular city, and you have a dataset showing the gradual increase over the past 20 years in that city's poverty rate. You could show that rate with a *fever line* — a line that charts the change in a single value over time. We show a fever line on the left in Figure 4-3. Or you could create a full bar chart, but that's not ideal for this information because the gradual increase won't *look* dramatic.

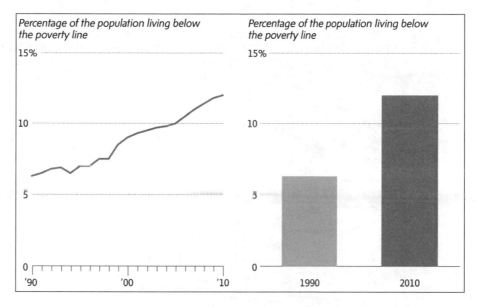

Figure 4-3: Heighten the impact of a chart by focusing on the end points of your data.

The best option for this graphic is using a bar chart with just two bars (shown on the right in Figure 4-3): the first showing the percentage of the population living in poverty for the first year of the dataset, and the second showing the same population in the last year of the dataset. (You may want to experiment with your visuals to see which approach is most effective in your situation.) The rise in poverty will be stark and instantly apparent, making the need to act more urgent. You can see the difference between the two approaches in Figure 4-3, and you achieve that impact by actually cutting all the data in between and using visuals to emphasize the change.

Favor individual stories over statistics

Research shows that appealing to people's emotions rather than their intellects is more effective in getting them to act, and stories about individuals tap into readers' emotions more powerfully than statistics. The reason is that statistics are abstract. They deal with people and events *en masse*. But individuals, including the ones you're trying to incite to action, don't identify with whole populations: They identify with other individuals.

The point is particularly apt if you're creating a graphic for a nonprofit or charity that's soliciting donations. Showing readers the plight of a nation in charts doesn't generate the same response as showing them the plight of one identifiable victim. In fact, a 2007 study by a University of Pennsylvania professor was titled "Sympathy and callousness: The impact of deliberative thought on donations to identifiable and statistical victims." You can find the study here:

```
http://opim.wharton.upenn.edu/risk/library/J2007OBHDP_DAS_
sympathy.pdf
```

The researchers found that even including statistical information beside the story of an identifiable victim resulted in fewer donations. The takeaway: Charitable giving isn't based on reason, so appealing to reason won't work. Avoid the head (logic); go right for the heart (emotion), as shown in Figure 4-4.

Figure 4-4: Clearly state the issue, the goal, and how viewers can help.

Appealing to the Target Audience

What one person finds fascinating can be completely different from what draws another person's interest. Getting your readers' attention and then hanging onto it first requires that you have some sense of who your reader is or who you want your reader to be. That reader is your target audience, and to make your graphic as compelling and amazing as possible, you need to tailor it to appeal to that audience directly.

To use two extremely different audiences to illustrate this point, think of what you'd want an infographic on rockets to be like if your target audience were a group of rocket scientists. Now think of what you'd want it to be like if your target were children. Everything in the graphic changes, from the information to the appearance.

In some cases, your target audience could be described as captive. For example, if your graphic on flying buttresses is going to be handed out as a promotional item at an architecture conference, your target audience is (or probably should be) architects, and you're almost guaranteed to get their eyes on your work. If the same graphic will appear in a brochure at a museum, something about it must be compelling enough to make people want to pick it up.

No matter who your audience members are, or whether they're sitting in conference seats or running around town, you still have to grab their attention. You want your graphic to draw readers in and hold their interest — and doing that requires a targeted approach. We write about this in much greater detail in Chapters 5 and 6.

Here's a brief rundown of different factors to consider as you tailor your infographic to appeal to a specific audience.

Complexity

One aspect of your graphic you need to be aware of is the *complexity* of the information you're presenting: how much data is packed into each chart and how difficult that data is to understand. Including a large amount of data in a single chart increases the effort needed to untangle it, so you need to determine what amount is acceptable for your target audience. Figure 4-5 (left) shows an example of a chart containing a great deal of data and a comparative version (right) that's been pared down.

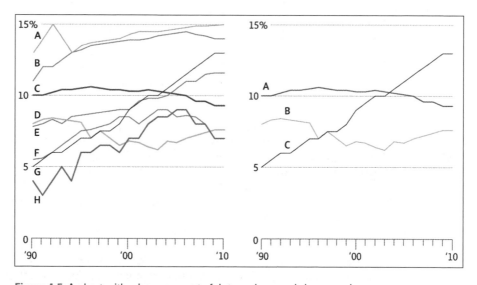

Figure 4-5: A chart with a large amount of data and a pared-down version.

Say for Figure 4-5, the infographic on the left is focused on France, but you're including data for other countries as context. Well, maybe you don't need to include data for that many other countries. Focusing on just a few key countries (the simple version on the right of the figure) might be enough to get your point across.

Your audience is also important to consider when you think of whether to use data that requires some work to understand. For the general public, a simpler approach is more suitable. Figure 4-6 shows charts using real data that demonstrate this point: The chart on the left shows the ratio of people age 0–14 to those 65+ in a population over time. The chart on the right shows the actual populations of each age group.

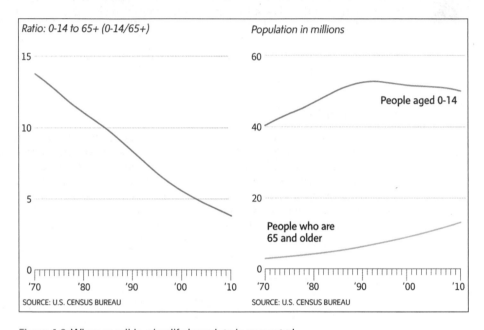

Figure 4-6: When possible, simplify how data is presented.

If your audience is the general public, you typically want to keep the complexity to a minimum. The data needs to be accessible to everyone, including people who may know very little about the subject. That doesn't mean you need to dumb-down anything. On the contrary, one of the joys of a good graphic is exploring the visual representation of a large, intricate set of data. But there is a line beyond which exploring becomes struggling to understand. Knowing the difference is a matter of judgment. (A notable exception to this point is when the goal of your graphic is to demonstrate the complexity of a topic.)

On the other hand, highly complex charts may be desirable if your audience is a group of specialists. Telecom engineers, for example, may enjoy working through a flow chart on the evolution of cellular standards through the years. As the designer of the infographic, you decide the appropriate level of complexity for your target audience.

Density

As opposed to complexity, *density* in this context refers to how many charts are in your graphic as a whole. To a great degree, design principles will govern how many you pack in and don't forget your all-important white space! (We talk about white space and design in Chapters 7 and 8.) But ultimately, you determine how data-dense your graphic is.

The rules on density follow the rules on complexity: If your audience is the general public, keep the density a bit lower than it would be if you were creating something for an audience of specialists. An infographic that looks like a wall of data can be alienating rather than inviting. An audience of specialists, on the other hand, can be more willing to engage with a very dense graphic if it covers their area of expertise.

Appearance

The look of your infographic, from the layout to the style of your drawings to the colors, should also be tailored to your audience. Earlier in this section, we touch on the example of a rocket infographic that appeals to rocket scientists versus one for children. You would expect a clear contrast in how each version looks. The graphic for scientists might feature cutaway photos or drawings detailing the rocket's engines. It would probably feature a relatively large amount of text, written at a college reading level. By comparison, the art for the children's graphic would be simple, perhaps even cartoonish, with only the major parts of the rocket labeled. You'd want to keep the text extremely simple.

Obviously, most infographics don't face such a stark choice between audiences, but the point is that you need to think of what's going to attract — and please — your reader's eye.

To use another example, a chart showing the performance of the U.S. stock market that's running on an irreverent news site isn't going to look the same as it would if it were running in a venerable financial journal. The whole visual feel of the two charts should be different even though they contain the exact same information.

Getting the Logistics

How you intend to distribute your infographic is another matter to consider. Most graphics today are published online, which is relatively inexpensive and immediate, making your work easily shareable with a wide audience. In some cases, however, printing your graphic may be the preferred way to distribute it, like if you want to release it as a flyer or poster, or are publishing it in a newspaper or magazine.

Each format comes with its own set of variables to think about as you prepare to publish, and in this section, we go over some of the basics you need to know. Being aware of your size specifications now can help you focus your work.

Why do you need to worry about this while you're determining your thesis? Well, remember that infographics must explain information as clearly and concisely as possible. One of the smartest ways to make sure your graphic gets to the point without taking up unnecessary bandwidth is to continuously review whether all graphic components support your thesis.

Printing considerations

Unless you have professional printing equipment in your home or office, creating a professional-quality print of your graphic is a little more complicated than just clicking the Print command on your computer or printer. You have to take your work to a printing house, which entails being able to explain to the printer exactly what you want. This section will cover some of the variables you should be prepared to contend with.

One note before we move on: Speak to the folks at your printer ahead of time to see whether their shop has specific requirements for the digital file you're printing from or certain limitations regarding what they're able to do. You may want your infographic printed on a long banner for a medical sales booth, but they don't have a printer that can handle the job. Or, you may be banking on heavy card stock that they don't have. You can save a great deal of time and effort if you're prepared for such issues *before* you try to print your work, so the first step is always to talk to them about your needs.

Print size

Obviously, the size of your poster or print can vary quite a bit. If you don't have a specific requirement or a particular size in mind, you may find it helpful to consider one of the standard poster sizes you'll find at most copy shops that do digital printing. The sizes in Table 4-1, which includes both inches and millimeters, are typically available.

Table 4-1		Common Paper Sizes for Digital Printing
Inches (in)	*Millimeters (mm)*	*Details*
8.5 x 11	216 x 279	Basic letter size; used for flyers
11 x 17	279 x 432	Ledger size; good for small posters
18 x 24	457 x 610	Popular medium size for posters

Inches (in)	Millimeters (mm)	Details
24 x 36	610 x 914	Common size for large posters used in marketing
27 x 40	686 x 1016	Called "one sheet"; standard size for movie posters in North America
36 x 48	914 x 1219	Very large poster (used for banners and the like)

By no means are you limited to the sizes in Table 4-1. In fact, if you're hiring a professional printing house, the size you can print at is limited only by the size of its presses. Most will have no problem printing a poster up to 40" (1,016mm) wide, not to mention any increment up to that width. Also, because the paper for these presses comes in a roll, you can make the length essentially anything you want (with limitations, of course; talk to your printer).

If you find that neither digital printing nor a printing press suits your needs, and you require something capable of printing even larger, you can always seek out a large-format inkjet printer. In North America, commercial copy centers (such as FedEx Office and Staples) often have them, and they can print up to about 60" (1,524mm) in width. And again, because the paper used comes in a roll, the length available to you is virtually endless. Depending on the colors you use and what material you print on, price can range from about $7 to $30 per square foot.

These larger shops, or local sign-making businesses, are also a good option if you're printing your work on a medium other than paper, such as mylar, canvas, or film positives.

Image size/resolution

You need to size your graphic according to what the actual print size will be. You also need to know the print resolution in dots per inch (dpi) that you want to print at. A publication like a newspaper typically prints at a resolution of 200 dpi or less, a regular magazine might print at 300 dpi, and a glossy magazine or photography book could print at a resolution of 2,400 dpi. The decision depends on where your graphic will appear and how crisp and clear you want or need the image to be. Again, this is yet another topic to discuss with your printer before you send a file.

After determining the final print size and resolution, the graphic should be sized at 100% in the document for printing.

File format

Check what file types the printer accepts. Among the most widely used are AI, EPS, JPG/JPEG, and PDF files. The GIF format is good for basic web graphics with simple animation.

Several other types include PNG, which is good for smaller file sizes, as well as TIFF and BMP files. These less-common file types might have to be converted before you submit them.

Fonts

One variable you should check with your printer is any nonstandard font that isn't embedded in your infographic. If your printer doesn't have that font, they can't print your infographic as you designed it. If the font is embedded like an image, though, it won't be an issue. You don't have to worry about this with rasterized files, for example. We explain more on this subject when we discuss Photoshop and Illustrator in Chapters 9 through 11.

If the font isn't embedded, you may have to include it with the file containing your infographic that you send to your printer. Be aware, however, that many nonstandard fonts are under license, which means that you're technically not supposed to distribute them, regardless of whether you paid for the font. Sometimes it's a good idea to have a backup font in mind in case the printing issue can't be quickly resolved.

Bleed

If your image goes to the edge of the poster or print, you need to be sure to extend your image past what will be its actual size. That extended print area is called "bleed," and the printer trims off the extra, leaving a clean edge. What you don't want is to end up with blank space between your infographic and the edge of the page or poster. Bleed requirements vary by printer, but 3mm — about one-fifth of an inch — is generally the minimum.

Web dimensions

The challenge of sizing a graphic for the web is design sizes are now so variable, there are no standards to speak of. The "responsive design" brought about with the advent of HTML5 changed the web design landscape permanently. Unlike a printed graphic, where everyone who sees it experiences it in the same size, the actual size of a web graphic changes depending on the readers' devices. A device screen can range from 27" for a desktop computer to 5" for a smartphone.

Always optimize for *your* audience. Use web analytics software to determine how people are accessing your site and base your decisions on that data.

That said, you do need to think about a few elements when you're publishing work online.

Screen aspect ratio

Responsive design is the web design principle that tries to make visual images clear and legible across a wide range of devices. For an infographic designer, the beauty of this approach is that your work will automatically fit itself to the screen it's viewed on. As a designer, you don't need to come up with one aspect ratio for work that will be seen on a laptop and another adapted to smartphones. The increasing use of HTML technology has made responsive design a standard. We touch on HTML and CSS in other chapters; just know that you don't have to be a programmer to use and benefit from these technologies. Phasing this technology into your work will make it much more accessible and readable and will certainly be a valuable job skill for you as an infographic designer.

If you're not using responsive design, think of where your target audience will be viewing your infographic and work backward from there. If most of your readers are getting your material on a specific platform or screen proportion, you design with that in mind.

Users don't always want to scroll down to see more, so think of what information you want your readers to see when they first look at your infographic.

For work that needs to be scaled for concurrent print and web use — say you work at a newspaper, and your infographic will run in both the print edition and online at that website — stick to using vector files. They'll make it easy for you to scale your work.

Screen resolution

One of the most common and basic questions asked in website design is what monitor screen resolution to use. The somewhat unhelpful answer is that your work should be optimized for the most common resolution, but it should work for all of them. On the other hand, no design exists that looks the same in every resolution, platform, and browser, so creating one isn't a realistic goal. What you're aiming for is a balance — something that looks perfect under the most common conditions and still looks really good in less typical conditions.

The website StatCounter monitors statistics on a variety of factors you may find useful, including the top screen resolutions, mobile resolutions, and browsers in use. You can find those statistics at `http://gs.statcounter.com`.

Always check your work by looking at it in different browsers and resizing the browser windows to see how your work looks under different conditions. And always design with your audience in mind. For example, if you know the target audience mostly uses mobile devices, design with mobile in mind.

Type point (size)

You always need to be aware of how legible the type in your work will be when people view it. Text has to be large enough and clear enough that people can read it. Common design standards dictate that body type shouldn't be smaller than 10 points (pt), and it's recommended in most cases to use 12pt or 14pt type. Many web design purists are now even calling for a 16pt minimum.

If your body type is between 12 and 16 points, scale up and down from there to determine the size for headlines, footnotes, and other features. So, your headline might be about 24pt type (or larger if it's a big graphic and needs a large headline). Footnotes will probably be 8pt type.

In Illustrator, you can test what your work will look like before exporting. From the View menu at the top of your Illustrator window, choose the Actual Size option to get a good sense of how your work will look when published. That way, you can check whether your type will be large enough to see clearly. You can also choose File➪Save for Web for work you intend to publish online. You find out much more about Illustrator in Chapter 9.

No matter what the characteristics of your infographic, you should keep these three questions in mind:

- ✔ Is my key information visible when readers first navigate to my graphic?
- ✔ Can readers easily read the text on the page?
- ✔ Does it look right under a variety of conditions, on different screen sizes and resolutions, and when viewed through different browsers?

New technologies debut all the time, and keeping up with them is virtually impossible. Getting some working knowledge of HTML and CSS can help designers make sure that their content continues to be legible and attractive even after technology marches on. If you had to answer "no" to any of the preceding questions, head back to the drawing board.

5

Gathering Your Data

In This Chapter

▶ Finding data on the Internet

▶ Making sure data sources are reliable

▶ Turning data into relevant information

A good infographic can visually tell a story or make some abstract or numerical point easy to understand, but none of this happens without a good base of data. Data is the underlying structure that gives shape to everything else — the skeleton on which hangs the flesh of design. It's the — well, you get the idea.

In his hugely influential first book, *The Visual Display of Quantitative Information*, famed infographic guru Edward Tufte wrote that the "overwhelming fact of data graphics is that they stand or fall on their content, gracefully displayed." In his philosophy, visual ornamentation, no matter how skillfully done or meticulously realized, should never get in the way of a graphic's real purpose: conveying information. He even coined the term *chartjunk* to refer to all that extraneous visual noise that can clutter up a graphic and distract from the point.

Being an efficient researcher is its own skill, but it's not a difficult one to hone. For the most part, researching involves knowing where — and how — to look. This chapter covers some of the best ways to gather and pull together the data you need to create the foundation of your infographic — and you'll find much of what you need online.

Searching Online

The single most powerful tool in a researcher's toolbox today is the Internet. That fact may be obvious to everyone, but not so long ago, you needed a trip to an actual office or library to find the data you wanted. So no matter what information you're looking for — whether it's a government database, a newspaper article, or an academic paper — make the Internet the first step in your search.

The Internet runs a large number of search engines, including some specialized ones that could benefit you if you're doing very targeted research. For example, quora.com is a terrific search engine that focuses on technology; artcyclopedia. com provides a wealth of information on art and artists. General-purpose search engines include Bing, ask.com, and Yahoo. But, king of them all is Google.

Doing simple Google searches

The Internet search market still bows before Google. The name itself has become a verb — as in, "*Just Google it*" — placing Google alongside the likes of companies like Xerox and Band-Aid whose brands are synonymous with a whole category of product. And for good reason, too, because Google is still widely considered the best online search option available.

Perhaps the best thing about Google is how easy it is to use. It ignores capitalization and punctuation, so no need to worry about that. It also has a built in spell-checker and will automatically search for the correct spelling, which can be helpful if you're looking for, say, statistics on appendectomies and forget that the word is spelled with two *p*'s. Google doesn't do all the work for you, though. To use it effectively, you need to keep a few basic principles in mind. Here are some helpful tips that will get you the search results you're looking for:

- ✓ **Keep it simple.** Avoid using unnecessary words. You don't need to search on a complete sentence. In fact, doing so can result in Google looking for words that aren't important. Also, the simpler your search, the broader the results will be. If it turns out to be too broad (too many hits), you can later add additional terms to narrow the results. Another highly effective way of narrowing your search is to put quotes around the exact term you're looking up. For example, a search for "John Quincy Adams" will prominently display information specifically about him. Typing *john quincy adams,* without quotes, will get you some of the information you need, but it will turn up lots of extraneous information, too.

- ✓ **Use linguistically appropriate search terms.** In other words, think about the sources most likely to have the information you want and what terminology and jargon they use. Those are the terms you need to search for. A government or medical database, for instance, will probably use more technical language: for example, searching on "influenza" rather than "flu."

- ✓ **Be exact in your phrasing.** If you want to know how many people are murdered each year in Hawaii, *murder* is one of the terms you need to search for. Using terms that are close may not actually get you the data you want. For example, looking for *death rate* is much too broad; *crime* is better but still too general given the very specific figure you are looking for.

- ✓ **Employ some creative thinking.** Ask yourself whether there are ways to find what you want by using other terms. If you're looking for data on murders in Hawaii, you could also search with the term *by state*. What you find may not be restricted to just Hawaii, but Hawaii's figures should be included.

The rise of Internet advertising and search-engine optimization calls for some critical reading skills. When you do a Google search, "results" at the side of the page are advertisements. The "results" that have tiny yellow boxes with the word "ad" in them? Those, too, are ads. Some of them may, in fact, turn out to be decent sources, but bear in mind that someone paid to put them there. Google is good about sniffing out the best content to display high in its search results, but you need to be on the ball, too.

Here are a few examples of searches you might enter to find that information:

- *How many people are killed per year in Hawaii:* Not good. This string isn't exact enough. People are killed by causes other than murder, so this search doesn't focus on murder. In fact, the top results are all about shark attacks.

- *How many people murdered per year Hawaii:* Getting closer. At least now the search specifies "murder." But it's still too wordy and isn't using the best language possible.

- *Murder rate Hawaii:* Great. The search string is simple and directly to the point, using the terminology likely found in a government database, which is the best source for this sort of information. Compared with the previous two search strings, this one returns the best results.

- *Murder rate by state:* Also great. The same merits of the preceding bullet apply here as well, only this version uses a little creative thinking to come up with different search terms that will still get you the information you want.

Talk the talk

Many fields (think medicine and economics) have their own jargon that will be helpful to know when conducting good web searches or understanding what you're looking at when you find a data set. For example, in medicine, the number of new cases of a disease in a given time frame is its *incidence,* and the proportion of a population that has the disease is *preva-lence.* Luckily, good glossaries are available online (and here are three) that can help you decipher this sort of language. If you need a glossary for a different field, usually searching on "glossary *field* terms" will find it.

- **Medical terms:** Centers for Disease Control and Prevention (CDC)

  www.cdc.gov/excite/library/glossary.htm

- **Economic terms:** Organisation for Economic Co-operation and Development (OECD)

  http://stats.oecd.org/glossary/index.htm

- **Demographic terms:** U.S. Census Bureau

  www.census.gov/glossary

Refining your Google searches

You can use the filter options Google gives you on your search results page to search for images, include maps, and find items available for sale. Additionally, you can employ specialized search terms to refine your searches and further narrow your results. Figure 5-1 shows the toolbar on the Google search results page with the following filter options:

- **Web:** This shows you all the results Google was able to find on the Web.

- **Images:** Shows pages of only images from your regular search, including photos and logos.

  Note: Google has a "usage rights" feature that shows you whether images are acceptable for public use or protected by copyright. Use it carefully — sometimes, an image that Google thinks is appropriate for reuse was actually stolen or misrepresented.

- **Maps:** With this filter selected, Google will place your search results on one of its satellite maps. For example, searching for preschools in a particular city will show several preschools on the map.

- **Shopping:** This organizes search results in terms of retail possibilities. For example, a search for used Mac computers will show a list of various products, with links to the websites where you can purchase them. If you were trying to research used Mac computers, but not purchase one, this type of search probably wouldn't be your best bet.

- **Books:** This filter turns up a list of books about your topic, which could be very helpful if you're working on a long-term project and have time to buy and read a book.

- **More:** This drop-down menu lets you choose from a few other filters, including apps, videos, news coverage, and more.

- **Search Tools:** Within any search results page, Search Tools further refines your search results by additional factors. For example, while using the Images filter, clicking Search Tools provides choices that let you specify the size and color of the images you want to see.

At the top right of the Google search results page, you'll see a few additional features, which let you set some privacy and web safety standards. Spend a little time experimenting with these, and you'll find the setup that works best for your needs.

Google is so vast that it can be very helpful to learn a few tricks to target your searches. By adding some select phrases or commands, you can help Google narrow the results so that you're more likely to get exactly the information you need.

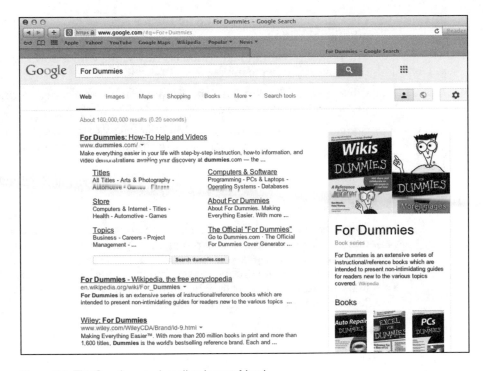

Figure 5-1: The Google search toolbar is your friend.

✔ **Search for an exact phrase.** Put quotation marks around your terms to search for that exact phrase with the words in that exact order. So, in our running Hawaiian crime example, typing "'murder rate' Hawaii" may be even better than "murder rate Hawaii."

✔ **Exclude or include words in your search.** If you want a specific term omitted from your search results, place a hyphen (-) in front of it. If you want Google to find a particular word that it normally ignores — such as *and* or *the* — put it in quotation marks, such as *murder rate Hawaii "and" 1985*. You may already be familiar with some advanced Google Search options, but if you happen to be a novice, here's a couple we find unique.

Searching within a time range

Follow these steps to search within a defined time period.

1. **Do a simple search for whatever you're looking for.**

   See the previous section for information related to a simple search.

   Just below the search box, on the page showing your results, is the Google search toolbar (refer to Figure 5-1).

2. **Click the Search Tools option (at the far right of the toolbar) to see additional options.**

   The first of the additional options is Any Time, with a down arrow indicating a drop-down menu.

3. **Click to open the Any Time drop-down menu and choose a time period to limit your search.**

   Google offers various options, including Past 24 Hours and Past Year. Or you can choose the Custom Range option and set a custom time frame.

The refined search results appear automatically after you choose an option.

Searching for page types

Yet another type of advanced search allows you to search for specific types of pages. For instance, you can search just U.S. patents or limit your results to scholarly papers on a topic. You can find all these search options, as shown in Figure 5-2, on the Google Products page under the Specialized Search heading. To reach the Products page, click the About Google link at the bottom of any Google page and then click the Products link. The URL for the Products page is

```
www.google.com/intl/en/about/products/index.html.
```

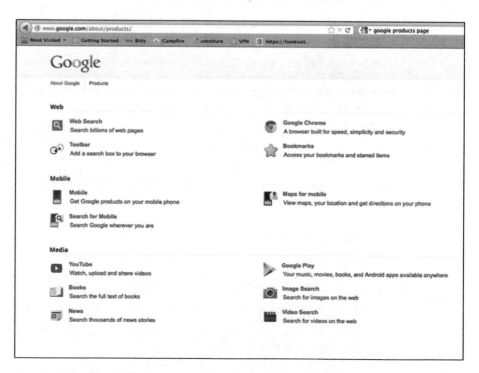

Figure 5-2: The Google Products page offers a variety of different search options.

Finding Additional Sources

Just because Google (or whatever search engine you choose) lists a page as its top result doesn't mean it's the best source for the information you want. Don't misconstrue its search ranking as an endorsement of its content. Google has taken steps to reward great websites with prominent placement, which in itself weeds out sites that rely on search-engine trickery. But the system is far from perfect, so you'll need to train yourself to find other accurate and relevant sources.

Watch out for *content farms,* or *content mills,* that exist specifically to game the online searching system. They generate huge numbers of articles on all sorts of subjects and use headlines, keywords, and other tricks to get their articles into the top search results. All the clicks they earn from that prominent placement bring in revenue. Not every article from a content farm will be full of falsehoods, but being accurate is not their top priority, so they're generally best to avoid. It helps that Google works constantly to weed them out.

A word on Wikipedia

Wikipedia ranks among the top results for many searches, but the accuracy of its information has been the subject of a great deal of debate over the years. In fact, countless news organizations and publishers have strict policies in place that prohibit reporters using Wikipedia as a source. Pretty much anyone can write or edit an article on Wikipedia, so there's no way to ensure that what you're reading is accurate. In theory, letting just about anyone edit pages allows inaccuracies to be corrected as soon as they're spotted — but that doesn't always happen.

In a somewhat bizarre incident in 2012, Philip Roth took to the pages of *The New Yorker* to address an error in Wikipedia's entry on his novel "The Human Stain." Roth, through an official intermediary, had previously petitioned Wikipedia to delete the error. Wikipedia responded that although Roth was obviously an authority on his own book, his word was not enough. They needed secondary sources as well. Evidently without any other recourse, Roth made his grievance public.

Still, studies have found that Wikipedia's error rate isn't significantly greater than that of supposedly authoritative encyclopedias. And, in some instances, Wikipedia may (in fact) offer a thorough and accurate overview of a topic. The problem is that you just can't be sure, and rather than trust Wikipedia more because its error rate is commensurate with those of other encyclopedias, we should really trust those other encyclopedias less. No matter your source, checking your facts is absolutely crucial, and having more than one reputable source is a good way to guarantee the accuracy of your work.

Wikipedia does have its uses, however. The site does a good job of allowing its authors and editors to link to the sources of their information in footnotes, and those links can offer a researcher valuable leads. So if you do use Wikipedia, think of it as an avenue to get to the information you want — just not a source unto itself.

So, how to do your own weeding? Well, there's no simple way to know whether a page is reliable — although, if you see the same text word-for-word turn up on a few pages, that's usually a good indicator it was created by a farm. You have to use your discretion. If you have any doubts about any source, read up on it. If you find good data but aren't sure you can trust it, try to find another source to verify it. If you still have doubts, follow your gut and don't use the information.

Discovering government databases

The world's governments and intergovernmental organizations maintain databases on all sorts of statistics. Demographic, economic, health, and cultural data for countless countries are available online for anyone interested. Assuming the information you're seeking isn't too obscure, you can probably find it.

Here's a list of useful governmental and intergovernmental databases and where they can be found online. A select few university pages have also been included. The University of Florida's library, for instance, has compiled links to the central statistical offices of many countries, organized by region.

- **African Union Economics Division:** Economic statistics for the African Union

  http://ea.au.int/en/statistics

- **Asian Development Bank:** Economic statistics for Asia

  www.adb.org/data/statistics

- **Asia-Pacific Economic Cooperation:** Economic statistics for several countries bordering the Pacific Ocean

  http://statistics.apec.org

- **Bureau of Justice Statistics:** U.S. criminal justice data

  www.bjs.gov

- **Bureau of Labor Statistics:** U.S. labor data

  www.bls.gov

- **Bureau of Economic Analysis:** U.S. economic data

  www.bea.gov

  U.S. Census Bureau: Statistical data on the U.S. population

  www.census.gov

- **U.S. Census Bureau, International Data:** Statistics on the world's countries

  www.census.gov/population/international

- **U.S. Census Bureau, Statistical Abstract of the United States:** Statistical portrait of the United States, compiled each year

  www.census.gov/compendia/statab

- **Census of Population and Housing:** Census information in the United States, dating back to 1790

  www.census.gov/prod/www/decennial.html

- **Centers for Disease Control and Prevention (CDC):** U.S. disease and illness data

  www.cdc.gov/datastatistics

- **CDC, National Center for Health Statistics (NCHS):** U.S. health data

  www.cdc.gov/nchs

- **Congressional Budget Office (CBO):** U.S. budget information

  www.cbo.gov

- **U.S. Energy Information Administration:** U.S. energy information

  www.eia.gov

- **European Commission (Eurostat):** Statistics on Europe's nations

  http://epp.eurostat.ec.europa.eu/portal/page/portal/eurostat/home

- **The Federal Bureau of Investigation (FBI):** U.S. crime statistics

  www.fbi.gov/stats-services/crimestats

- **Federal Reserve System:** U.S. financial statistics

  www.federalreserve.gov/econresdata/releases/statisticsdata.htm

- **FedStats:** "One-stop shop" for U.S. public data

  www.fedstats.gov

- **Food and Agriculture Organization of the United Nations:** Data on world food and agriculture

  www.fao.org/statistics/en

- **U.S. Department of Health & Human Services:** U.S. healthcare data

  http://healthdata.gov

- **Historical Census Browser:** Data browser for U.S. census stats going back to 1790

  http://mapserver.lib.virginia.edu

- **Inter-American Development Bank:** Stats on Latin America and the Caribbean

  www.iadb.org/en/research-and-data/statistics-and-databases,3161.html

- **International Energy Agency:** World energy data

  www.iea.org/statistics

- **International Monetary Fund (IMF):** Global economic and financial data

  www.imf.org/external/data.htm

- **International Labour Organization:** World labor stats

  www.ilo.org/global/statistics-and-databases/lang--en/index.htm

- **Inter-university Consortium for Social and Political Research:** Public data curator

  www.icpsr.umich.edu/index.html

- **Statistical, Economic and Social Research and Training Centre for Islamic Countries (SESRIC):** Economic data on the world's Islamic nations

  www.sesric.org/databases-index.php

- **United Nations Children's Fund (UNICEF):** Information on the well-being of the world's children

  www.unicef.org/statistics/index.html

- **United Nations Economic Commission for Europe:** Assorted data on Europe, including economic and infrastructure stats

  http://w3.unece.org/pxweb

- **United Nations Economic and Social Commission for Asia and the Pacific:** Economic and social information on Asia and the Pacific

  www.unescap.org

- **United Nations Educational, Scientific, and Cultural Organization (UNESCO):** Global data on education, science, technology, and culture

  www.uis.unesco.org/Pages/default.aspx

- **United Nations Industrial Development Organization (UNIDO):** Stats on global economic growth and business

  www.unido.org/resources/statistics/statistical-databases.html

- **The United Nations Refugee Agency (UNHCR):** Information on the world's refugees

  www.unhcr.org/pages/49c3646c4d6.html

✔ **United Nations Statistics Division:** Main database of the U.N., containing a variety of global stats

`http://unstats.un.org/unsd/default.htm`

✔ **University of Florida George A. Smathers Libraries:** Aggregated links to many country's databases organized by region

`www.uflib.ufl.edu/docs/int_statistics.html`

✔ **The World Bank:** Data on global industry, business, and trade

`http://data.worldbank.org`

✔ **World Health Organization (WHO):** Statistics on health and disease around the world

`www.who.int/gho/en`

The greatest obstacle in your search may be navigating the database itself. For example, the website of the U.S. Census Bureau can feel maddeningly mazelike to the uninitiated. It contains so many pages filled with so much information that knowing where to start can be daunting — particularly difficult if you're looking for historical data and need to compare reports from various years. When that happens, sometimes there's no recourse but to call the U.S. Census Bureau and ask for assistance. Its public relations department can often connect you with an expert who can lead you through the virtual hedge maze.

Using company resources

A number of private companies and nonprofits exist that specialize in data. Some focus on a particular topic, such as the income gap between the world's rich and poor, and others are generalists. Many of these sources use information from the government or intergovernmental databases in the previous section, but they sometimes offer analysis or a different perspective on the information. They can also make what you're looking for easy to find.

As opposed to the many government databases that can seem geared toward specialists or people within the government, these sites are intended for public use. That means they're designed to be accessible, and they can prove a valuable resource to a journalist, especially on a deadline. Here's a sampling of some of the best:

✔ **datacatalogs.org:** Links to the open data catalogs for various cities and towns around the world. If you want to know how to find the public database of Ann Arbor, Michigan, or Venice, Italy, this is a great place to look.

`http://datacatalogs.org`

✔ **DataMarket:** Aggregates public data and makes it easily searchable. The site organizes data in a few ways, including by country and industry, which is useful if you're looking for stats on a sector (such as retail or the auto industry) but aren't sure what's available.

`http://datamarket.com`

✔ **Gapminder:** A terrific resource if you're looking for anything related to development. You can sort data in several ways and look at what's available on subjects such as causes of child deaths, poverty and inequality, and population growth.

`www.gapminder.org`

✔ **Harvard WorldMap:** Run by the Center for Geographic Analysis at Harvard University, it allows users to create maps of any location in the world or to view maps submitted by other users.

`http://worldmap.harvard.edu`

✔ **Influence Explorer:** Tracks money as it flows through Washington, DC. It allows users to search detailed records on topics such as lobbying dollars, earmarks, and who has received what contracts.

`http://data.influenceexplorer.com`

✔ **Knoema:** Lets you search for stats on a wide variety of topics, from African tourism to European patent applications. You can browse by topic, data source, and region, or use its search engine if you know what you're after.

`http://knoema.com`

Sometimes the issue isn't finding data but analyzing it. If you have a vast spreadsheet of figures in front of you, the hard part is often making sense of it all. Thankfully, websites specialize in performing statistical calculations and offer users ways to organize and analyze messy datasets. The following sites are worth checking out to see whether they work for you:

✔ **Stanford University DataWrangler**

`http://vis.stanford.edu/wrangler`

✔ **StatPages**

`http://statpages.org/javasta2.html#Freebies`

✔ **StatCrunch**

`www.statcrunch.com`

Reading company reports

If you're making an infographic that involves information on a specific company, sometimes your best source is going to be the company itself. Say, for instance, you're making a chart about a public company's sales or financial performance. Public companies must make that information available, and you can get it by simply reading the company's latest financial report (available on virtually every public company's website). Or, if a drug company has just released an exciting new drug, and you're assigned to put together an infographic showing how it works, your best source is obviously going to be the company that created it.

The best place to search for this information is a company's online newsroom, alternatively called a "press room," "media room," or something in that vein. That's where many companies house public info that might be useful to a journalist. There's no single location where all companies put their newsroom on their website, but there are some general guidelines to finding it.

✔ **Go to the company's home page.** You may get lucky and find a link right at the top of the page, but if not, scroll to the bottom. Many websites have an assortment of links to less frequently accessed parts of the site all the way at the bottom of their home page.

✔ **Look for an About page.** If you still don't see a link to the newsroom, try to find a link to the company About page. Most company websites have one that functions as a catchall for general info about the company. Often you can find corporate information there as well as a link to the company's newsroom.

✔ **Search for the company name with the term "corporate."** When searching for the newsroom of certain types of companies, particularly retailers or companies that sell a product, it helps to search the term *corporate* along with the company's name. Otherwise, you'll usually come up with the company's e-commerce site or a promotional page all about its products.

Gap Inc. is a good example. A web search for *Gap* brings you to the Gap e-commerce site. If you search *GAP corporate*, the first result is its corporate page with information relevant to investors and media.

What you'll find in the newsroom is anything the company wants to share with the press, such as press releases. Some companies include a wealth of information in their newsroom, particularly if they have a product they really want to promote, so you might find everything you need for your infographic. Other companies, especially those that are privately owned, keep the data they release to a minimum, which doesn't mean the data isn't available. You'll probably have to call or send an e-mail to their press contact to get what you need.

If you can't find the name and contact information of a press contact in a company's newsroom, try looking at a few of its press releases, which frequently offer contact info for reporters looking for information.

With public companies, one resource you can usually access online is the company's financial records. Knowing how to find these statements is crucial for business journalists. For the most part, locating them is the same as locating a company's newsroom, but the page you're looking for may be called something like Investor Relations. It helps to know that large companies, such as the Ford Motor Company or General Electric, often have a dedicated corporate website (as opposed to one for consumers) where this information is readily available.

Reaching out to experts

Sometimes your best resource is going to be an actual human being with a specialized area of knowledge — in other words, an expert. That can be particularly true if you need help understanding a highly complex topic, such as quantum mechanics. Even if you're dealing in more obscure subjects, an expert can often tell you where to go if you've hit a wall in your search for information.

Finding experts isn't difficult, and generally they're willing to help. Try looking at the following sources when you find yourself in need of an authority on your topic:

- **Books:** An author who has written about the subject you're researching can be a great source of information. He may have the data you're looking for, but even if he doesn't, he'll likely know who does. If you can't find the author's direct contact info from a web search, the media relations department of the book's publisher can often get you in touch.

- **Research institutes and think tanks:** These organizations are filled with subject matter experts. Find one that has done research on your subject and contact their press department. The PR team will find the right person for you to speak to.

- **Universities:** The website of a university will have dedicated pages for their different departments, typically listing the faculty and staff within that branch. Find the department that's relevant to you, and you can often find an expert, as well as her contact information, directly through the site. If you're not sure who is your best contact, call or e-mail the department and explain what you need to see whether you can get in touch with the best person.

Placing It All Together

Finding the information was the hard part. Assembling it into a coherent infographic is just a matter of focusing it. Depending on the size of the project you're working on, that process can be very simple or take a little more effort. The guidelines that follow apply whether your project is large or small.

The larger the project, the more you'll probably find you have to work to maintain that focus.

Getting back to your thesis

The amount of information available to you can seem nearly unlimited. Not all of it, of course, is relevant to your project. You may find some surprising statistics that rock your world while you're researching; if those numbers aren't directly pertinent to the topic at hand, get rid of them. When evaluating what information to include and what to exclude from your infographic, ask yourself the following questions:

- ✒ **What is my thesis?** In other words, what point are you trying to make with this information? Hopefully, you've kept this in mind as you've collected data, but it doesn't hurt to reiterate it as you consider what should make it into your infographic.

  Read more about setting a thesis in Chapter 4.

- ✒ **Is this information directly relevant to my thesis?** Keep the data that supports the point you're making, and jettison the rest. If your thesis is that child mortality rates are higher in the developing world, including a chart on malaria rates among adults might not make sense.

- ✒ **Does this information help explain my thesis?** Statistics that don't necessarily prove your point but help explain it may be worth including. For instance, if your thesis is that child mortality is higher in the developing world, it would help to include information showing the top causes of child mortality. If one of those causes is the unavailability of clean drinking water, it may even make sense to include a chart on what percentage of the population has access to clean water.

- ✒ **Does the information bear out my thesis?** If in the process of gathering data you find statistics that contradict your thesis, you may need to revise or qualify your thesis. Keep in mind that you're acting as a journalist, and your commitment is to accuracy — not necessarily proving a foregone conclusion.

Citing your sources

Always make sure you give credit where it's due. You should name the source of every piece of information in your infographic. After all, without sources, you wouldn't have a graphic, and you could infringe on someone's copyright. When dealing with experts, ask them how they would like to be cited. Some may prefer not to be listed by name and just give their organization instead.

The standard is to list sources in order of how much information they contributed. The source that provided 90 percent of your data should get top billing over the source that contributed 10 percent. Sources can go anywhere unobtrusive, but standard practice is to put them at the bottom of your infographic and to format them in a small type point.

6

Discovering the Story

. . . .

In This Chapter

▶ Putting information in context through trend-spotting and comparing

▶ Using facts and statistics to show patterns

▶ Exploring the visual and written pieces of the narrative

. . . .

*I*nfographics traffic in data. They're made up of charts and graphs and drawings, all filled with facts and statistics and more facts. For all this data to be meaningful to readers, however, it has to tell them something worth knowing about its subject. What readers learn can be something surprising, something new, something disturbing. The graphic can show how something has changed or how the subject is likely to change in the future. The possibilities are endless. Without a story to tell, though, a fact unto itself isn't notably significant.

This chapter explores how to find the story in your facts as well as how to frame that story in your infographic. We look specifically at why trends and patterns are important, how to present data so it provides the reader with insight about a subject, and how to begin crafting a narrative flow — which has both visual and textual pieces — with your information.

Analyzing and Organizing Your Information

In Chapter 5, you can read how to gather data. Now it's time to analyze your information, pulling out the most interesting, relevant facts for your infographic. Digging through the data to find the best nuggets of information will help you craft a graphic that truly tells a story.

Looking for trends

One way to make a fact more meaningful to readers is to place it in context. For example, telling readers that the May unemployment rate in the United States is 9.4 percent doesn't provide much education or illustration on its own, as shown in Figure 6-1. Is that rate good or bad? Is unemployment getting worse or easing up?

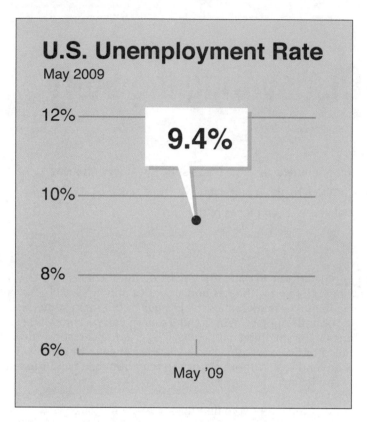

Figure 6-1: A statistic on its own doesn't help the reader understand the news.

When you place that rate on a bar graph with the unemployment rates of an entire year, though, a picture of economic health begins to develop: a trend (see Figure 6-2).

Some trends reveal themselves easily. Any numbers collected at regular intervals — such as state or national economic data, education statistics, demographic information, and certain medical and scientific data — can be used to show a trend. Here are some examples of data that can easily reveal trends:

- Government spending
- Voter turnout
- Birth and death rates
- Employment rates
- Household and individual income

- ✔ Mortgage rates
- ✔ College enrollment
- ✔ Recycling rates

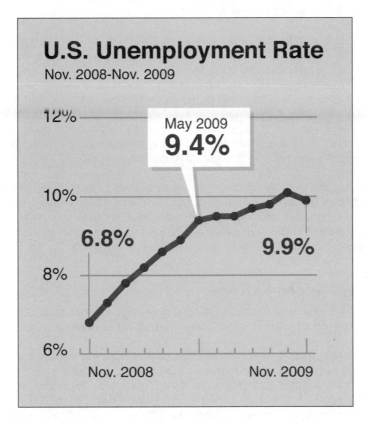

Figure 6-2: By charting statistics over time, you can see a trend developing.

Government agencies are a rich source of this type of data, and many of them update their statistics every month, making it easy to see trends developing. As a de facto reporter, though, you can and should seek out information from more than one source. At times, you'll be able to find links between the data offered by various agencies. You might need to create your own database to compare these two seemingly disparate figures.

For instance, the U.S. Federal Reserve System releases information on consumer debt each quarter. Referring to the unemployment rate example in Figure 6-2, correlating that chart with consumer-debt statistics may reveal something interesting about Americans' spending habits. Are Americans spending less as unemployment rises or are they resorting to debt because more people are without regular paychecks? Or is there no apparent relationship?

Don't try to force a relationship into your infographic. Let the data prove your point, not the other way around.

The big takeaway here is that looking for trends and charting them graphically can help a researcher craft a compelling narrative by posing and answering questions based on data.

When you present a correlation between two trends, be sure that a concrete link actually exists. Just because two trends occur at the same time doesn't necessarily mean that they're related. Do your research and make certain what you're saying has a basis in fact, using clear language so the reader knows exactly the relation between two trends.

In that vast sea of data out there, navigating it isn't always easy. When you're looking for patterns and connections, make certain that your comparisons and correlations are accurate. When in doubt, interview an expert. All those agencies we mentioned have media relations officers who can clear up your questions or connect you with experts who can help you.

Employing comparisons

Context is everything. Readers can't form opinions about issues and won't feel well informed without having information for comparison.

Here's an example. How much does the United States spend on elementary education each year? Say the total is $250 million. To the average person, that's a lot of money, and to be sure, if you found this deposited into your checking account, you'd be having a pretty good day. But on the scale of a government with 300 million citizens, is $250 million *really* a lot of money? To figure that out, you could compare education spending in America with spending on other areas, such as defense, healthcare, and more. Say you found out that America spends $500 million yearly on healthcare. That's twice the amount spent on education. Now, in context, the amount spent on education seems smaller.

And take a moment to think about why comparing these budgets adds meaning. These numbers aren't just dollar amounts — they're about priorities. Comparing how much a government spends on different sectors suggests something about where that government places value. If you compare the budgets of different presidential administrations, you wouldn't just have a picture of their financial behavior; you'd also have a sense of what each administration thinks is important. That level of meaning — that *story* — isn't evident without making a comparison.

Using the right comparison

You need to think of all the variables potentially involved in any comparison you make. Otherwise, you run the risk of saying something misleading or inaccurate. You can avoid that mistake, however, by making sure you use the right comparison.

To give an example, put the hypothetical U.S. education budget into a global context. How does the $250 million spent annually by the United States stack up against other countries? If you found out that Japan spends only $200 million annually, it would seem that America spends — and thus, by suggestion, also *values* — education more than Japan does, which is what Figure 6-3 implies

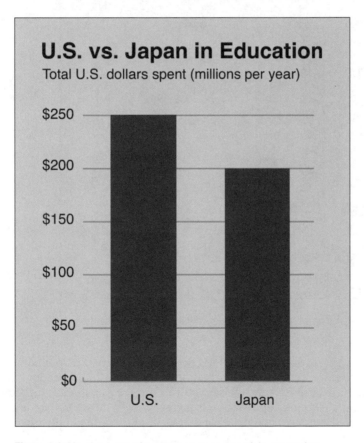

Figure 6-3: Numbers out of context present an unfair comparison.

But is that really a fair comparison? After all, Japan's population is about one-third that of the U.S. population. So, although the Japanese government spends less on education in *absolute terms,* it actually spends far more *per person* (per capita), which is shown in Figure 6-4.

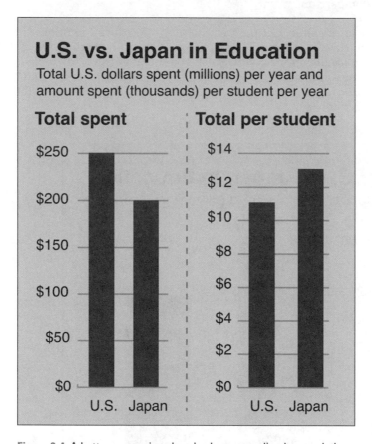

U.S. vs. Japan in Education

Total U.S. dollars spent (millions) per year and amount spent (thousands) per student per year

Total spent

Total per student

Figure 6-4: A better comparison breaks down spending by population.

Always strive to use numbers that take context, such as a country's population, into account. That way, the information you present to the reader offers real insight and doesn't create a false picture. Using per capita information rather than absolute totals, for instance, is a great way to create a more accurate comparison between two countries, or states, or cities. You get the idea.

Many databases keep per capita figures. Even if they don't, determining this data isn't difficult. The formula is simply the amount in question divided by the population.

amount/population = amount per capita

Here's a simple, real-life example to figure out the U.S. national *gross domestic product* (GDP), which is the total value of all goods and services produced by a given country.

Follow these steps to calculate a per capita figure:

1. **Find the amount in question for which you want to find the per capita figure.**

   In this case, the U.S. GDP is $15,600,000,000,000, according to the World Bank.

2. **Determine the population of the given country, state, or city.**

   The U.S. population is 316,000,000, according to the U.S. Census Bureau.

3. **Apply this formula:**

   amount/population = amount per capita

   $15,600,000,000,000/316,000,000 = $49,367 per capita

Understanding why the right comparison matters

So what story does this per capita figure have to tell, and why is it more revealing than absolute GDP? Well, America has by far the world's largest GDP, but it has only the tenth highest per capita GDP. This means that relative to other countries, the American economy is not the strongest. Without figuring out the right number to use and then employing a comparison, this story wouldn't be at all evident.

Thinking about history

The biggest cause of death of Americans since 1921 is heart disease (see Figure 6-5), according to the Centers for Disease Control and Prevention. In that same time frame, pneumonia and influenza (combined) fell from the second-leading cause of death to ninth. The riddle is discovering why. Did humans suddenly become less susceptible to such infections or more susceptible to other infections? Or did something else intervene?

Of course, scientists have developed effective treatments that have vastly improved doctors' abilities to treat and cure those conditions. Now, a bout of pneumonia is no longer a death sentence for most people.

Top Ten Causes of Death
United States, 1920 and 2011

1920	2011
❶ Pneumonia and influenza	❶ Heart disease
❷ Heart disease	❷ Cancer
❸ Tuberculosis	❸ Chronic lower respiratory disease
❹ Stroke	❹ Stroke
❺ Nephritis	❺ Accidents
❻ Cancer	❻ Alzheimer's disease
❼ Accidents	❼ Diabetes
❽ Diarrhea and enteritis	❽ Nephritis
❾ Premature birth	❾ Pneumonia and influenza
❿ Puerperal causes	❿ Suicide

Source: Centers for Disease Control and Prevention

Figure 6-5: This infographic illustrates changes over time in causes of death in the U.S.

Any major shift over time should prompt you to ask, "Why?" On the 2011 list of causes of death, you can see multiple conditions usually related to age: cancer, stroke, and Alzheimer's disease. Is this change related to longer lifespans? More exposure to toxins in the environment? And note that premature birth dropped off the list entirely. Is that thanks to better family planning or better obstetric care overall? Suicide is now a leading cause of death. Are U.S. citizens becoming more depressed people? Considering historical developments can help you shape the graphic you're presently working on and generate ideas for future projects.

Asking "Why?" is how you find the story in this sort of data. The answers you discover can help you turn your infographic into an engrossing picture of historic changes that your reader can pore over at length. The feeling your reader gets of being both educated and entertained is one of the main charms of a great infographic.

Finding the outliers

Some data points — known as *outliers* — lay so far outside the norm as to call attention to themselves. In the most severe cases, they can even skew data and create a misleading picture of the subject. You need to recognize when you have an outlier and then decide what to do about it.

Table 6-1 contains a simple example to demonstrate this idea. The two data-sets represent a student's grades, for eight weeks, on two weekly exams; the numbers are the percent correct on the exam. The dataset on the left (the first exam) doesn't contain an outlier, but the dataset on the right (the second exam) does. The one outlier is shown in bold.

Table 6-1	Weekly Exam Grades	
Week	*Grades (no outlier)*	*Grades (one outlier)*
1	90%	90%
2	88%	88%
3	90%	90%
4	85%	**50%**
5	86%	86%
6	87%	87%
7	85%	85%
8	84%	84%
Average	87%	83%

The average in the middle column paints quite an accurate picture of that student's achievement in regular testing. The single (bold) outlier (50%) in the dataset on the right throws a wrench into the works, though, dropping the student's average by four percentage points and skewing the data.

What does a data journalist do in such a case? Here are a few options:

✔ **Throw out the outlier.** If you're using only the average in your graphic and are concerned that it's misleading, eliminate the outlier as an aberration and then calculate the average without that week, as shown in Figure 6-6. In this example, throwing out the outlier would mean this student's average test score jumps up to 87%, which (as the first column shows) is a better representation of achievement over the term.

If you go with this option, be sure to add a footnote explaining everything: in this case, the deletion of a data point. Always be as transparent as possible.

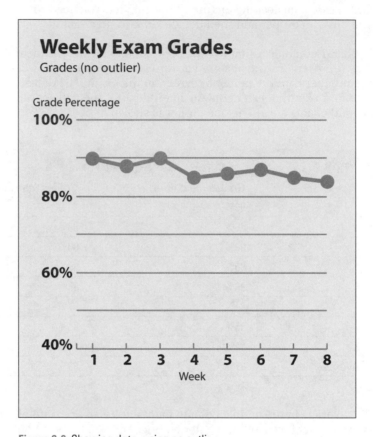

Figure 6-6: Showing data, using no outlier.

✔ **Show the data as-is.** Whether you're using just the average in your graphic or plotting all the data in a chart, you can always present the data exactly as it came to you, as shown in Figure 6-7.

In this case, we also recommend adding a footnote calling out the outlier so that your reader is fully aware of it.

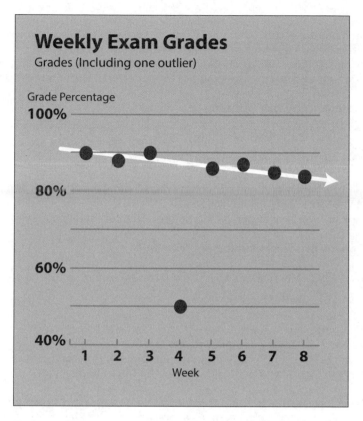

Weekly Exam Grades

Grades (Including one outlier)

Figure 6-7: Using an outlier can change the whole story.

> ✔ **Construct a "line of best fit."** This option applies only if you're going to create a chart showing all the data. A line of best fit — also called a *linear regression* — is a visual average of your data: literally the line that represents your scattered data points best.

Recognizing patterns

The human brain naturally seeks out patterns. Even your ability to read this sentence is thanks to your brain being trained to recognize letters arranged in particular patterns as words.

Spotting patterns is vital to creating compelling content for infographics because patterns point to a layer of meaning behind the data and suggest the presence of an underlying relationship or structure to investigate and unearth. In short, patterns are another important way that a data journalist finds the story in the facts.

Here's an example from professional American football. Say you're working on a simple graphic comparing the top ten current quarterbacks. You know, either from your love of football or from your research, that Peyton Manning dominated the NFL as an Indianapolis Colt before missing an entire season due to a neck injury. How did the Colts perform with and without him?

Indianapolis Colts' winning percentage

- 1998–2010 (with Manning): 68%
- 2011 (without Manning): 13%

Clearly, the Colts did much better with Manning on the field. Manning, however, moved to a new job with the Denver Broncos. Over the same time period, take a look at how Denver performed before and after Manning played with the team.

Denver Broncos' winning percentage

- 1999–2011 (with at least five quarterbacks, but not including Manning): 53%
- 2012 (with Manning): 81%

The pattern you see emerging is that teams led by Peyton Manning tend to be successful. To be sure, many other factors affected each team's winning percentage, but simply isolating this one pattern reveals just how instrumental Peyton Manning is in the success of the team he plays for.

You can take this ball and run with it. Now, perhaps your simple graphic on the top ten quarterbacks becomes a look at how one player can change a team's fortunes. Perhaps Manning becomes the focus of the graphic, and the top-ten data becomes supporting background information. Your entire visual story may change based on the patterns you find through your research.

Thinking of a Narrative

After you know broadly what story you want to tell with your data, you assemble that story. A good infographic needs a narrative flow that carries the reader from one point to the next, so how you lay out your graphic and arrange its various elements determines how the reader proceeds through the information. That structure can be as important as the data itself in determining whether your graphic is great or merely good. After all, even though you're using visuals and charts rather than just words, you're still telling a story.

Creating a flow

How the narrative of your graphic flows depends on a variety of factors. Because infographics are a visual medium, much of your decision-making will relate to the look and function of the graphic. You'll use some combination of drawings, photos, charts, and text, and each element has a specific role to play. We talk more about this in Chapter 8. For now, here's how you can start thinking about turning your terrific information into a coherent final product.

This section focuses on a few of the factors that determine the flow of a graphic, and how to make sure your graphic is functional as well as eye-catching.

Purpose

The purpose of your graphic is perhaps the most fundamental aspect to consider. After all, that purpose tempers virtually every decision made about the overall approach of your graphic. Always bear in mind the interaction of two factors: content and audience. In other words, what's your purpose in sharing this content with this audience? Is the infographic meant for general online consumption? Is it a print piece being distributed to the news media? Is it going to be part of a corporate presentation? The answers to these questions will factor into every element of your graphic.

A good way to ground yourself before you begin designing is to create a basic outline after your research is complete. Doing so allows you to get an overview of your information and forces you to consider how you want to move from one point to the next.

Here's an example. Say you're developing an infographic for the Internet aimed at informing the general public about breast cancer. Your outline could look like this:

TOPIC: Breast cancer
FORMAT: Online, vertically oriented infographic
AUDIENCE: Health bloggers, women's health sites, health reporters
CONTENT FLOW:

1. **History of breast cancer awareness, from ancient times to modern era**

   Arrange in horizontal timeline starting with older dates.

2. **Health-related statistics**

   How many women will be diagnosed this year? How many will die? How many women are at risk? Which states and/or countries have the highest diagnosis and death rates? Look at trends over time. Are more women being diagnosed, fewer, or the same? What racial/ethnic/other demographic differences can be seen in the rates?

3. **Diagnosis and treatment**

   How is breast cancer discovered and treated? What are the stages and the survival rates? How can women detect breast cancer on their own? What new advances have been made in recent research?

4. **Research and fundraising success**

   To end on a positive note, how much money has been raised for research over the years? Perhaps there are state-by-state figures to be revealed here.

Now change the purpose of your graphic. Say you're creating the piece for a nonprofit entity trying to raise funds for research. You may switch the order of the preceding sections to 2-4-3-1, or you may drop sections 1 and 3 entirely. You may also start with the story of a real woman who survived breast cancer.

Format

Your infographic can exist in one of two forms: print or electronic (published online). Each format has some common features as well as advantages and disadvantages.

Web graphics

Web graphics let the reader scroll down through the information, but print graphics are usually designed in a single, wider block. (See Figure 6-8.)

Most graphics published online have a long, vertical orientation. Readers start at the top of the web page and scroll down to discover information "below the fold."

The term "the fold" is borrowed from newspaper publishing, when the whole newspaper is folded in half, like in a newsstand. What you first see — only the top half of the front page — is "above the fold." In an online or mobile device setting, *above the fold* is simply what a visitor sees when first visiting a site — or in this case, the first section of information.

What you place above and below the fold is something to keep in mind as a designer because you can control your graphic's effect on the reader by changing the order in which you reveal things. As readers scroll down the page, they're following a storyline in which new facts come to light.

One disadvantage of web graphics is that the width is limited to the size of the reader's screen (the viewport), which can be particularly narrow on a smartphone. In this case, think of your graphic in terms of sections the reader will pause on while scrolling through. The flow of your graphic becomes determined by what information you put in each section, like chapters in a book.

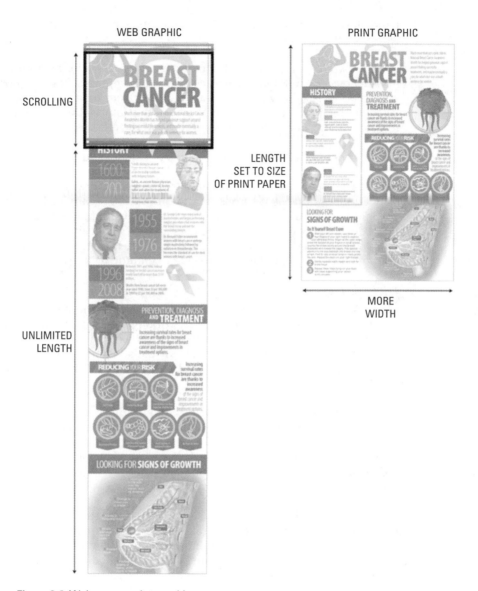

Figure 6-8: Web versus print graphics.

Because technology never stops evolving, it can be challenging to stay on top of the best ways to design infographics for mobile devices. Presently, we recommend using HTML or CSS to deliver your text content. You don't have to become an expert — you just have to ensure that your infographic is as user-friendly as possible. Using HTML or CSS to create a graphic with fewer bells and whistles can make the infographic faster to load. It also sucks up less bandwidth and removes some of the sluggishness if the viewer is in a place with a weak connection.

Going forward, you may be asked to design infographics for multiple formats — mobile devices and tablets as well as personal computers. Exploring web-based solutions can also provide new ways for getting your point across, such as using interactivity, providing links to supporting information, or including calls-to-action that wouldn't be possible with printed materials.

On the other hand, one of the great advantages of using web graphics is that you have nearly unlimited length (height), which allows you to incorporate a great deal of information. We don't recommended, of course, that you construct your graphic so it scrolls on and on with no regard for keeping your graphic concise and focused. The point is simply that height dimensions don't decide how much data you can include. As long as your information is compelling and relevant to your main point, the flow of your narrative can continue beyond what you may be able to include on a printed page.

Print graphics

In terms of width, a printed graphic may offer a little more space than a web graphic — or even a lot more if you're working with a poster-sized print. Moreover, a printed graphic is more likely to be contained in a single page (refer to Figure 6-8) and therefore fully visible all at once compared to a web graphic where some information becomes visible only when the reader scrolls down.

The flow of a printed graphic functions differently as a result. You're not restricted to a vertically oriented layout, which can be a great advantage, and controlling the flow of your narrative is mostly a matter of design. You can direct the movement of your reader's eye by thinking of the sizes of the elements on the page (larger ones tend to draw attention), their locations, and the colors you use.

A graphic showing how nuclear fusion works in the sun, for example, could be organized around a large, central image with information arranged around it. The flow of your graphic begins at the center and radiates outward. Some graphics — such as timelines — are better horizontally oriented, flowing from left to right (in Western cultures).

At least in the global West, readers are accustomed to reading top-to-bottom and left-to-right. That doesn't mean that every graphic has to be structured that way. However, using a design approach that's too unconventional — say, a graphic that begins in the bottom-right corner and directs the reader to the top left — can feel forced and unnatural.

Perhaps the greatest disadvantage of print graphics is a strictly defined size, which limits the amount of data you can include. This limitation becomes very noticeable when you have precious little space in which to explain the nuances of a complex topic. Creating a narrative flow under these conditions can be difficult with the temptation to squeeze in information wherever it fits.

With practice, you'll get the hang of creating that flow. In the meantime, here are a few potential solutions:

- **Bulleted lists:** Instead of writing large blocks of text, break out important elements into bullet points. Like this one.

- **Transitional elements:** Use your visual design to create transitions instead of writing them out. For example, arrows are an obvious but effective way of guiding a reader through an infographic.

- **Focused, streamlined design:** Edit relentlessly. Ask yourself whether every piece of your infographic is necessary and effective. If it's not, cut it.

Desired impact

The flow of your graphic strongly influences the effect your work has on its reader. The choices you make as the designer can alter that effect. Some graphics, for instance, seem to explode off the page from the moment you look at them, and every bit of information is treated like a major element. Other graphics reveal themselves slowly. They may have a few primary elements and then a great deal of subsidiary information for the reader to explore.

Figure 6-9 shows two infographics, one with each approach. On the left is an infographic that highlights a smaller amount of information but makes a bold visual statement. The second infographic (on the right) is more subdued and packs a lot of information into its subtle design.

Each approach has its place. The former can be great if you don't have a lot of complex information to present and you need to make a statement as quickly as possible, like in a brief sales presentation. The latter may be more appropriate for an academic journal, where readers expect detailed data and will have time to consider it.

Look at another example. Say you have information you think is quite surprising, and you want to use the flow of your graphic to heighten that surprise in the reader. In this instance, you'll likely want to find a way to build some suspense and then reveal this surprising information at the end.

Using this structure properly can be a little tricky. You really need the right information to support it. First, you have to grab your reader's attention at the beginning, so you need relatively compelling data to start at the top. Second, you need information you can then use to build to your surprise in much the same way a thriller builds suspense before a shock.

EXPLOSIVE   SUBTLE

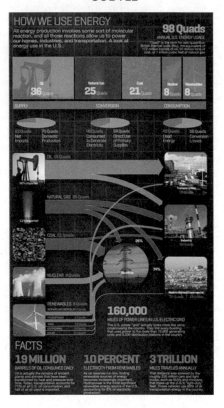

Figure 6-9: Two good graphics; two different approaches.

To give you an example, say you're creating an infographic for a company that has found several ways to modify a standard home so it uses dramatically less energy than a typical home. Here's a hypothetical structure outlined step by step:

1. **Draw in readers.**

   Begin with a detailed drawing of a home and point out the modifications.

2. **Build suspense.**

   Go through the energy savings of each modification.

3. **Reveal surprise.**

   Show the (ideally quite dramatic) collected total energy savings of these various tweaks, as shown in Figure 6-10.

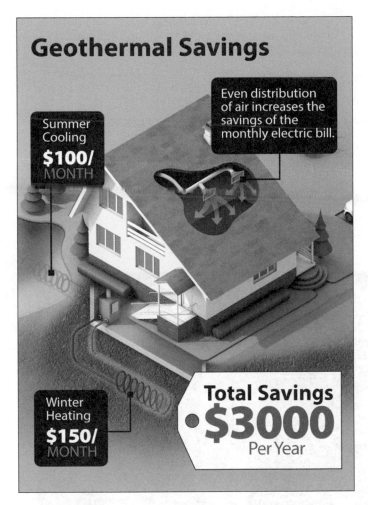

Figure 6-10: The price tag clearly shows a key statistic, which can make a reader feel satisfied.

You can see how the flow here works to a climax to create the desired impact. Now as a mental exercise, imagine the impact on a reader if you were to place the total energy savings at the top and then break it down piece by piece. Our original approach feels dramatic, while the second feels more analytical. Again, each has its place.

Writing copy

Because infographics are a visual medium, the amount of *copy* — text — is minimal in most infographics. The general rule is that if a piece of text doesn't add to a reader's understanding of the topic, get rid of it.

Of course, including copy can be extremely useful. And because copy is so minimal, each word becomes all the more vital. Some different types of copy that you'd see in a typical infographic include the following, as shown in Figure 6-11:

- Title
- Introduction
- Section subheadings
- Chart and graph labels
- Data explainers
- Sources and footnotes
- Branding and copyright information
- Supporting narrative

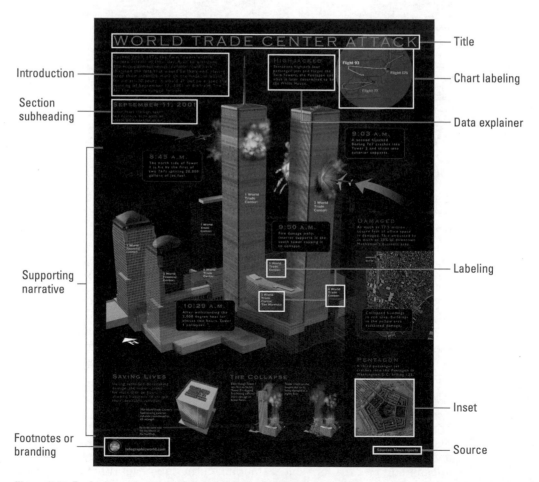

Figure 6-11: Each piece of copy in an infographic plays an important role.

The following sections discuss each type in more detail.

Title

Your title tells your reader very quickly what the infographic is about. As such, a title should be informative yet also draw in the reader. Good titles are often catchy and creative, but they should also match the tone of your infographic. Here's an example of how the tone of a title can vary:

- ✔ Straightforward and serious: *The Importance of Small Business*
- ✔ Clever and catchy: *Small Business, Big Impact*
- ✔ Provocative and funny: *It's Not the Size That Matters*

The approach you choose depends largely on the audience you're hoping to attract and also where your infographic will be published.

Introduction

The first full sentences in your graphic explain to readers what they're about to see. In essence, you want these few lines to sum what your graphic is as clearly and succinctly as possible. Of course, the approach you take for your intro matters quite a bit because you ideally want to draw readers in right from the start while also striking the right tone.

Section subheadings

Subheadings are used to identify different topics within the graphic as a whole, and they also help guide the reader from one section to the next. They serve the very practical purposes of directing the reader's eye and providing visual breaks.

Chart and graph labels

Labels accompany data tables to help explain what's being shown in the table. They generally consist of only a few words or even just one word.

Data explainers

Close cousins to chart labels, data explainers do just what their name indicates: They explain data, much like a caption explains a photograph. For instance, you might not want to literally use the following: "99.7% of employers are considered small businesses." Instead, you might present the information as follows:

99.7%

Employers considered small businesses

The line of text is the data explainer. Presenting information this way — rather than as the earlier sentence — gives you more design freedom and allows you to heighten the impact of your data. Generally, a data explainer is treated as a standalone phrase, so the first word in the phrase is capitalized, and the phrase does not use a closing period.

Sources and footnotes

Some infographics provide footnotes for each particular piece of data. If you choose to do so, how you cite data is really a matter of following a house style or even just your preference. In some cases, you may need to use a specific academic citation style, such as MLA or APA. Typically, in a web graphic, simple superscript numbers follow the data point and correspond to a URL at the bottom of the infographic that links to the source of that figure.

Alternatively, you may choose not to use footnotes at all to avoid distracting the reader. In this case, just list all your sources at the bottom of the infographic, generally starting with those that provided you with the most information.

In either case, listing sources is absolutely vital to ensuring credibility. Readers should be able to verify your data.

Branding and copyright

If you're designing infographics for a specific client, that client will probably require you to publish its name in some way. It may also want to ensure copyright protection. Often, the company name appears with or near source information at the bottom of an infographic. Follow all orders set out by a client's brand guidelines.

If you're working on your own, chances are good that you'll *want* your infographic to be widely copied and shared. Still, you can protect your work from being stolen, inappropriately altered, or plagiarized by setting up some simple guidelines for reuse. One way to do this is to create a Creative Commons license. It's simple to set up via `http://creativecommons.org`.

Supporting narrative

Supporting narrative copy frequently appears in text boxes that run alongside your visual elements, and here is where the amount of text will vary greatly depending on the topic and how you choose to illustrate your information. Some supporting narrative comprises only a few words, but the text you write for another infographic could include a great deal of context and analysis. What you don't want to do is simply put in writing what's already evident from your visuals. You need to ask yourself frequently: Is the text adding value?

Writing this type of copy certainly requires a deft touch. Often, you need to condense complex information into a small space without sacrificing accuracy or basic grammar. The key point to remember is that you don't need to explain everything. Let your visuals do the heavy lifting.

Part III
Depicting with Delightful Design

Visit www.dummies.com/extras/infographics for information about working with Adobe Illustrator's gradient mesh tool.

In this part . . .

- ✔ We'll show you how to create a wireframe to organize your ideas and set the tone for your infographic design.

- ✔ We'll delve deeply into Adobe Illustrator, the preeminent tool for creating awesome infographics.

- ✔ We'll also take you through Photoshop, which provides some excellent technical tools for adding finesse to your work.

- ✔ We'll help you determine which program to use in which case.

- ✔ We'll talk about some online options for trying out infographic design.

7

Creating Wireframes and Managing Mood Boards

A wireframe is nothing more than a visual representation of your info-graphic's structure — actually a simple conceptual tool that can make your job as an infographic designer much easier. Like the outline of a term paper, the wireframe process will help provide structure to all the elements of your infographic. This is where you map out the best way to combine your graphics, text, and data into a strong, coherent visual plan.

The wireframe can help you determine how various text and data points will be illustrated and will reveal a visual roadmap of sorts. Which data points are most important? Where will the reader's eye be drawn first?

This process can reveal flaws with data or problems with the narrative. Will the infographic be top-heavy? Boring in the middle? Lacking an ending punch? Maybe your wireframe seems light on details, which is a clue that the graphic is light on substance and might need some more research. A good wireframe also doesn't give too much away; you don't want to hamstring yourself or another designer by committing too heavily to a specific visual scheme.

If your infographic is being created for a client, the wireframe process is vital. Your client might want to have some approximation of the design before giving the green light to proceed with the project. And a good wireframe will help keep you from redoing work down the line.

This chapter delves into all these topics to help you start down the right path to creating your infographic.

Outlining Your Wireframe

There is no single best strategy for designing a wireframe. Depending on the size and simplicity of the graphic, a rough sketch on paper or a whiteboard will do just fine. If your project is more complex (or you love working at your computer) you could use Microsoft Word or go right to Photoshop or Illustrator. Although more expensive and more high-tech than most projects would require, Microsoft Visio (a sophisticated diagramming software program) is useful for mapping out more complex projects.

And how much time should you allot? Well, that's really tough to quantify. It could really be a few minutes' work on the back of an envelope, or it could take a couple of days. It depends on complexity, client relationship, deadline pressure, and more.

Regardless of the medium used to create your wireframe, it should consist of the following elements (see Figure 7-1):

- Spots for title and introduction
- Rough renderings of charts, graphs, and other data visualization
- Approximations of illustrations in use (whether you sketch something out or use a service like Shutterstock to find placeholder images)
- Spots for section headings (if you're using them)
- Rough placement of data, particularly if the data will relate or connect to an element within the background of the visual itself
- Fonts and color palettes (optional)

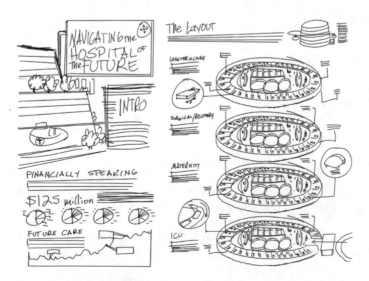

Figure 7-1: Most infographics start with a sketch.

Most infographics will follow, more or less, the same structure as a news article: Each infographic needs a title, a beginning (the introduction to the infographic), a middle (the body), and an end (generally, a call to action). Crafting your wireframe at the start of your project can help you guarantee that your infographic has those basic elements, which we discuss next.

The title: Creating the viewer's first impression

Whether your infographic is for a print publication (newspaper, magazine, corporate report) or a website, information generally begins at the top and then trickles down. Either format has some advantages and presents some challenges to the designer.

The title of your infographic works like a newspaper headline. You have to grab the reader's attention, and you have to set the stage for the content that follows. That means that language should be clear and your *thesis* — your main idea — must make sense. (Read more on theses in Chapters 4 and 5.) This is also the place to set a visual tone for your graphic, whether it's whimsical or purely informational.

Some readers never go any farther than the headline, so the title of your graphic is really important. The title should be clever and catchy, and the illustrations with it should serve the title and theme in some way.

A well-planned title area could take one of several approaches:

✔ **An illustration that encapsulates what's being described in the title:**

- *I Wrecked My Car — What Should I Do Now?:* This title area could show a drawing of a person in a car crash with a quizzical look on his face.

- *The Wired World of Sports:* This title image could be a collection of sports imagery (basketballs, footballs, baseball bats) rendered as computer chips.

✔ **An illustration that fits with an overall visual metaphor:**

- *Navigating the Hospital of the Future:* This title could be rendered as the sign atop a hospital building, as shown in Figure 7-2. It would set the tone nicely for a graphic that displayed its data as parts of a hospital — beds, rooms, surgical equipment, and so on.

- *Science of Sleep:* This title could be part of an overall theme that calls to mind antique medical books, with pencil-type sketches and ornate typography, as shown in Figure 7-3.

✔ **A functional, utilitarian title with or without visual embellishment:**

- *What the Boss Doesn't Know:* The title for this could simply be large type of a font used throughout the graphic with color treatment that reinforces the palette selected.

Figure 7-2: The hospital's sign is the title of the infographic.

Figure 7-3: Make your title fit with the overall theme of the infographic.

Title are important, but they don't have to be huge. While you're mapping out your project, reserve about 80 to 90 percent of the physical space for the body of information. The title will take up roughly five to ten percent, as will the conclusion.

The introduction: Presenting your most important data

Most infographics have some introductory text that sets the scene and delivers the most important information. Many principles of news writing come into play here. Taking a page from journalists, we provide some do's and don'ts for effective infographic introductions in Table 7-1.

Table 7-1	Writing Effective Infographic Introductions
Do	*Don't*
Be concise and to the point.	Give too much away.
Tease the reader with a fact that encapsulates the infographic's purpose.	Use information readers already know or present it in an unsurprising way.
Provide sufficient reason for readers to explore your infographic.	Use marketing jargon. Readers know when they're being sold something.

By the time you're sketching out this part of your wireframe, you should have truly absorbed all the data you're using, and you should be able to answer a simple question: *Why should anyone read this infographic?* You've done a good job making a title that lures viewers in, but now you need to hold their interest. Your introduction should do just that. If you find that the words just aren't flowing, take another look at your data and ask yourself, "What's the point?"

Your intro must be supported by the remainder of the information, so if an angle isn't really illustrated in the infographic, don't bring it up in your introduction. For instance, don't tell readers that your infographic will help them choose a college if the rest of the information is about college education in general but doesn't provide any analysis about specific areas to consider when making a college choice.

The visual treatment of the introduction should generally follow the same principles as the title. You could weave it into an overall visual metaphor; you could render it in a style that fits with the overall tone of the infographic; or you could simply treat it as text.

Whatever the visual treatment, make sure that the introduction is connected somehow to the title, whether it's through using a visual metaphor or simply placing the intro close to the title.

The body: Building the content of your infographic

After you construct a clever title and insightful introduction, the fun can begin. With 80–90 percent of the visual space in the infographic being devoted to the body of the piece, ensuring a smooth flow of visuals and information is key.

Every bit of information included in the infographic should serve to reinforce the title, intro, and basic premise of the graphic. If a bit of data is interesting but ultimately doesn't help you make your point, get rid of it. Your readers will appreciate a tightly focused infographic that tells them only what they need to know to understand the point.

Make sure the body of the graphic supports and is supported by the title and intro. At the top of the graphic, you introduce the topic; but the middle of the infographic is all about proving your point.

One major benefit of using a traditional, vertical arrangement of an infographic is that you can easily lead the reader through your information. Using a horizontal graphic can prove more challenging, forcing readers to go in the direction you desire. Either way, you must ensure the flow of information is logical. People should learn one bit of information before they learn the next, and each subsequent bit of data should naturally build on what came before.

Organizing information, like the following, does *not* create a logical, effective flow:

Incorrect flow of information

Title, intro

Offer solutions to problem

Introduce problem

Explore history and context of problem

Here is a much better approach to organizing information that creates a logical, effective flow:

Correct flow of information

Title, intro (lead-in text)

Introduce problem

Explore history and context of problem

Offer solutions

The job of an infographic designer is clear: You do all the work as the writer/designer/developer to make sure readers get the information they need and nothing else. In the previous example, it may be tempting to reveal the solution to the problem first, particularly if that's the newest bit of information you have. But that would mean that you wouldn't be building your case for the solution first: rather like knowing the end of a book before you read it.

Proper flow can also help eliminate any misinterpretation of the data. By placing data in proper context, you ensure that readers get an accurate, complete picture of the thesis of the infographic. When you're working on your wireframe, consider any of these elements to help you organize your data:

- ✔ Section headings and subheadings
- ✔ Clearly labeled charts and graphs
- ✔ Consistent use of color throughout
- ✔ Illustrations that connect accurately to data

The call-to-action: Drawing a strong conclusion

When your reader reaches the end of the infographic, what do you want him to do next? Or, how do you want him to feel? These are questions you should answer while you're compiling your data and writing your narrative. Often, the answer will reveal itself as you are sketching out your wireframe.

Here are a few common takeaways from infographics:

- ✔ I now see a problem (in the field of education, economics, business, science, medicine, and so forth) needs to be addressed.
- ✔ I agree/disagree with a political standpoint.
- ✔ I have a better understanding of the nuances of a problem.
- ✔ I learned something about the history of a topic that changes/reinforces my opinions on that topic.
- ✔ I will buy a particular product.

If readers get to the end of the infographic and realize they've learned nothing and no new information or position has been revealed to them, they'll consider their time wasted.

Some infographics feature a clear *call to action* that might motivate readers to do something, such as quit smoking, vote for a certain candidate, or support a charity.

As you're working on your wireframe, think about whether the content flows logically to the conclusion you intended. If it doesn't, this is a good time to revise earlier sections: Add more information, take out data that doesn't support your point, or perhaps add an illustration to reinforce your message.

Regardless of whether your conclusion is obvious or subtle, the most important thing is that you hint at it in the intro and that every bit of data reinforces it and naturally leads readers to that destination.

Editing Your Story

Wireframing is a preliminary process, and you'll probably have plenty of time to change your plan as you build your infographic. Perhaps your research will lead you to rewrite your title. Maybe you'll decide to emphasize a new element of the story, requiring you to redesign at least some of the infographic.

Still, it's never too soon to start editing your story. Infographics must present information as clearly and concisely as possible. So, while you're mapping out your graphic, make sure that everything you include — text, art, charts, and so on — supports your main idea. While you're sketching out your ideas, ask yourself whether every component supports your main idea. If it doesn't, ditch it. This can prevent you from wasting time later.

Clarifying the "big idea"

Your infographic no doubt will have a variety of subtopics, sections, and types of information. But in all those various elements, there should always be one nugget of information or one conclusion that's more important than everything else. If a reader had to tell a friend what your infographic was about, have you given that reader the tools to do so?

That single big idea doesn't always have to be groundbreaking; in many cases, you won't be revealing brand-new information. But that doesn't mean the core of the infographic can't still be new and surprising to people.

Say you have information on how much time the average person spends watching TV. By itself, that's probably information your reader doesn't have, so it is new even if it's not particularly interesting. What if you were able to compare that information with another piece of data, though? For instance, the Bureau of Labor Statistics conducts an American Time Use Survey, which shows that Americans spend 18 minutes per day reading, and 2.7 hours watching TV. Now a picture is revealed about the relative value people place on various activities.

As an infographic designer, you can connect the dots in ways that illuminate the numbers while tickling the readers' sense of humor and curiosity. By doing the math, you see that people watch TV for nine times as many minutes as they read. So, perhaps you could play around with one drawing of a book and nine drawings of TVs.

The point is that having data isn't enough: You need to provide context and analysis of that data. That will allow you to present that one big idea that resonates with readers long after they finish your infographic.

In your wireframe, now it's time to consider which type of graphic element — pie charts, bar charts, among others — provides the best support for your main idea.

For instance, if you have groups of numbers totaling 100 percent, using a pie chart may seem like the logical choice. But other ways of representing 100 may be more visually interesting and just as accurate. Say, for example, your percentages are 25%, 25%, 40%, and 10%. Using 100 people-shaped icons, as shown in Figure 7-4, you could shade them appropriately and create a more memorable but still totally accurate chart.

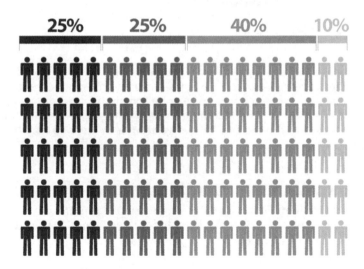

Figure 7-4: Show percentages in creative ways.

Figure 7-5 is another creative way of showing the same data.

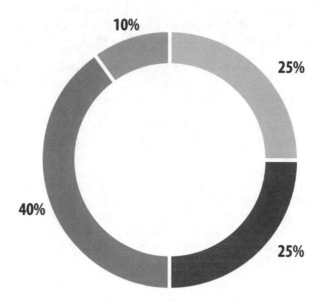

Figure 7-5: A modified pie chart.

A pie chart seems as easy as . . . well, pie. It can be a fine way to show a very drastic difference between a large percentage and a small percentage. But for more complex surveys, a pie chart may be too simplistic. For example, if a survey breaks out results in ten different percentages, the text required to label each piece of the pie may clutter your infographic and may be hard to read.

Conceptualizing an overall layout

Having a theme in mind as you work can be helpful, but it's not mandatory. After you have your information together and have some idea of the types of charts and illustrations you'll use, you may have several ideas for an overall theme or particular layout.

The topics shown in Table 7-2 are all broad topics that have obvious, familiar, and well-known visual imagery that people associate with them.

Table 7-2	Broad Topics and Their Associated Imagery
Topic	**Associated imagery**
Environment	Trees, animals, leaves, water, Earth
Technology	Smartphones, laptops, computer chips, circuitry
Education	Books, teachers, students, pencils
Economics	Currency, coins, dollar signs, green colors
Food	Food items, drinks, culinary tools, eating utensils
Sports	Balls, players, coaches, fields, arenas
Space	Planets, rockets, comets, stars

If your topic doesn't lend itself immediately to attractive visual images, you may want to run a quick Internet search to see how others have illustrated your topic. Or, rather than trying to brainstorm specific images, you may want to think of your topic in general terms. For example, if you are working on an infographic on the consumer price index, broaden your focus to economics.

Some topics lend themselves to integrating the data into the background imagery, as we describe in this list:

- If you have information about forest health, use the background of a forest and create illustrations that play off that. For instance, use leaves and tree trunks to illustrate percentages, or make your bar graphs look like branches.

- If your infographic is about gasoline consumption around the world, create a street scene that depicts cars painted with the national flags driving down a street. Or, you could make the cars sized proportional to their consumption, so the real gas-guzzlers are larger than the cars from countries that use less gas.

- A cutaway of a house could give you a fun way to depict spending and budgeting. If the family spent $1,200 on their TV, show the TV displaying that dollar amount on its screen. Maybe they spend $300 a week on groceries; have a family member open the refrigerator door to reveal a milk carton with the dollar amount on the carton.

You may have ideas on a theme well before you begin researching and writing, and the wireframe is a great way to get them down on paper before committing. The risk of planning a theme before you do a bit of research is that the data you reveal may not fit into that plan, and you will have to rethink things if you paint yourself into a corner.

In the end, allow the data to guide the visual, not the other way around.

Visualizing transitions

In writing, transitions help content flow logically from point to point. Without transitions, content can become terribly stilted. The same is true for good design. You should be as thoughtful in creating visual transitions in your wireframe as you are in crafting your narrative.

Section headers can provide natural transition points, but don't rely on them completely to reinforce your theme. Consider varying colors of the backgrounds of section headers or creating unique imagery that fits within the overall visual to go with each one, so that readers have subtle visual cues leading them through the infographic.

The layout of your infographic should work with the way the human eye functions. We naturally read from top to bottom and from left to right. At the same time, our eyes subtly seek out transitions that lead us from one piece of information to another. Without them, your infographic can appear choppy, or can seem to be a random assortment of charts.

Sometimes, you'll see obvious cues, like a timeline or arrows. Other times, a simple change in color provides the cue. Here's an example, in Figure 7-6.

Figure 7-6: Use clear transitions in your infographic.

Some graphic elements will lend themselves naturally to transitions between points of data and between sections. Those include

- ✔ Flowcharts
- ✔ Process illustrations
- ✔ Themes with roads or paths
- ✔ Timelines
- ✔ Side-by-side comparisons
- ✔ Growth charts

Use of color is helpful, too, providing a subconscious transition from one section to another. A change in color, even if it is subtle, can help the reader's eye make the transition into the next part of the graphic. See Chapter 8 for more about developing a color palette for your infographic and incorporating patterns and textures.

Mapping your illustrations

After you have a solid idea of all the different types of illustrations you'll need, lay them into your wireframe. Exact placement isn't critical at this stage, but you do want to begin to get a feel for overall size and distance around each illustration. Use placeholders — rough sketches or dummy type (refer to Figure 7-1) — to stand in as needed.

Arrange the illustrations or their proxies according to the vision in your mind. Place the intro and title illustrations (if they exist); otherwise, leave adequate space for them. Place subheadings, whether the font is chosen yet or not.

Then, when you get everything arranged according to your vision, look at the picture as a whole. Is one side too heavy or light with charts? Do you have too many of the same types of illustrations in one section? If so, consider changing placement or rethink the type of illustration.

Blocking: Creating a visual roadmap

Placing text and art elements — a simple process known as "blocking" — will give you a good visual plan. The amount of detail in your wireframe will vary depending on the type of graphic. A timeline probably won't be highly detailed, but a more complex infographic in which you are weaving information into a visual theme will be.

As always, step back. Make sure to look at your wireframe with a critical eye. Are you putting too much emphasis in the wrong section? Does the flow seem natural?

Here are a few things to avoid:

- Sparse areas
- Overly busy areas
- Juxtaposed illustrations that might create inaccurate impressions
- Overly long subheadings
- Too many chart types in one area or overall
- Charts that are too long or too short to provide the best context

By this point in the process, you should really start to see the piece come together. Ideally, your work on the wireframe will make the final design go more quickly and smoothly.

Working with Fonts

One last component of your wireframing process should be choosing — or at least thinking about — font choice. As we discuss in Chapter 3, sometimes clients will require you to use certain fonts. If that's the case, just jot them down on your wireframe, and perhaps do a quick review of your computer to make sure you have all the fonts you'll need.

If you're not working with preordained guidelines, the wireframing phase is a great time to plot out your own font choices.

A wireframe is really a rough draft, and you can always revise as you go.

Choosing text styles

As with any type of design, there is a hierarchy in fonts. Appropriately sized typography shows the reader which information is most important. The same way a news page designer wants the top headline to be the largest and most dominant, infographic designers want the title font to be the largest.

Effective design varies font size and weight in smart ways. Here are some of the different elements that will need typographical consideration, including overall font choice, size, and weight:

- Title and intro
- Section headings
- Section intros

- Body text
- Body text with special emphasis
- Chart intros
- Chart labels
- Image captions
- Callout bubbles
- Ending text/call to action

Not only will organizing the text into general guidelines by size help guide the reader, but it will help speed up the work you'll need to do to finish your graphic. You will be able to look at any given piece of text and know immediately what size it needs to be.

Text sizes in general should follow some sense of hierarchy and proportion. You don't want to call too much attention ("highlight") text by making it larger if it's not all that important.

Following the three-font rule

Variety is the spice of good design, but when it comes to fonts, the wise designer knows when enough is enough. Choosing more than three typefaces puts you at risk of making your infographic look like a ransom note or community newsletter.

Choose font families that have several options for weights to help you to create a seamless flow because your typefaces will fit together. This will keep you from needing to choose another typeface for a specific purpose. In general, opting for a serif, sans serif, and special display typeface should provide you with plenty of variation to make your infographic eye catching.

When combining typefaces, don't simply pick randomly or choose fonts that you personally prefer. You should have a good reason for choosing the fonts you choose. To that end, these guidelines can help you pick fonts:

- Use typefaces that provide complementary moods to reinforce the overall feel of your infographic, whether it's upbeat or more somber. For example, don't use a whimsical font for a serious topic.
- Avoid using fonts that are too similar to each other; this creates visual dissonance and can be seen by readers as a mistake. By the same token, don't choose typefaces that are wildly disparate. See an example in Figure 7-7.

Figure 7-7: Not the best font choices.

✔ Use distinctive fonts, but not everywhere. If you want to use a very dramatic font, make sure the typefaces around it are more neutral.

✔ When in doubt, stick with two typefaces that provide a huge range of weights and choices. A well-chosen pairing should give you all the fonts you need. See Figure 7-8.

Chances are that your boss, or the client who hired you, is willing to take a look at your wireframe at this point, too. Take the opportunity to find out whether you're on the right track, and whether all those elements you've sketched out are leading the reader to the right conclusion. If you aren't, it's a lot easier to make changes at the wireframe stage than during the creation of the infographic itself.

If you're working with a client, you may want to establish early whether she wants to approve your wireframe. Taking a little extra time to share your vision and make sure it's in line with the client's needs can save hours of work later on.

Figure 7-8: Font pairings should work harmoniously with each other.

Putting Your Mood Board to Work

As we talk about elsewhere in the book, a *mood board* is a collage or collection of images, colors, typography, and other art elements that allow you to show the direction you're headed — and that's a really useful thing in the early stage of a project to help you organize your thoughts. Knowing what you want the overall effect to be, or the style you want to use, will focus your efforts.

Your mood board can also be used in early discussions with your client. The mantra "Show, don't tell" should be pinned up somewhere in your studio. (After all, it applies to much of the infographic process.) Verbally describing the style you plan to use leaves room for confusion. Using visuals, displayed neatly for a client to study, can provide a much clearer sense of your ideas.

You don't have to reveal every element of your finished product in a mood board. They're simply a way to organize your preferences and test what works.

Some art departments make a conscious practice of keeping inspiration, from a variety of sources, visible for the team. That's a great idea. But you can develop your own mood boards, whether they're as old-school as images stuck to a bulletin board or as modern as a Pinterest site.

Now, what's the difference between a mood board and a wireframe? In some cases, they may be very similar. But in general, mood boards loosely organize your preferences for design, while a wireframe is a true rough draft of a specific project. You can draw on your mood boards as you create your wireframe. You can also add to a mood board at any time, and come back to it for inspiration for many different projects. It may be part of your quest to develop your custom style, as we discuss in Chapter 8.

By contrast, you'll be done with your wireframe as soon as you've turned it into a finished infographic.

Working with mood boards in the digital age

Keeping a mood board in a digital space is easy and fun. Flickr (www. flickr.com) is a suitable vehicle, and a variety of other programs are available in which artists and clients can work collaboratively in a shared visual space. Pinterest (www.pinterest.com) has become one of the most frequently used ways to keep mood boards organized. It's an intuitive and elegant way to keep track of great ideas.

To work in Pinterest, sign up and create a profile. It's free. Then create as many boards as you like, perhaps one for each project. Or, you could create boards for "color palettes," "favorite fonts," "amazing infographics I've seen," and so on.

In the upper right of the Pinterest interface, look for a plus-sign (+) symbol. Click that, and the resulting drop-down menu gives you choices to upload a pin from your hard drive, add a pin from a website, or create a new board.

So, create your mood board and add collaborators if you like. That could be co-workers or clients — whoever you want to be able to see and add to the board. By default, boards are public and searchable on the web.

We recommend "following" people or companies with content that inspires you. If you follow enough good contributors, you'll get fresh inspiration every time you log onto the site. When you see something you want to keep, "Like" or repin it to one of your own boards.

8

Designing Around a Theme

- -

In This Chapter

▶ Choosing visual elements that match your topic

▶ Learning to work with a client's brand guidelines

▶ Choosing a custom style for your graphic

▶ Getting inspired from outside sources

- -

There's a fine line in infographics: They must be eye-catching enough to attract readers yet subtle enough to maintain clarity and fit in with the style guides of the newspaper, magazine, or website that will publish them. Establishing a theme can be a great way to enliven a pie chart or bar chart, and marry art with data. And in complex graphics with multiple parts, a theme often unifies the package.

USA Today uses lots of themes in its infographics. Their artists turn an ordinary pie chart on pitching averages into a baseball. It's simple, effective, and eye-catching. Or, a bar chart on smoking trends to look like . . . what else? Cigarettes spilling out of a pack.

In this chapter, we will talk about how to use those whimsical thematic elements without distracting readers from the content. We talk about how to design creatively while working within a client's brand guidelines and color palettes. We'll show you how choice of fonts and graphic style and the use of textures and patterns can spotlight the most important information. And we give you some suggestions on how and where to find inspiration when your creative well runs dry.

Matching Visuals to Your Topic

By now, if you have secured your assignment and gathered your data, you may already have a brilliant idea for a theme. Be careful, though — creating a theme should take up only about five percent of your creative power. Making it work with your information will be another 91 percent. (That leaves about three percent for hand-wringing and one percent for excuse-making when you have to start over.) Your brilliant ideas may not sit well with those that are waiting for you to produce. To please a client, an editor, or an art director, you may need a backup plan.

Have five good ideas for a theme. It helps to put your big idea down on paper, and then physically move it aside. Then brainstorm another four ideas. Some might be better than your original thought. Some might be boring to you but exactly what your client wants. Or, maybe you got it right the first time, and your initial sketch does become the final theme. Either way, the brainstorming process really helps stimulate creativity. Getting your first idea out of the way — literally and figuratively — gives you the space to generate new ideas.

You are setting the tone for this graphic. Don't think of anything as a bad idea. Only think in terms of better ideas, and ultimately, the best.

As we discuss in Chapter 7, doing rough sketches of your graphics is a powerful way to organize your information and make sure that your graphic is well thought-out. It can also help you generate ideas for a theme. You can consider a wireframe or opt for any other organizational scheme. Drawing nothing more than boxes on a sheet of paper can help you map out an infographic and drum up ideas for a theme. Here's one way to use a sketch to lead you to your visual theme:

1. **Organize information by including the following items in roughly this order:**

    a. *Branding logo or company name, if applicable*

    b. *Headline*

    c. *Major point, with a chart to show statistics*

    d. *Major point breakdown; perhaps another chart to illuminate an interesting subtopic*

    e. *Outlook for future, and any additional charts*

    f. *Branding logo, if it works better here than at the top*

2. **Now ask yourself some questions about your topic:**

   • *Does your subject and storyline have something in common?* A famous song? Sporting event? Holiday? Saying? Cliché? Nursery rhyme? It doesn't have to be a perfect fit, but thinking of these links can spur creativity.

   • *Does your storyline have a logo or iconic symbol associated with it?* For instance, breast cancer research uses a pink ribbon to identify the cause. Can you implement that in your design?

   • *Does your storyline have a pop culture connotation?* If your infographic is about the top-grossing movies of the year, you might tie in movie reels, popcorn, or an Oscar statuette.

   • *Can you design around a headline?* Sometimes a catchy headline will allow you to play out a theme by simply breaking it down. For instance, "A Stitch in Time" could be used as a theme in a graphic about wedding gown designers.

3. **Sketch out the basic theme to see how the information from Step 1 fits into the theme from beginning to end.**

   At this point, you may really be sketching your artistic elements. They'll still be very rough, but doing some actual drawing will help you make sure that your artistic theme is clear and supports the main idea of your infographic.

Figure 8-1 is a piece of our graphic with a personal finance theme showing how Americans are trying to get their finances back into shape. To represent the American people, a stylized Uncle Sam is used in a gym training scenario to illustrate multiple financial statistics. For instance, Uncle Sam's jump rope is a fever line chart that tracks revolving debt and bankruptcy filings.

Ever shut your eyes to concentrate and come up with an idea only to get zilch? It's happened to us, too. Thanks to the Internet, though, inspiration can come with a few keystrokes. For a quick kick in the creative behind, take a look at online photo sites such as Shutterstock or Depositphotos. You can search by theme and get a wealth of new ideas to inspire you. Also, check out the "Finding Inspiration" section, later in this chapter, for a wealth of sources — both online and off — to get your creative juices flowing.

Your graphics should reflect the information, *not* the other way around. The information is the most important thing here, so visuals should come second. Many times, a great artistic idea may not work with the information, or may even distract from it. If that happens to you, throw out that idea and start again, perhaps saving it for a future project.

Figure 8-1: Use a consistent theme throughout several elements of your graphic.

Following Brand Guidelines

A typical assignment for our graphics firm is to create infographics for a corporate interest or business that will publish them on a company website. In some cases, the graphic will be used for an internal company publication. These graphics usually have to follow a specific set of design parameters so that the company's identity can easily be recognized.

Sometimes, the client company provides brand guidelines. In a case like this, your theme has been chosen for you — to support and promote the company or its cause. The company may have provided some of the art elements, too. Regardless, everything you design must fit with their mission.

Depending on the size of the company, these design rule books can be as long as 200 pages, filled with strict regulations meant to corral wayward designers into the company pen. This is understandable. Companies rely on consistency of color, font, tone, and more, to establish and protect their brand image and copyrights. Designers are artists, innately geared to rebel. Brand guidelines are a useful tool in uniting the two parties.

Using guidelines for logos, color, and font

In general, brand guidelines provide specifications for these elements:

✔ **Logo treatment:** How a logo can look and should look. Guidelines on the logo may include how it should be displayed, how to resize it with the correct ratios, or how to use alternate versions, such as a darker reverse. (Take a look at Figure 8-2 to see Infographic World's logo; this is how we would expect to see it reproduced in any publication.)

Figure 8-2: Using brand guidelines to maintain consistency in logos.

✔ **Color palettes:** Many companies spend millions of dollars to have their branding designed by a "colorist" or "packaging designer." The simple fire-engine red bulls-eye of Target department stores is unmistakable. Small children learn very quickly that red and yellow means McDonald's. And, not to toot our own horn, but readers looking for the best how-to books on the market know to seek out the yellow and black of the For Dummies franchise.

To ensure consistency of their brand identity, companies mandate the range of colors a publication should use when reproducing their logos. You will often see the colors of the corporate logo, plus a range of secondary colors that the client uses in its marketing materials and publications. Figure 8-3 shows a swatch of colors, which is what you typically receive when designing an infographic for a client with specific brand guidelines.

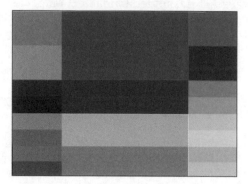

Figure 8-3: Providing specifications on colors and tones.

✔ **Font usage:** Many companies use a certain font to cement their brand identity. They've done the hard work of choosing a recognizable typeface for their company; it's your duty to carry it throughout their graphics. Many times a font included in a brand guidelines package is designed for that company and no one else. (See Figure 8-4.)

Figure 8-4: Maintaining consistent fonts in infographics.

Keep it in the font family

You can't use artist's drawings or writer's words without proper attribution. If a piece of work is protected by a copyright, it cannot be reproduced without permission. Fonts present a similar situation and a bit of a gray area.

A little-known difference between fonts and typefaces. A typeface is the artistic treatment of letters, numbers, and symbols, applied consistently. A font is the computer file or program that tells the computer to use a certain typeface.

In the United States, typefaces are not covered by copyright law. Courts have determined that they are basic "utilitarian" objects that don't need protection. However, courts have ruled in favor of protecting fonts. The most common copyright protection comes in the form of End User License Agreements, which may state that the font is licensed for use on only one computer. If that's the case, do not start swapping and copying fonts with friends or colleagues.

While you are starting out as an infographic designer, stick to the fonts that come with your design software. Nowadays, the choices are pretty extensive. Plenty of fonts and font families are also available for purchase, but you might find that most projects are well-served by fonts you already own.

Working with your client's specifications

Following brand guidelines can make your job easier, dramatically cutting down on the time you'd spend searching for the "perfect" font or color. Sometimes, guideline booklets even suggest a specific type of illustration or graphic that the client likes. Follow their lead, and you'll probably have a happy client.

1. **Discuss brand guidelines with your clients.**

   Most clients will be happy to send their guidelines to you as a PDF, via e-mail.

2. **Have the client send you the fonts they prefer.**

   Fonts can be costly. Buying an entire family of fonts can run into the hundreds of dollars. Often, clients will send you their fonts for your one-time use in creating their materials.

3. **Keep in mind the sizing of the graphic and its usage.**

   Printed material, advertising, animated content, and web graphics have varying size requirements, all of which can affect your design. For instance, a graphic used in a newspaper may call for a certain height and column width, whereas an assignment for a web graphic may specify pixel size.

Give the client a rough draft of the graphic showing their guidelines clearly applied to your work. This will signal the client that you were aware of the rules and implemented them.

Designing a Custom Style

If information is the engine that drives a graphic, style is the Porsche 911 body of the car. The style grabs the reader, excites the senses, and makes you want to spend time checking out the product. The information is the only reason this baby is running, but the style of the graphic can make it fly.

Style is relative to the audience. Readers of *The New York Times* will expect their infographics to look different than the graphics published in *USA Today*. Both create great graphics, but you'd never confuse one for the other. That's what style is all about.

While creating your own style, you focus on four main design elements: colors, fonts, illustrations, and textures or patterns, all of which are visible in Figure 8-5. You won't use all of these elements every time. For example, some graphics will feature plain backgrounds, without any texture. Some simple charts, such as an infographic showing the latest unemployment figures, may not need illustration. But in general, the relationship between those elements is what ultimately creates your style as an infographic artist.

The key to styling a graphic is to make it attractive to look at while not distracting from the information. Graphics have to be legible and compelling. The reader has to want to read the graphic and get your desired message. So, again, simple rules can make your graphics more effective and more attractive.

The red, white, and blue in the client's logo (refer to Figure 8-5) helped the designer pick the Uncle Sam theme, keeping with the patriotic colors; whereas, the green adds contrast and draws attention to important items. Texture (the dotted backgrounds) helps to visually organize the sections, and the digital font on the statistics looks as though they're coming right from Uncle Sam's calculator. Finally, the clear, legible font in the body and headline copy is Arial.

Creating color palettes

There was a time when many infographics were designed and printed in black-and-white only. Most newspapers reserved color for the front page, and (of course) the Internet didn't exist.

Today, most graphics are designed with the potential to work across media platforms. That means that the whole world of color is available to graphic designers. Color is an easy way to enhance the artistic elements of your graphic — and when done well, can make a graphic leap off the page or screen.

Approach using color as systematically as you approach the rest of your design. An editor once told us that adding color to an illustration that didn't enhance the accompanying text was "Putting lipstick on a pig." All the color in the world won't make up for a graphic that doesn't work.

Here are a few tips on color that will work with your custom theme.

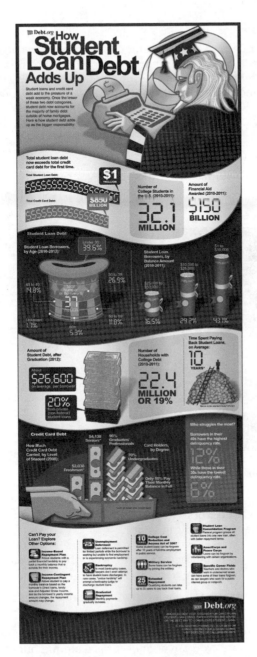

Figure 8-5: Colors, fonts, illustrations, and textures reinforce the theme of an infographic.

Using color to set a tone

Every story has a tone or level of emotion that needs to be conveyed. If the information is a call for action, consider more exciting tones in the yellow and orange range. If the information is more somber and muted, so should the colors: Think blues and muted violets. At times, the theme can really help determine your color palette. For example, an infographic about economics might feature green, black, and gray tones, calling to mind dollar bills.

Developing a color palette

Whether to satisfy a client's guidelines or to solidify your own style, you may want to create a color palette (as shown in Figure 8-6) for your work.

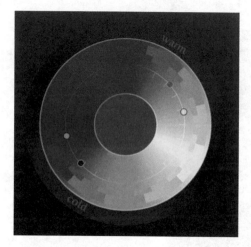

Figure 8-6: Using a color palette.

Remember the color wheel you worked with in childhood art class? All the rules you learned back then still apply. In short:

- Colors opposite each other on the color wheel complement each other, creating visual appeal and excitement. See Figure 8-7.

- Colors next to each other match each other, and can be used together to create harmonious design.

- Red, yellow, and orange are warm colors; green, blue, and purple are cool colors. Choosing one group over another is a simple but effective way to create a certain mood.

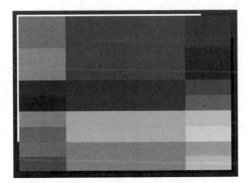

Figure 8-7: Blue and orange sit opposite each other on the color wheel.

You will naturally prefer some colors and come back to them repeatedly. Over time, using your favorite colors and others that complement them can become part of your signature style.

A neat way to devise your own personal color palette to revisit for each project is the Adobe Kuler tool (`https://kuler.adobe.com`). The Kuler tool is a color inspiration community where you can browse color schemes other users have uploaded. You can also create your own color themes. Then, if you save a color palette on the Kuler website, it will automatically import to your Kuler tool in Illustrator.

Several other color palette websites can help you choose the perfect palette for your graphic. Do a Google search for *"color palette generator"* or *"color palette creator."* You will get a host of tools for developing functional color palettes.

Sampling colors

We delve deeply into the wonders of Adobe Photoshop in Chapter 10, but for now, here's a cool trick that can help you while you're working with color. If you have a photo you plan to use in your graphic, Photoshop's Eyedropper tool lets you sample colors from it. It's easy and fun; you use an eyedropper-shaped tool to click a color from the photo. The eyedropper takes that color and makes it the foreground. This helps your design in two ways:

- You can match the tones of your graphic with those of the photo.
- You have a standard that you've already found appealing.

And, don't be afraid to experiment. Particularly if you have some time before your deadline, why not try your infographic in a few different colors? This will show you how color choice can affect the entire look and mood of an infographic.

Feeling out the right fonts

In the early days of infographic design, artists sometimes got a bit carried away by all the exciting possibilities for illustrating the news. Much of the work was drawn by hand, including our headlines. We used the fonts we saw in magazines, on album covers, or on billboards. Our fonts looked great at the time, but now make our graphics look as dated as a 1950s magazine.

Today, technology has given us many more options (so it's highly unlikely you'll be crafting any headlines by hand) that add elegance and consistency to prevent your work from looking dated in another 20 years. Adobe Creative Suite offers hundreds of font faces. Regular, Medium, and Bold-faced fonts have given way to Light, Light Extended, and Light Condensed. The number of fonts has multiplied dramatically, and if your software doesn't offer a font you want, thousands more are at your digital fingertips, available for download. Here are some tips on choosing a font that will work for your project:

- **Take stock of the fonts you have in your personal library.** It pays to look around and get a feel for what you have in your computer's font library. You will be surprised at the variations and styles that are at your disposal.

- **Keep a font favorites list.** When designing a graphic, we have a list of go-to fonts we love to work with. Some fonts lend themselves better to headlines; others are great for body text. We like to keep track of a few headline and body-text pairs as go-to choices for any infographics project. Figure 8-8 shows some of our favorites.

HEADLINES	BODY TEXT
BANK GOTHIC	Myriad Pro Regular
SALVO SERIF	Salvo Sans
MYRIAD PRO BLACK COND.	Myriad Pro Regular
BENTON SANS COND.	Benton Sans Book
ELECTROLIZE	Myriad pro Light
MYRIAD PRO LIGHT	Myriad Pro Regular
TRAJAN PRO	Helvetica Regular

Figure 8-8: Maintaining a list of favorite fonts.

- **Consider your preference for sans fonts or serif fonts.** Sans fonts — also known as sans serif fonts — are typefaces that do not have a little toe or spike on the ends of the letters. Serif fonts have a toe or spike on the ends. For instance, Times is a serif font. Helvetica is a sans font. In general, we tend to use sans fonts, but sometimes a headline just works with a serif font. If the headline is a serif font, we generally make the body text a sans font.

✔ **Decide whether your projects call for bold, light, or regular fonts.** This is normally an easy choice. Bold fonts are most often used in headlines and portions of the graphic you would like to call attention to. Regular or light fonts tend to be body text and labels that need to be played back in a design.

✔ **Remember to read the branding guidelines to see whether the client insists on using a specific font.** Brand guidelines will spell out font usage and many times, include the font with the guideline package.

✔ **Experiment with fonts that are unfamiliar.** Take a moment to try out a font that you may not have run across, but remember to strike the right chord with the tone of your graphic. For example, a Black Extended font may not work with a story or project about yoga. It may look too leaden and heavy; whereas, a lighter but equally elegant script font may help illustrate the theme. (See Figure 8-9.)

Figure 8-9: A stylized font looks right at home in a yoga-themed graphic.

✔ **Don't overdo it:** Sometimes in an attempt to add visual excitement, a graphic's design can fall short because of bad font uses, overly busy sections, or odd font alignments. In Figure 8-10, a skewed effect to the headline, a 3D tilt, and contrasting angles make the information hard to read.

Figure 8-10: This infographic fizzles because of an over-attempt to dazzle.

Take a tour of some font sites on the web. Just searching for *fonts* will generally be enough to peek at what's out there. While looking, keep a wish list of fonts you would like to work with. When times are tough and you're tired of the same-old look and feel, consult the list.

When searching for the right font for your theme, try several font websites. Many sites will let you try the font out by typing it and seeing how your headline looks in that font. You can then take it to your graphic and see how it plays with your design before buying.

Including illustrations

A good infographic (obviously) should include good art. Illustrations promote the storyline, define elements visually, and brighten a page that might otherwise be filled with gray type. An illustration can be a physical drawing, some sort of chart or graph, or even a time line. Our everyday lives are filled with examples of how illustrations entertain and inform: Consider simple elements like the icons on a TV remote control or the capital S and the P on salt and pepper shakers. Infographics rely similarly on clear, intriguing visual elements.

Your illustrations will be a major part of your infographic theme. They will help you carry home your message, cement the seriousness or humor of your work, and will attract and delight your readers.

The illustrations used in the infographic must reflect — not distract from — the information that the graphic is displaying.

To help you choose and use the right art in your graphic, follow these tips:

- **Consider which type of art element can best present the information in your infographic.** If your graphic depicts a scene, like devastation to forest trees after a storm, you'll probably want to draw an illustration. If the information uses numbers to show a trend, a fever line chart might work. If the graphic breaks out percentages, a pie chart is effective. A comparative list of numbers over time may call for a bar chart.

- **Sketch your graphic to help the client or your editor see what you're going for with your design.** Most people need help to see what you're envisioning. After all, that's why graphics are around in the first place: They break down elements of a story to increase the readers' understanding. A quick sketch and explanation of the sketch will assist you in your presentation to the boss or client who may have to sign off on it.

- **If you're not producing the art yourself, include examples of the artist's work when presenting your graphic to a client or editor.** You may know what kind of work the artist produces, but the editor/client won't.

- **Keep a file of graphics that you like.** Refer to these when you need help generating ideas for future projects. Also, when dealing with a potential client, using sample illustrations to accompany your custom-themed graphic can help you share your vision.

Testing out textures and patterns

Sometimes you can't rely on just the right information, design, and fonts. Texture and pattern can pack a punch in graphic design, subtle though they may be. Adding a texture or a pattern can provide a more polished graphic that adds visual appeal for the reader. These design elements can support your theme, by developing the mood of the piece and enhancing your art. For example, a light-hearted graphic on expenditures for a baby in its first year of life might have a background of pale blue and pink polka dots.

Adding textures and patterns to your infographic can also help you highlight different sections of the graphic or to spotlight the most important facts. Take a look at the subtle textures we show in Figure 8-11. Using one of them to highlight the thesis of your graphic can help ensure that the reader's eyes go there. Using a different texture on other information (or no texture at all) can create a visual signal to move on to the next section.

Follow this cardinal rule when choosing texture, pattern, or background for your graphic: *Will this help communicate the message of this graphic, or will it hinder it?* In general, these features must be used sparingly. A light touch can enhance, but a heavy touch can make your graphic virtually unreadable.

Metal plate   Splatter   Scratches   Patterns

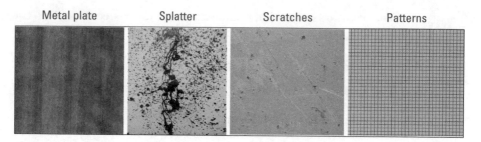

Figure 8-11: Creating background textures in a graphic.

Textures and patterns are available in Photoshop and Illustrator (more on these in Chapters 9 and 10). When you choose a texture or pattern, the programs also allow you to choose the percentage of density. Opt for a low percentage — 30 percent, for example — and see whether you like it and whether you can read all the text. Then scale it up or down as you like. Using a lighter touch allows texture and pattern to play a subordinate role in the graphic and highlights the important parts of the information.

In a more complex graphic, adding a background pattern can unify the final product. Again, you'll want to be subtle. In the segment of the graphic shown in Figure 8-12, the pattern doesn't distract the eye — all the information remains fully legible — but the pattern adds a little depth and visual interest to the graphic, helping to draw in the reader.

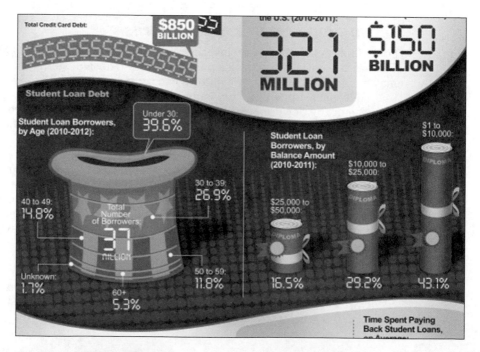

Figure 8-12: Adding patterns to increase visual appeal.

Finding Inspiration

Customizing anything — a car, house, room, T-shirt, or web page — is nothing short of a message from the heart. The customized piece leaves an impression of you when the work is done. Custom style is all in the name of the project, of course. But who is to say it's for the client or editor alone? Ideally, your readers will connect with and embrace your customized infographic's theme.

When planning your theme, if you reach deep down into your very existence and come up with cobwebs, don't panic. Sources for inspiration abound. When you need inspiration immediately, a few sources of graphics genius can be your best friend.

 Targeted web searching can provide you inspiration. Try using specific search terms to find images that pertain to your subject. For example, try "life insurance icons," or "term life insurance images" instead of simply searching "life insurance."

For less-targeted searching and general browsing for ideas, take a tour of websites run by the graphics greats:

✔ http://nigelholmes.com

Nigel Holmes, former head of the graphics department at *Time* magazine, now turns out some fabulous freelance projects.

✔ www.nytimes.com/interactive/2012/12/30/multimedia/

The New York Times is a go-to for graphics with a strong news component. Even its more feature-oriented graphics, without a strong news peg, will surprise you with their brilliance.

✔ http://infographicworld.com

Hey, what can we tell you? You're in our house.

✔ www.shutterstock.com

Perusing a stock photo sites can jog your cramped creativity. Running a simple search of a subject will produce large numbers of images that may spark your own idea. For instance, you may need an idea for cyberbullying. A search of visual images on cyberbullying may inspire your depiction of angry digital arrows attacking you from a computer monitor. Other good photo sites include Depositphotos (www.depositphotos.com) and Getty Images (www.gettyimages.com).

✔ www.xocas.com/blog/en

This is the interactive graphics blog of the *The New York Times* own Xaquin Gonzales Viera. Xaquin's infographic work spans a good portion of the last decade. He is well known for his great interactive information graphics. He also cooks a mean paella.

✔ www.johngrimwade.com

John Grimwade has been Condé Naste Traveler's information graphics specialist for long enough to compile a portfolio of exceptional graphics.

✔ http://juanvelascoblog.com

Juan Velasco is the veteran art director of *National Geographic* magazine.

✔ http://jzarracina.com

Javier Zarracina, formerly of the *El Correo* newspaper in Bilbao, Spain, is the graphics director of *The Boston Globe.* His work combines 3D, pencil drawings, and a lush array of beautiful infographics.

✔ http://dailyinfographic.com/sitemap

This site, featuring a new infographic every day, is a great place to stroll through its archives for ideas.

Or look in a book:

✔ "Information Graphics" (Taschen Books) by Sandra Rendgen and Julius Wiedemann. London-based blog Urban Tick describes this book as "a tasteful framework to showcase the many awesome examples of the data narrative." It's great.

✔ "The Wall Street Journal Guide to Information Graphics: The Dos and Don'ts of Presenting Data, Facts, and Figures" (W. W. Norton & Company) by Dona M. Wong. This book is organized into mini workshops. You will learn what works and what doesn't.

✔ "The Functional Art: An Introduction to Information Graphics and Visualization" (Peachpit Press) by Alberto Cairo. We believe that Alberto Cairo is the twenty-first century's Nigel Holmes. Cairo describes his book as "an introduction to Information Graphics and Visualization, the communication of facts and data by means of charts, graphs, maps, and diagrams." It includes a DVD featuring 90 minutes of video lectures.

✔ The Society for News Design's "Best of News Design" annuals. These design annuals always come to mind for quick inspiration, particularly if you are focusing on news-oriented infographics. They are stocked full of amazing design ideas and graphics. www.snd.org/join/the-snd-store.

✔ "The Visual Display of Quantitative Information" (Graphics Press) by Edward R. Tufte. Ask any graphic artist from the past two decades who fathered present-day information graphics theory, and they will probably cite Edward Tufte. This book, along with Tufte titles "Envisioning Information" and "Visual Explanations," are the top three must-reads in the graphics realm.

9

Designing Infographics in Adobe Illustrator

. . . .

In This Chapter

▶ Arranging your workspace

▶ Getting to know basic Illustrator tools

▶ Working with common Illustrator effects

. . . .

*W*hen completing a graphic or illustration, it's important to keep the details as simple as the information will allow. This way, the artwork gives way to the message you are trying to convey. The message is forever the most important objective.

That said, there is plenty of room left for a good drawing. Many times, simple shapes can bring home the point better than a photograph.

Adobe Illustrator, which debuted in the late 1980s, is the gold standard for graphic design across print and digital media. Graphics created in Illustrator are easy to resize, which makes it appealing for web graphics. Illustrator features allow you to polish and improve your art, lending your infographics some added polish and visual appeal. This full-featured and robust program can appear overwhelming, but with some practice, you'll come to appreciate its many user-friendly features.

Setting Up Illustrator

Opening an Illustrator document can be pretty overwhelming. Upon first glimpse of this powerful program, it almost feels like a David and Goliath standoff. (You're David, by the way.)

Illustrator can be intimidating, yes, but with a little patience and a goal, you can surely tame the giant and get it to work to your benefit. Taking the time to arrange your workspace can dramatically improve your efficiency. Illustrator includes a lot of tools that you can tailor to your own work habits and preferences. Start off by taking a look at how to use them.

Navigating the workspace

Arranging the workspace (work area) simply means arranging panels and other workspace elements to best suit your needs. The Illustrator workspace allows you to organize elements so that your favorite tools are the most accessible. You can even make your own custom workspace; read how in "Making your own workspace." And, if you are working on multiple projects at one time, you can run more than one workspace.

Windows and tools can be moved, deleted, or added to match the way you work. Spending some time upfront getting to know your way around Illustrator's workspace can save you time down the line.

The first window you will see has a configuration that is straight-out-of-the-box standard. After you open the program and start a new document (by choosing File➪New), a standard, letter-size page will appear.

Working with toolbars and palettes

Illustrator organizes its tools into a few bars. Here's a look at where you can find some of the program's main features.

The tools panel

This area is a one-stop-shop for creative tools you need to produce art on the *artboard,* which is the blank white space that functions like a piece of paper. It has the selection tools, the Pen tool, and the Shapes tool. As you work, you'll have to select a tool before you can use it. More on Illustrator's tools later in this chapter.

The application bar

Across the top of the screen are application controls, including a workspace switcher. You can hide it by opening the Window menu and deselecting Application Bar.

The panel title bar

You can organize, stack, and rearrange palettes and panes in this area (typically on the right side where palettes sit) to best suit the requirements of each project. For instance, if you're drawing, you could put the Color pane on top because you'll be using that frequently. Or, if you're working on something like a newspaper graphic, you could put the Text pane on top.

Determining the essentials

One of the charms of Adobe Illustrator is that its developers really try to anticipate what users will want. Check out the Essentials Switcher, accessible by clicking the Essentials button at the top-right of the window.

This drop-down menu holds a list of several workspace presets: Automation, Essentials, Layout, Painting, Printing and Proofing, Tracing, Typography, Web, and a lower menu that we talk about later. These are preset configurations for what Adobe thinks would be some typical workspace arrangements.

Choosing a preset workspace

When you click and hold the Essentials button in the upper-right corner of the Illustrator window, you see the list of preset workspaces. Here is a rundown:

- **Automation:** This workspace arranges the palette menus down the left side of the window in a way that concentrates workflows on automated commands like the Actions palette (automatically performs commands by assigning quick keys); Links palette (allows you to keep track of imported items); Variables palette (where a linked image, a text object, a graph, or an object can be made dynamic or changeable); and Layers palette (content can be arranged on separate layers to allow for easier editing).

- **Essentials:** This is just the basics. The palettes bar on the right is collapsed, but any of the palettes are available from the Window menu.

- **Layout:** This workspace has the essential editing palettes for any single or multi-page layout you may have to perform. It includes the Artboards palette (allows for added artboards for multi-page layouts); the Stroke, Swatches, and Graphic Styles palettes (for line editing, quick color swatches, or background patterns); the Color palette (for editing line, text, or fill colors); the Transform palette (for editing size of objects); and the Type palette (for text editing).

- **Painting:** For the artist who loves to draw, paint, and create. This workspace features the Color, Swatches, and Kuler palettes (for finding color palettes through a web-hosted community); the Color Guide palette (some preset color schemes); the Brushes, Stroke, and Symbols palettes (for choosing brush tools, line editing, and quick symbol generation); and the Layers palette.

- **Printing and Proofing:** After you complete a project, you can switch to this workspace to help usher your way through the production process. This workspace offers the Layers palette, the Info palette (you can view attributes on any object in the work area), and the Links and the Artboards palettes. It also contains the Swatches palette, Appearance palette (for quick editing of stroke, fill, and opacity in an object), the Transparency palette (for another quick opacity edit), and the Color palette. After those, you have the Separations Preview palette (for viewing preproduction cyan, magenta, yellow, and black layers of an artwork or photo), the Document Info palette (for a quick rundown of various objects in the project), and the Attributes palette (for adding overprint options or fill options).

- ✔ **Tracing:** This workspace offers the Image Trace palette, which allows for photo tracing or quick and easy autotracing. This workspace also has the Navigator palette (you can quickly view where you are on the project by pushing the navigation box around the work area in this palette), and the Info palette. It also includes the Color, Swatches, Color Guide, Layers, and Links palettes.

- ✔ **Typography:** This workspace gives the user the most important palettes for editing text color and editing, plus the Open Type palette (gives the user the ability to change Open Type fonts within the fonts list).

- ✔ **Web:** When designing projects for the web, this setup comes in handy for preparing files for interactivity.

When working on a project, you may end up with a lot of palettes strewn across the work area. You can easily get back to an organized workspace by clicking a preset workspace above or a new customized workspace of your choosing.

Making your own workspace

Getting used to Adobe Illustrator is a bit like moving into a new neighborhood. You slowly learn who likes to chat, who likes to keep to herself, who keeps his yard nice, and who practices opera at 6 a.m.

Imagine if you could move into a new neighborhood and customize your neighbors. Well, that's pretty much what you're doing with Illustrator's workspace customization. Here's how to make this program livable for you:

1. **Choose Window➪Workspace➪New Workspace.**

2. **In the New Workspace dialog box that appears, name your workspace.**

3. **Open the Window menu at the top and select the palettes you'd like to add to this custom workspace.**

    Those palettes will appear on the artboard.

4. **Drag any palettes to the right side of your artboard. You can repeat this addition with as many palettes as you can fit.**

After you arrange your customized workspace, you can always switch to it from any other workspace by choosing it from the workspace switcher, found under the Essentials button.

As an example of Illustrator's tools and palettes we'll show how we can put together an information graphic on personal finance. Figure 9-1 is a sketch for a client of a graphic dealing with financial matters.

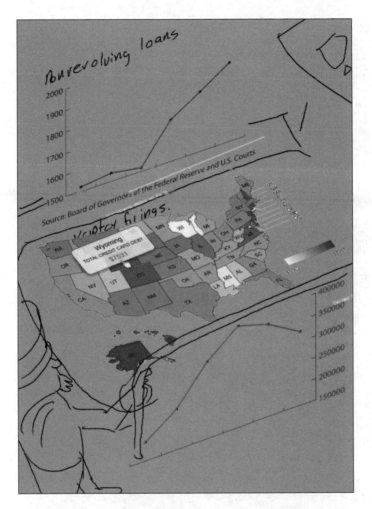

Figure 9-1: Starting with a sketch.

The graphic uses a fitness theme to show how the U.S. economy was beginning to inch back to life after a dismal few years. As a theme, Uncle Sam (representing the U.S. economy) is training for the fight of his life (recovery from economic recession) by running on a treadmill (charts showing recovering economy). Figure 9-2 shows the finished infographic.

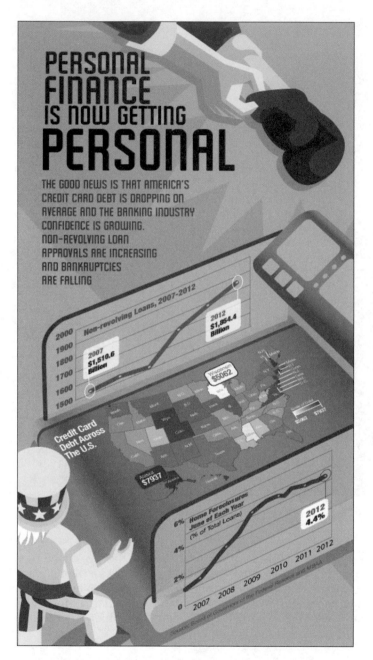

Figure 9-2: Finished Uncle Sam infographic.

Mastering Illustrator Basics

Adobe Illustrator has some unbelievably cool features you can use to add all sorts of flourishes to your graphics. Before you get into those, however, take a look at some of the basic features of the program for a little taste of the technical wizardry you can add to your infographic.

Glitches can arise at a moment's notice. Save your artwork frequently by pressing ⌘+S (Mac) or Ctrl+S (Windows). The first time you save your work, the computer prompts you to name the file and place it in a certain folder on your computer.

Using the Selection and Direct Selection tools

While you work, two "selection" tools allow you to perform certain functions to each element of your infographic. You'll experiment with them later in this chapter, but the Selection tool (the black arrow in the tools panel) allows you to move or resize an object. If you have objects grouped together, the Selection tool allows you to move the entire group.

The Direct Selection tool (the white arrow to the right of the Selection tool) allows you to grab points on an object and manipulate them individually. Or, if you click a line that's between two points, you can manipulate the whole line.

Maximizing the Pen tool

The Pen tool is one of the most basic components of Adobe Illustrator. You use it to draw straight and curved lines, forming the foundation of almost anything you'd want to include in an infographic.

When you open Adobe Illustrator, on the left side of the window is a thin row of tools called the *toolbar*. The fifth tool down the toolbar is the Pen tool, which looks like the nib of an old-time fountain pen.

Just click the Pen tool to activate it. It will turn dark to show that it's high-lighted and active.

You can also press P (on your keyboard) to select the Pen tool.

Now have some fun. With the Pen tool selected, try a few clicks on the empty artboard to the right. You'll probably end up with a random shape, filled with black and surrounded by blue lines and dots. The lines are *paths,* and the dots are *anchor points,* which all have handles. The handles on the anchor points allow you to change and control the bend in the line.

To begin drawing Uncle Sam, select All on your artboard by choosing Select⇨All on the main menu or pressing ⌘+A (Mac) or Ctrl+A (Windows). Then hit Delete to clear any experimental points you just made. In this example (Figure 9-3), I used the Pen tool to draw the hat brim, stripes, and top. In the first example (left), I filled with white to show the shapes. In the second, I filled the shapes with color.

Perhaps you want to outline your shape. You can choose Stroke to outline the edge of your shape in any width and color you'd like. Both commands are accessible from the Tools panel.

You might also wish to do one of the following:

✓ **Fill your shape with a different color (or none).**

There are several ways to add a color. You can click a color in the Control panel, the Color panel, Swatches panel, Gradient panel, or the swatch library. Additionally, you can double-click the Fill box and then select a color from the Color Picker.

You can also fill your shape with no color by selecting the check box with the red hash mark through it in the lower left.

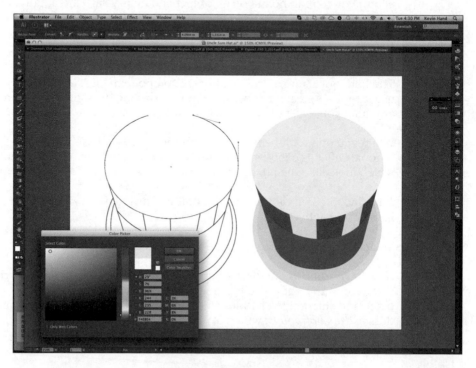

Figure 9-3: Use the Pen tool to outline your shape.

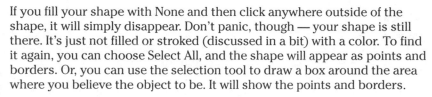

If you fill your shape with None and then click anywhere outside of the shape, it will simply disappear. Don't panic, though — your shape is still there. It's just not filled or stroked (discussed in a bit) with a color. To find it again, you can choose Select All, and the shape will appear as points and borders. Or, you can use the selection tool to draw a box around the area where you believe the object to be. It will show the points and borders.

✔ **Add a stroke to your shape.**

a. Reselect your drawn shape.

b. Go to the color fill menu as before and select the box shape under the color fill box. This is the Stroke color box.

You can toggle between Fill and Stroke color by pressing X on your keyboard. This will save you time clicking the actual color boxes.

c. Click the little black box in the lower-right corner of the color menu to stroke your shape with a black color.

✔ **Make the shape a closed image.**

a. Use the Pen tool and click one of the handles with the Pen.

A small hash symbol appears near the tip of your Pen tool. Now the Pen is ready to add to your existing shape.

b. Select that point and then go to the opposing end handle with your Pen tool.

c. When a small circle appears at the tip of your Pen tool to show that the additional point will close the shape, click there to close the shape.

✔ **Edit your shape.**

a. Click and hold the Pen tool.

Four tools choices appear: the Pen tool, the Add Anchor Point tool, the Delete Anchor Point tool, and the Convert Anchor Point tool.

b. Move any point in your shape. Activate the Direct Selection tool (the second arrow down from the top of the Tool palette: a hollow, NW-pointing arrow) to move the points.

With this tool, just select and drag points to edit the shape as you like.

c. (Optional) Choose the Delete Anchor Point tool to delete points you think are unnecessary for your artwork.

d. (Optional) Try using the Convert Anchor Point tool to add arches or curves to your art by simply clicking and dragging the point you wish to be curved.

Use this tool to turn a corner point to a curved line. It works from the center of the point and curves the line outward. It takes a little practice to master this tool.

Use these quick keys to toggle between Pen tool options:

P   Pen tool

+   Add Anchor Point tool

-                          Delete Anchor Point tool

+C   Convert Anchor Point tool

Continuing with the Uncle Sam drawing we can add stars to his hat by either drawing them with the Pen tool (by clicking and adding anchor points in a star shape) or by using the Shape tool. This tool is in the tools palette farther down than the Pen tool. The star Shape tool resides under the Shape tool icon (a square box). Click and hold the Shape tool and a fly out menu will appear. Scroll down to the star Shape tool. Simply click and drag the star shape onto the artboard. (See Figure 9-4.)

Figure 9-4: Use the Shape tool's star shape rather than using the Pen tool.

The rest of the hat can be completed by drawing curves with the Pen tool. Here's how to draw curves:

1. **With the Pen tool, click the artboard.**

   That creates an anchor point

2. **Moving slightly to the left or right, click and drag.**

    The line creates a curve.

3. **Move slightly again and complete the arch with a single click.**

4. **You can repeat these actions over and over to complete the hat brim or to add curves to the stripes in the hat.**

Always save your artwork every time you think of it. The computer, the program, and your work are all built by humans. Glitches can arise at a moment's notice, so saving your work is imperative.

Placing a text box

Text boxes organize all the type in your graphic, from headlines to blocks of text that tell your story to the tiny type that gives credit to your sources. By the time you are building your infographic with Illustrator, you should have all your research complete, and you should have written your text (also known as *copy*). Now, it's time to lay it out like you planned in your wireframe, and make sure that your text and art support each other.

To create a text box, click the Type tool on the Tools palette and then click anywhere on your artboard. Then type your text. You can create a specific size for your text box by clicking the Type tool on the artboard, then holding and dragging in a diagonal fashion downward. After you create a text box and fill it with copy, you can move this block of text around the infographic by using the Selection tool and then clicking, holding, and dragging the text box around your layout. You can also click any text box handle to drag that side of the box in or out. Because text boxes are so easy to move and resize, they can help you as you modify and edit your infographic.

Changing fonts with the Type tool

The Type tool in Illustrator is a quick and easy way to find the best font for your graphic. With just a few clicks, you can find a typeface that suits your project — anything from an infographic on revenue for a company's annual report to a diagram of a race car's engine for an infographic on Formula One racing.

You'll find the Type tool on the Tools palette (down the left side of the screen). It's the big letter T (for Type). (By the way, this is an excellent example of a simple icon!)

When you click and hold the Type tool, options for type formatting pop up. For now, though, just concentrate on the first option: the Type tool itself.

Here's a simple exercise to get you started using the Type tool:

1. **Select the Type tool and move the cursor to the artboard.**

2. **Click in the empty text field.**

   This sets the incursion marker or cursor in the middle of the field. In essence, you're selecting a place to begin your text.

3. **At the blinking cursor that appears, enter some simple sample text.**

   The font doesn't matter at this point. See Figure 9-5.

Figure 9-5: Start with a simple font.

4. **Press Esc (the Escape key) on the keyboard.**

   This releases the Type tool and automatically returns you to the black Selection Tool.

With your basic text entered, you can now adjust your text.

In the Uncle Sam Personal Finance Graphic, I used a special font called Featured Item. I wanted something that reflected the Industrial-style look I was going for.

Along the top of the artboard are several options that Illustrator places when you choose the Type tool including the font name, style, and font size. You can change the font by clicking the Character drop-down menu and scrolling to any font. It is always interesting to see how each font may enhance the theme in your graphic. (See Figure 9-6.)

Figure 9-6: Investigate other font options.

Start experimenting by changing the font.

1. **Choose the font (the first drop-down menu).**

   a. Click and hold the small white arrow of font family to open its drop-down menu.

   b. When the array of Illustrator fonts appears, scroll and select the one you want.

2. **Set the font style (the second drop-down menu).**

   a. Click and hold the small white arrow to open this list of font styles that come with that particular font.

   b. Scroll and choose the style you want.

      In most cases, your choices are limited to Regular, Italic, Bold, and Bold Italic. Some fonts, though, come with more variety, such as Condensed and Bold Condensed.

3. **Set the font size (the third drop-down menu).**

   You know the drill by now. Font size, by the way, is set in points (pt). For reference, 72pt is one inch.

Using the Direct Selection tool

The Direct Selection tool is the second tool down on the Tools palette. Some folks call it the "empty arrow" (in comparison with the black-filled Selection arrow). Whereas you use Selection to select an object or group of objects, you use Direct Selection to select individual handles or points on a vector drawing or Pen drawing in Illustrator and edit them. You can work with any object that is a vector or AI Pen-drawn shape.

Repeating yourself is good sometimes

Here's how to duplicate an object or text box.

1. **With the black Selection arrow active, click/hold the object.**

2. **Press and hold Option/Alt.**

3. **Drag the object anywhere on the artboard.**

4. **Release the mouse.**

You have a clone!

5. **Repeat as often as you wish.**

This duplication trick comes in useful quite often. In the Uncle Sam example, I used this duplication maneuver to create a second hand rail for the treadmill.

Try this. Start by creating a simple shape:

1. **Activate the Shapes tool (the eighth icon down on the Tools palette, that looks like a basic rectangle with a little shading in the SE corner).**

2. **From the menu of shapes that opens, choose something simple, like a basic rectangle (opt for the Rectangle tool) and then click the workspace.**

Now you can use Direct Selection to manipulate the shape:

1. **Activate the Direct Selection tool (press A for a shortcut).**

2. **Click and hold any anchor point and then drag it.**

If you select the upper-left anchor of a rectangle and drag it toward the center, you get a trapezoid. For fun, do the same with the upper-right anchor point: Select it and move it to the same place as the first point. That gives you a triangle.

If you hold down Shift while doing these movements, it will constrain them to parallel, vertical, or 45-degree movements.

The direct selection tool has a really useful "marquee" feature that allows you to draw a box around a portion of your work and then drag or move everything that's inside the box.

You can also use the Direct Selection tool to move only selected lines between two points. Just click any line in a shape, holding and dragging.

Grouping objects

Grouping objects (choose Object⇨Group) can help you move them around a design or piece of art. A group combines objects into a single unit, which can then be moved or altered as one, without having to change the qualities of every single component. These components can be polygons, text elements, rasterized images, or any combination of the above.

When you click and hold the Direct Selection tool, a menu appears holding the Group Selection tool. Use this tool to select items within a group one item at a time.

Toggle between the Direct Selection tool and the Group Selection tool by holding down Shift. When Direct Selection is selected and then you hold down Shift, a small plus sign (+) appears below the tool's icon.

Use this technique to move an entire grouped object without leaving anything behind. Try it out.

1. **Activate the Group Selection tool.**

2. **Click some artwork you've created.**

   • Click the object. One of the items will be selected.

   • Click the object twice. All items within the group are selected.

3. **With the objects selected, you click and drag to move them en masse.**

If you hold down Shift while using the Group Selection tool, you can deselect objects within the group.

Discovering the beauty of the Brush tool

The quintessential image of the artist is a picture of a painter with a paintbrush. The brush is an old tool, but even in the digital age, it's not obsolete — but instead of paintbrush and paint, you use a paintbrush and pixels.

The Brush tool (a paintbrush icon) is located nine icons down on the Tools palette. Here are basics of how to use it.

1. **Activate the Brush tool.**

2. **Take a swipe on the artboard to the right.**

   The tool paints a thick line in black. The default setting is 5pt Round.

In the area above your drawing is a series of options and menus. From left to right, here's a rundown.

   ✔ **Path:** This tells you the object type you have selected.

   ✔ **Fill:** Your path won't have a fill at this time, which is denoted by a white box crossed with a red line (universal in CS for "no fill").

   ✔ **Stroke Color:** Click and hold this menu to open a color picker for the desired color.

   ✔ **Line Size:** Here is where you can change line width. Click and hold this menu to see line width options. Try a few to see the effect.

Another way to change path line width is to select the path, and then press the left bracket ([) to decrease the width of your line or the right bracket (]) to increase it.

✔ **Variable Width Profile:** This option is interesting when dealing with the Pen tool but not particularly useful for the Brush tool.

✔ **Brush Definition:** As we mention earlier, the default setting is 5pt Round. Click and hold this menu to open a list of great brush definitions: for example, 5pt Flat is great for calligraphic lettering, and Charcoal Feather is good for a painterly look.

To try different brush definitions from this option, duplicate your path several times (selecting the path and press ⌘+D/Ctrl+D) and then choosing different options.

There is a whole library of brush options to play with. On the right side of the workspace, click the fifth icon down to bring up the Brushes Options dialog box. In the upper right of this dialog box, click the a little "list" icon to bring up another list of options to use. If you scroll near the bottom of this list, you will find Open Brush libraries, which provides a bevy of brush types.

You can also call up the brush library by clicking the little Library icon on the lower left of the Brush Options dialog box.

Getting geometric with the Shape tool

Other than the Pen tool, the Shape tool is one of the most widely used Illustrator features. You use it to create rectangles, rounded rectangles, ellipses, polygons, stars, and flares.

The Rectangle tool

The Shape tool is located eight tools down on the Tools palette. Just click the Rectangle tool and then click and drag on the artboard to create the shape.

The shortcut for the rectangle tool is pressing keyboard letter M.

Remember your geometry teach saying how all squares are rectangles? This is where you will use that math in real life. To create a square, hold down Shift while creating the rectangle. You will get a perfect square while dragging on the artboard.

To open a dialog box where you can set strict measurement parameters for your object, select the Rectangle tool and then click once on the artboard.

The Rounded Rectangle tool

As you might surmise, a rounded rectangle is a regular ol' rectangle but with sloped shoulders. To use it, click and hold the Rectangle tool in the Tools palette. A fly-out menu appears with an array of shapes to choose from.

1. **Drag the pointer to the Rounded Rectangle tool.**

2. **Click and drag on the artboard.**

   When you release the mouse, you see an object that looks a bit like a bar of soap — great for text boxes, picture frames, a corner on a neighborhood block. The possibilities are endless!

   While clicking and dragging the shape of the rounded rectangle, adjust the rounded corner radius by pressing the up- and down-arrows keys on the keyboard. Pressing up arrow increases the radius, and pressing the down arrow decreases it.

   To open a dialog box where you can put in your own specific measured parameters (radius of the corners and size of the sides on the rectangle), activate the Rounded Rectangle tool and simply click on the artboard.

The Ellipse tool

Just like using the Rectangle and Rounded Rectangle tool, click the Ellipse tool and then drag to create an ellipse or oval on your artboard.

To create a circle at any size your monitor will allow, activate the Ellipse tool and hold down Shift while creating the shape.

Edit a circle shape by activating the Direct Selection tool and then clicking and dragging any of its points to reshape the circle. When you click a point, notice that the selection produces two more handles on either side of the point. These arc-editing handles can be used to reshape the arc within that circle.

The Polygon tool

Moving on to the next tool in the Shapes menu, click and hold the Shape tool icon to find and select the Polygon Shape tool. Click and drag on the artboard, and a hexagon appears.

To edit the polygon while creating it, use the up and down arrows on the keyboard to change the number of sides on the shape you're creating. Pressing the up arrow adds more sides; pressing the down arrow decreases the number of sides. You can make something as complicated as an octagon or as simple as a triangle by simply tapping the up and down arrows on the keyboard.

The Star tool

Find the Star tool icon in the fly-out menu that opens under the Shape tool. To make (and tweak) stars, select the Star tool and then click and drag on the artboard to create a star shape.

To edit a star, use the arrow keys on the keyboard. You can create a sun shape by pressing the up arrow or go as far as a triangle shape by pressing the down arrow. This comes in handy for making light flashes or just stars for a flag.

While clicking and dragging to make the star shape, hold down ⌘/Ctrl to pull out the points on the star shape to make for more pronounced shine spikes.

If you activate the Star tool and click the artboard, a dialog box appears where you can add more precise measurements for your star artwork: for example, the size of radius 1 (the inner points of the star) and radius 2 (the outer points of the start) as well as the overall number of outer points. (See Figure 9-7.)

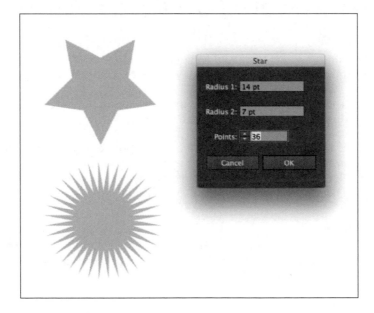

Figure 9-7: Edit your star shape.

The Flare tool

The Flare tool is a specialty item with dramatic properties: not really a shape but kinda. Think of a photo you've shot or seen that has lens flare, when it's not well exposed and is marred with big balls and streaks of light. (Okay, sometimes lens flare is pretty cool.) The one drawback to using the Flare tool is that it must be used on a black background.

Making charts and graphs with the Graph tool

Illustrator has a very flexible Graph tool. You can make charts and graphs styled any way you want, while still keeping them "live." This means that you can change the look of the chart to fit your publication's style without changing your ability to add new numbers later.

Creating a chart

Activate the Graph tool on the tool bar. If you click and hold it, a menu appears of the various graphing options. Just for fun, choose the Line Graph tool. This format is useful for showing data over time, or for showing values that create a trend of some kind.

In the workspace, click and drag to define the size of the chart. (Don't worry, you can always adjust the size later.) When you release the mouse, a dialog box opens where you can save your data.

Populating your chart

You can start entering your data directly into it — or, even better, cut and paste already formatted data from a program like Excel. Comma-separated values (CVS) data flows neatly into a variety of programs without losing the essential column and row organization. So you can edit data in a powerful program like Excel (sorting, for example, so that the numbers go from biggest to smallest) and then just copy and paste your clean data into the Illustrator data field.

If your chart doesn't turn out the way you expected, or you see an error message, the problem is likely the data format. Illustrator reads numbers with commas in them as text. Likewise, if you have a column of dates that are just numbers, you need to add quotes for Illustrator to understand that those numbers are categories.

The second button from the left — Transpose Data — allows you to flip how your data is organized. Click it to see what happens; then click it again to toggle to the original orientation. When you close the data dialog box, it will query whether you want to save your chart. Assuming that you select Yes, you can get to the data again by choosing Object⇨Graph⇨Data or by right-clicking the chart and choosing Data from the context menu.

Get a head of yourself

Remember to add a title to your chart. State what is being measured as well as what quantities are being used in that measurement. And just like remembering to save your progress at regular intervals, the graphic artist should develop a habit of double-checking data. "Am I really showing thousands of dollars, or is it millions?"

Here's how to modify the look of your chart:

1. **Click and hold the Selection tool at the top of the Tools palette.**

2. **Choose the Direct Selection tool from the options that appear and then click the fever line (chart line) within your chart.**

   The Direct Selection Tool allows you to select only the fever line in your chart. Although it will only select a portion of the line, you can select the entire line by holding down Option/Alt while clicking the line.

3. **With the entire line selected, change the color of the line by choosing Window⇨Color and then selecting the color you want.**

   You can choose any color you like for the line color. You can also choose a different line width for the fever line by using the Window⇨Stroke menu.

   If you're working with a client, make sure your choices work with any required brand guidelines.

Now you can change the chart font and type size:

1. **Deselect everything by clicking an empty part of your pasteboard.**

2. **Click your chart once to select the full chart.**

3. **Change the type attributes from the top tool bar.**

Now you can choose different chart types to see what your data looks like expressed in different chart forms:

1. **⌘+right-click your chart without deselecting.**

   It's not uncommon to click and miss the target item, thereby deselecting the target object. If that happens, just click the target object again.

   That brings up a dialog box where you can change many more things about how your chart looks.

2. **Click Type to see a selection of options.**

   • *Chart type:* Along the top are icons for different chart types. If you want to see what your data looks like expressed in different chart forms, change it now. (You can always change it back.)

   • *Column/Cluster width:* At the bottom of that same dialog box are Column Width and Cluster Width, which control the width of the bar and how far apart the bars are, respectively.

   • *Graph options:* From the Graph Options drop-down menu at the very top of the dialog box, you can change aspects of the x and y axes, including the range of the numbers and the length of tick marks in your chart.

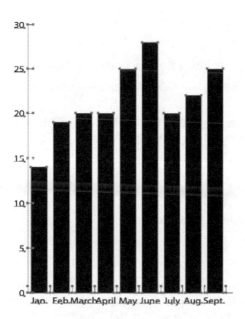

Time to save. Choose from

- ✔ **An AI (.ai) or a PDF (.pdf) if you want it to remain editable**

  If you choose to save as an Illustrator file, you (obviously) can open the file to edit it in illustrator. For a PDF file (.pdf), you can open the file in illustrator or a .pdf reader program (in case you don't have Illustrator). And that's a good thing in the case your client isn't graphic savvy or doesn't have the required software to view the graphic.

- ✔ **A rastorized JPEG (.jpg) image if you want to include it as an image for use in another program**

- ✔ **An SVG (.svg), a GIFF (.gif), or a PNG (.png) for web use**

If you choose the Save for Web & Devices option (just Save for Web in Adobe CC), you can specify the exact pixel size you want your chart image without physically changing the size of the chart itself or the pasteboard. This is handy if you're exporting the same graphic for use on multiple platforms.

Using the Eyedropper tool

The Eyedropper tool is one of the most useful in Illustrator's toolbox. Use it to copy attributes — for example color, font, or level of transparency — from anything in your document and then apply those attributes to virtually anything else in your document.

Say you have a photo with a shade of blue that you would like to use in your graphic. Here's how easy it is:

1. **Paste the photo into your Illustrator document by choosing File⇨Place.**

2. **In the file-browsing dialog box that Illustrator opens, search for the image you want.**

3. **Double-click the file in the dialog box and click the place within your document where you want to put the photo.**

4. **Activate the Eyedropper tool from the Tools palette.**

5. **In the pasted photo, click the color you want to copy.**

   The Eyedropper "picks up" the information. You'll see the color show up in the box at the bottom of your toolbar.

6. **Activate a drawing tool — say, the Pen tool — and draw a shape.**

   It will automatically have the color you just picked up.

   The picked-up color becomes a part of your working file, isolating/defining that color with the Eyedropper allows you to add the color to a shape or text, and you can also add it to your color swatches for use later.

   Press D on your keyboard at any point to return that box to your default color.

Here's how to change the color of a shape already in your design. For this example, assume you have a blue box and a red circle, but you want the circle to also become blue.

1. **Select the shape — in this case, the red circle.**

   You can change attributes for more than one shape at a time. Select as many polygons and type elements as you want, and change them all at once. Just hold down Shift while you click to select multiple items.

2. **Activate the Eyedropper tool and click the blue box.**

   The red circle takes on the same color and stroke as the blue box.

   If you hold down Option/Alt while clicking, the Eyedropper tool works the opposite way — turning the box red.

Custom Eyedropper

If you don't want the Eyedropper tool to pick up all the attributes of whatever you're copying, you can customize the tool. Double-click the Eyedropper icon in the Tools palette to bring up a dialog box where you can select what the Eyedropper will affect. For example, if you want it to use only the level of transparency, clear all check boxes but that one. The red circle in our example now picks up only the amount of transparency applied to the blue box, not the color or stroke. The same function allows you to copy font information.

Adding icons with the Symbols tool

Using the Symbols tool is pretty straightforward — an easy way to add icons, which are increasingly useful in the age of shareable graphics. To test-drive it, start by choosing Window➪Symbols. The Symbols tab will open empty.

To make a symbol, simply select a vector object or a photo and drag it into the box. It's that easy. Or go to the drop-down menu from the Symbols panel and choose Open Symbol Library. (Take a look around there first; there might be some fun stuff already made. Just click individual symbols to add them to your palette.)

Here's how to make a symbol from scratch. We'll star — um, start — with stars.

1. **From the Tools palette, click and hold the Rectangle tool and then select the Star tool from the menu that opens.**

2. **Make the star, select it, and drag it into your open Symbols palette.**

   A dialog box opens where you can name the symbol.

   Give it an easy-to-remember name in case you end up with a lot of symbols.

3. **Choose what kind of symbol you want it to be, as shown in Figure 9-8:**

   • *Movie Clip:* Movie Clip is important only if you plan to animate it later in Flash.

   • *Graphic:* This is what you want.

   You could also change the registration point of your object — the "center" that your object rotates around. You probably won't need to change that very often.

4. **Click OK to finish creating the star symbol.**

Preset symbols

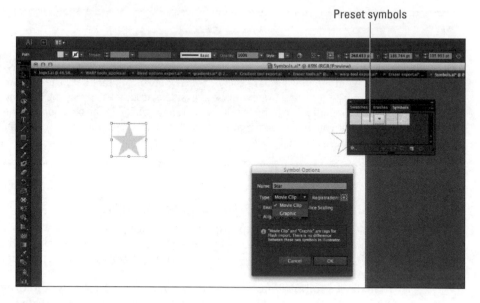

Figure 9-8: Creating symbols of your own.

Using your symbols

Activate the Symbol Sprayer tool, which is found in the Symbols panel and looks like a can of spray paint. If you click and hold it, a menu appears with all the tools in this set. Click the right edge of that window, and the tool will pop out into its own box. You can always just close it like any window in Illustrator.

With the star symbol selected, give the tools a test drive:

- ✔ The **Symbol Sprayer** tool acts like a can of spray paint. Click and drag for a heavy effect, or just dab for individual instances of your star.

  Use the Symbol Sprayer to (in effect) create clones of the same "shape," which makes using a symbol easier than a shape sometimes. (See Figure 9-9.)

- ✔ Use the **Shifter tool** to move entire sets of symbols. You can move the symbols after they have landed, pull in stragglers, or move whole sections.

- ✔ The **Symbol Scruncher** condenses areas, pulling the symbols more tightly together as you click and drag over key spots.

- ✔ The **Symbol Sizer** has you click and drag to change the size of your symbol. This makes the collection of symbols less uniform.

- ✔ The **Symbol Spinner** changes the direction of the symbols.

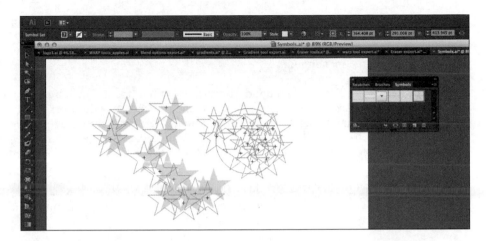

Figure 9-9: Spraying a shape creates clones quickly.

✓ The **Symbol Stainer** tool changes the color of the symbols. Select a color, and then click and drag over the stars to see how the color is applied.

✓ The **Symbol Screener** controls opacity levels. Like the Color Change tool, now your stars have varied levels of transparency.

✓ The **Symbol Styler** tool allows you to apply specific styles to your symbols from the graphics style palette. Just click and drag over leaves to change to whatever style you chose from the palette. You can find the graphics style palette by choosing Window➪Graphics. Look at the fly-out menu to find a library of styles that you can experiment with. Select a style and click the stars to see the results.

For more control, double-click any of these tools. The Options dialog box will open, giving you the ability to control the tools numerically.

Editing your symbols

The drop-down menu in the upper-right corner of the Symbols palette offers a full array of options for editing your symbols. Some of the functions are also available along the bottom of the symbols window. These are shortcuts to the most common actions.

Making the most of the Symbol tool

To swap a symbol with another, select a symbol on your pasteboard and then select the symbol icon in the panel that you want to use in its place. From the drop-down menu, choose Replace Symbol.

To change one instance of the symbol, select it. Then, from the drop-down menu, choose Break Links to Symbol. Now what you have are just regular graphics. When you make changes to those vector graphics, the symbol remains unchanged.

The Edit Symbol command opens the symbol itself. You can make changes to the vectors. You can add parts, change the shapes, whatever you like. Then when you go back to the main document (arrow at upper left of document), your changes will appear in that symbol. Those changes are not reflected in symbol libraries, though — just in the symbol within your document.

Saving your symbols

The Symbols panel shows what you're working with at the time, within any given document.

To save a group of symbols — for example, to share with other designers, organize them into themes, or to keep a version untouched by edits — choose Save Symbol Library at the bottom of the drop-down menu. Whatever you have in your palette will be saved as a new Illustrator document. The default will be to save your selection to the Symbols folder, but you can save it anywhere you like. For example, you could save it to your desktop and e-mail that document to other collaborators.

Using the Pathfinder tool to create shapes

The Pathfinder tool is a real workhorse tool. Use it to create shapes, even very complex shapes, without drawing them from scratch. This section shows you how to draw with the Pathfinder tool. Then, amazingly, you'll see how the Shapefinder tool does the same thing, only faster.

Pathfinder uses Boolean technology, which essentially uses one shape to change another. When you have two shapes, you can use the Pathfinder tool to "add" those two shapes together, "subtract" one from the other, or just cut them into separate parts.

Start by choosing Window➪Pathfinder. The dialog box that opens has several different pictograms of the actions that it can perform.

The top row — Shape Modes — are live effects: that is, you can position one shape over another, click the "action" of choice, and still move and adjust the individual shapes at will. When the shapes are where you want them to be, click the Expand button on the right side of the dialog box to complete the action. If you choose the Minus Front shape mode (second from the left), the shape that was on top will cut out the part of the lower shape where the two shapes overlapped.

The lower row perform similar cuts and adds, but they are immediate and can be changed only with the Undo command.

The Shapefinder tool is newer and can be found in the Tools palette. See Figure 9-10. You can select many shapes at once and, without ungrouping anything, just select individual parts of the group to merge or cut. This tool behaves basically the same way as the Pathfinder tool but in a much more direct way.

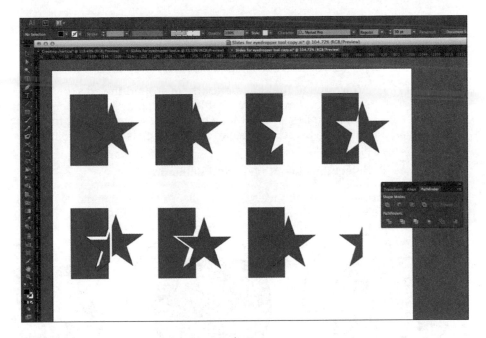

Figure 9-10: Using one shape to change another.

Editing paths with the Eraser tool

You can take a vector object — any vector object — and erase parts of it as easily as you can with the Eraser tool in Photoshop . . . perhaps even more easily than with pencil and paper.

The powerful Eraser tool does several functions at once. In essence, it draws a brushstroke, expanding that brush stroke to make an actual shape, and then uses that shape to cut into other vector shapes in the same way the Pathfinder tool works. Incredibly complex, but it's quite easy to use.

Getting started with the Eraser tool

Double-click the Eraser tool (about one-third of the way down the Tools palette, and looks like, well, an eraser).

Double-clicking any of Illustrator's tools opens a dialog box offering precise control over the way that tool behaves.

If you have a Wacom tablet, the Eraser tool gives you the ability to become "pressure sensitive." See the Fixed option? Check out that drop-down menu and marvel.

The Eraser is just as much fun if you're using a mouse, though. Here's something you can try.

1. **Draw an apple.**

2. **Select the shape, activate the Eraser tool, and start cutting.**

   For fun, draw a bite-shaped cut. See Figure 9-11.

   After you cut the shape, the stroke around the edge of the apple now goes around everything that hasn't been erased. If there is a stroke, the tool reapplies it to all of the edges. If there isn't, then the cuts are simply cuts. The Eraser cuts a narrow line because the size of the Eraser tool is small.

3. **Select the cut-out piece and delete it.**

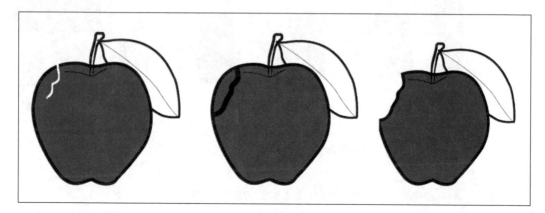

Figure 9-11: Working with the Eraser tool.

Working with straight edges and lines

Hold Option/Alt while you click and drag with the tool to create a cutting area shaped like a rectangle. Cut whole straight-edged chunks off anything you've drawn. Hold Shift+Option/Alt, and the Eraser tool constrains it to a square.

Another really excellent use of the Eraser tool is to refine drawn brush lines. Brush stroke lines can be cut or sculpted with the Eraser, as shown in Figure 9-12. If your line end is too rounded and blunt, select the line and shave away unwanted parts with the eraser.

Brush line

Cut with the Eraser tool

Expanded and then cut with the Eraser tool

Figure 9-12: Perfect brush lines with the Eraser tool.

Dealing with snafus

You may find that parts of your illustration are erased, while others are not. There are a couple of reasons why this may happen.

- ✔ **The Eraser tool works only on vectors.** If you have a rasterized image in your graphic, you can't edit it this way.

- ✔ **Maybe only part of your illustration was selected.** The Eraser tool works only on the part that is selected. Or, if nothing is selected, it will affect everything — except rasterized images (see the preceding bullet).

- ✔ **If you erase a part of a line and the result is surprising, you may need to "expand" the look of the line before you use the Eraser on it.** If your line has an effect applied to it (like an artistic brushstroke) and you cut the line with the Eraser, each new part of the line has the effect applied to it separately.

The results can sometimes be unexpected. If you want the Eraser tool to cut the shape as the shape is shown, use the "expand" option under the Object menu to turn paths into straightforward vector shapes that you can erase.

✔ **You may be trying to erase type.** You can't erase type unless you've turned it into a vector object (Type➪Create Outlines). You also can't erase charts or blends until they are ungrouped or expanded.

Experimenting with Illustrator Effects

With the basic functions of Adobe Illustrator under your belt, you may want to play around with some features that add extra artistic flair to your work. You certainly don't need all these features in your bag of tricks, but they're fun, and sometimes they add the perfect finishing touch to an infographic.

Gaining contrast with a gradient

Using the Gradient tool is pretty straightforward. A gradient is simply one color fading into another color. For example, filling a square with a gradient that goes from blue at the top to white at the bottom would create a quick-and-easy sky background in a drawing.

But, the fact that you can have multiple colors in a blend, can blend to 100 percent transparency, and can decide between a straight (linear) blend or a circular (radial) makes this tool one of the most powerful drawing tools in Illustrator's toolbox. The uses for the tool are limited only by one's imagination.

Gradients can be applied to any vector object as long as it's a closed shape.

You can apply a gradient fill to type, to shapes that you have drawn, or across several shapes at once. And, as of Illustrator CS6, a gradient can even be applied to a line or stroke. So if you try to apply a gradient, and it looks like it didn't happen, check that you didn't accidentally apply it to the stroke instead of the fill.

To understand how the tool works, here's a simple example to create contrast and depth in a drawing. Here we show you how to make two red circles and use a radial fill to make the first one look more 3D.

1. **Create two red circles.**

2. **Choose Window➪Gradient.**

3. **Select the first red circle and apply a blend.**

   Illustrator provides some default blends to start, which you can access from the Gradient tab or from among the swatches. (Note: Any blends that you create and want to keep can be saved to your swatches when you're done.)

4. **Now change the colors in the gradient. Change the white part of the gradient to red:**

   a. Select the white swatch.

   b. Adjust the color in your color window or by double-clicking the white square to open a color swatch list that you can select from.

At this point, the gradient is "linear," going from left to right. Changing it to a radial fill will make the shading look more ball-like. Follow the bouncing ball:

1. **With the circle selected, activate the Gradient tool found in the Tools palette.**

2. **Click and drag from a point within the circle.**

   The start point will be red, and the end will be black. Experiment with where you click and drag to get your gradient just where you want it. You can also physically move and rotate the gradient annotator bar with your gradient tool. See Figure 9-13.

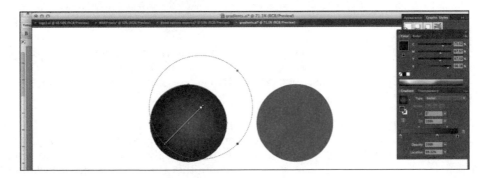

Figure 9-13: Changing the fill to alter appearance.

Add a third color:

1. **Hover the cursor underneath the gradient slider on the Gradient tab.**

   You'll get a little plus symbol.

2. **Click to add a third color.**

   Move the three color stops left and right to see how they change where the color transitions happen.

3. **Change the black swatch to a dark red.**

   Now the shading looks more subtle. You can add as many color stops as you want, including white at the far left if you want to create a really sharp contrast. See Figure 9-14.

Figure 9-14: Experimenting with shading.

Building depth with the Blend tool

The Blend tool is a robust function within Illustrator that can be used in a wide variety of ways. It's definitely worth experimenting with. It can blend lines, colors, shapes, and type, and it does each of these blends along a dynamic path that you can edit.

Locating the Blend tool

Blend is available on the Tools palette bar or from choosing Object⇨Blend.

If you access Blend from the Tools palette, the dialog box that opens gives you the ability to choose the following blending options: Smooth Color, Specified Steps, Specified Distance, and Orientation. (You need to double-click the option to open it.)

The Smooth Color option makes a seamless blend from one shape to the other. If that isn't what you want, choose the next option from the drop-down menu and set the number of steps manually. Fewer steps make a more abrupt transition; more steps make a smoother transition. Specified Distance is how far apart each of the objects in the transition are set from one another.

If you choose Object⇨Blend, you get a few additional options:

- **Release:** Undo the blend.
- **Expand:** Flatten your dynamic blend into a set of editable vectors.
- **Blend Options:** These are the same elements available from the Tools palette.
- **Spline commands:** Affect the path that the blend is following.

One more difference between accessing the tool from the Object menu versus the Tools palette is that from Object, you can choose Make Blend with both objects selected to make the blend. If you're using the Tools palette Blend tool, you select the tool, click the first object, and then click the second object.

Be careful: Where you click the objects can determine object rotation in the blend. If you click in the center of the objects, you get a standard blend. Clicking the corners and edges of the objects creates a rotation in the blend, which can be fun and useful — but a shock if you aren't expecting it.

Determining what you can blend

The good news is that you can blend anything that is a vector. All you have to do is select both items and then choose Object⇨Blend⇨Make. You'll automatically get a blend from one object to the other that will show a transition of size, color, and shape.

Blending shapes can mean creating a transition from a small circle to a large star, or a small square to a large piece of type. Illustrator now treats type as a vector object even without creating "outlines" of it, which can be really handy. See Figure 9-15.

Figure 9-15: Creating a simple blend.

The Blend tool can also be a quick way to create a set number of items, which can be handy in graphics with representations of large numbers. If you know you need exactly 50 of something, you can use the blend steps to create that number within a defined distance. Try blending one star to another of the same size. If you set the number of steps to 48, you know you have 48 plus the 2 stars you used to make the blend.

Using the blend's spline

The objects that you blend are treated as one grouped object if you're using the Selection tool. However, if you're using the Direct Selection tool, you can get into that blend the same way as you can any grouped object. You can select one of your blend objects and change the color, and the blend is updated instantly.

You can also see, especially when you're in preview mode, a line that shows up between the two objects. That line is the blend's spline. You can interact with it by clicking it with the Direct Selection tool. Select one end point, and you can move that end of the line. Turn that anchor point into a curve by using the anchor point information box along the top of your workspace. Using Convert (under the Pen tool) changes curve points to corners and vice versa.

Then, when your endpoint is a curve, you can use the handles to control the arc of your spline.

You can also swap out that "spline" line for any other line. If you suddenly want your blend to be in a zigzag line, the solution is quite simple. Draw your zigzag line, select it and your blended object, and then choose Object➪Blend➪Replace Spline. The blend is now attached to your new zigzag line. Cool!

Creating dynamic graphics with a warp

Illustrator has a set of warp tools that can add a dynamic flair to your designs with just a couple of clicks. Find these tools on the Tools palette, under the Variable Width tool. These tools all do basically the same task: distorting your vector elements, a lot or a little, depending on how far you click and drag.

Click and hold the Variable Width tool, located about halfway down the Tools palette. The warp tools will show up in the drop-down menu.

Click the tear-away bar at the right of the window to separate it from your Tools palette to see the tools all at once and access them easily.

The Variable Width tool affects only lines or strokes. If you click a line in your design, it will change the width as you click and drag. This tool is good for making your lines look like brushstrokes from a paintbrush, among other things. If you hold down Option/Alt while you drag, only one side of the line expands. If you like the kind of line you just made and want to keep it to apply to other lines later, add it to the Variable Width profiles drop-down menu, located along the top. There, you can choose from the menu of saved presets or add a new one.

So, to save your finished line, select it, and open the Variable Width profile menu in the control panel. Click the Add to Profile button at the bottom (looks like a tiny floppy disk). Then you can name and save the changes you made to your line into the Presets menu. It will be available to use later on any other line in your document.

The Variable Width tool is conceptually similar to the warp tools, but it's different in one key way. The lines themselves are not changed; it's just an effect that's applied and can be edited at any time. Look at your line in preview mode (⌘+Y/Ctrl+Y) to see that your line and its points are all still as you initially drew them.

The warp tools, however, actually change the geometry of the line or shape that you use them on.

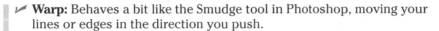

✔ **Warp:** Behaves a bit like the Smudge tool in Photoshop, moving your lines or edges in the direction you push.

✔ **Twirl:** Creates spiral shapes. Select the tool, and then click and hold a spot on your line. The longer you hold it, the tighter the spiral. If you press Option/Alt after you start the spiral, the spiral will spin in the opposite direction.

✔ **Pucker:** Pulls in parts of your drawing like cinching in a waistline or tightening a belt.

✔ **Bloat:** Does the opposite of the Pucker tool. It adds organic scaling or "bloating" to parts of your vector shape.

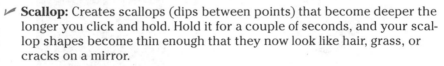

✔ **Scallop:** Creates scallops (dips between points) that become deeper the longer you click and hold. Hold it for a couple of seconds, and your scallop shapes become thin enough that they now look like hair, grass, or cracks on a mirror.

✔ **Crystallize:** Similar to the Scallop tool but jagged. The effect looks a bit like how explosions are drawn in comic books.

✔ **Wrinkle:** Also similar to the Scallop and Crystallize tools but smoother. The distortions to your edges look more like waves.

All these tools can be adjusted and controlled numerically for really precise handling. Double-click the tool icon itself, and an Options dialog box appears where you can change size, angle, intensity, and more.

Multiple effects can be applied to the same vector object or line. You can start with the Bloat tool, for example, and add scalloping to it for a paint splatter effect. Or create spirals and then further distort those spirals with one of the other tools. The results of these tools are quite complex and can really add a lot of visual interest to your work.

Joining objects with a compound path

As you likely have figured out by now, there's often more than one way to complete a task in Illustrator. For instance, to draw a circle, you can use the Ellipse tool, or you could draw a circle manually with the Pen tool, or you could draw a square and reshape the corners to rounded arcs. Any of these techniques would be fine. You might notice subtle differences, but the end product will be a circle.

Some designs are a little more complex, with really only a couple of options for completing them. For example, take a shape that needs to be edited to include a "see-through" hole, like a donut. Illustrator's Compound Path selection is your best bet (choose Object⇨Compound Path). Compound Path turns several grouped polygons into what the program recognizes as one polygon. It can also take one object and subtract it from another.

If you make two circles, one inside the other, you can punch a hole out of one in the shape of the other. See Figure 9-16. For the best results, be sure to make the circle on top smaller than the one behind. Choose Object⇨Compound Path⇨Make. This will produce a donut shape. Then, Illustrator sees this as one object — not as a grouped object — which makes it simple to move around your design.

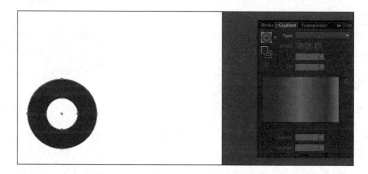

Figure 9-16: Creating an object with the compound path.

With Pathfinder, you can also produce compound paths. First, select the donut and choose Object⇨Compound Path⇨Release. This will ungroup the donut polygons and become two separate shapes again. Duplicate these three more times by copy/pasting the pair (choose Edit⇨Copy, Edit⇨Paste). You can use these as examples for the Pathfinder tool.

Move them into a configuration that will best show the Pathfinder results. That is, place them in a line — not atop each other.

With the Pathfinder selected, select the first group of circles. With both small and large circles selected, go to the Pathfinder and select the first pathfinder option — Unite — which will combine the two shapes into one shape.

With the second group of circles selected, click the Subtract function in the Pathfinder. This, much like the Compound Path tool, will subtract the top from the bottom shape.

The third option — Intersect —leaves only the areas that overlap in the selections. The fourth option — Exclude —does the opposite of the Intersect option (leaves out overlapping sections of the shapes). See Figure 9-17.

Figure 9-17: Detailed work with the compound path.

Use the Pathfinder and the Compound Path tools to help create drawings where you need a hole in a wall, bites out of a sandwich, or a key hole in a door lock. They are immensely useful and will be a great addition to your drawing tools.

Cropping illustrations with clipping masks

Illustrator, like Photoshop, allows you to mask elements of your design. Illustrator has two types of masks: clipping and opacity.

The Clipping mask allows you to mask any shape with any other shape simply by selecting them all (hold down Shift to select multiple items) and then choosing Object⇨Clipping Mask⇨Make. The object on the top (the other shapes are behind it) becomes the mask, or window, through which the bottom layers are seen.

For example, make a red rectangle. Then for a little excitement, put some white stripes across the top of that rectangle. Draw a white line, make it nice and thick (say, 10pt). While holding down Option/Alt, drag the line down a little ways. (If you hold Shift down as well, the movement is constrained to a single direction.)

Now you should have two lines.

Press ⌘+D/Ctrl+D to get a third line evenly spaced from the second. Do this a couple more times, and you'll have a bunch of stripes.

Now draw another shape on top. It could be a circle, a star, or even just the word "stripes."

It doesn't matter what color that object is because the color won't show. It's just important that this last shape be on top of the others. Select all those elements and choose Object⇨Clipping Mask⇨Make or press ⌘+7/Ctrl+7. (See Figure 9-18.)

You should have a masked version of your stripes now. You can choose Object⇨Clipping Mask⇨Release to undo the mask at any point, and use the Direct Selection tool to select and move any masked object, leaving everything else untouched.

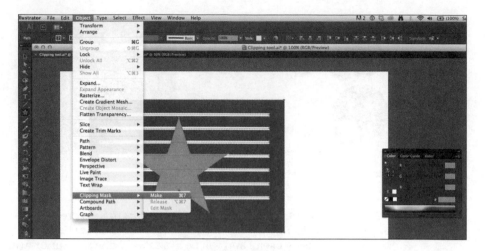

Figure 9-18: Experimenting with the clipping mask.

The Opacity mask works basically the same way but uses tones to establish what shows through and what doesn't. This allows for a more subtle transition between visible and not visible.

Give it a try:

1. **Take the same red rectangle and stripes and draw a new shape on top.**

2. **Fill that shape with a gradient fill: say, a black and white gradient.**

   It doesn't matter whether you choose a radial or linear style of fill. Either will work.

3. **With all the shapes selected, choose Window⇨Transparency.**

4. **Click the Make Mask button in the Transparency dialog box.**

   What you masked shows through in the white parts and less so where the gradient was darker.

   If you select the Invert Mask box, the opposite happens: The lighter parts will be hidden, and the darker parts will show through.

Here's another example. Draw another shape and fill it with a color — say, black — and then move it behind your image (choose Object⇨Arrange⇨Send to Back). You can see that the edges of your image really are being masked in a gradual way.

You can use either technique to mask vector shapes, text, and photographs. Illustrator also allows you to create masks within masks, allowing you to create complex designs very quickly.

Importing sketches into Illustrator to use as a template

Even in our wired world, artists still love to sketch. Great news! Your rough sketches can be easily worked into your drafts of infographics. You can scan sketches or snap a picture of your sketch with your phone and e-mail it to yourself. They don't need to be color, just clear enough for you to work with.

You can also import your sketch directly into Illustrator. To use a sketch as a template, open your Illustrator document and simply place the image the way you would any photo. Put it on its own layer so you can turn the visibility on and off to check your progress. You can lock that layer or make it a "template" layer, which will enable you to dim the image, making it easier to draw on top of.

Sketches can also become part of your infographic. You can colorize a pencil drawing in a number of ways. Most simply, you can draw color layers and then set the transparency on your traced image to Multiply. This will make the black-and-white image combine with the colors to create a Photoshop-like result, as illustrated in Figure 9-19.

Figure 9-19: Apply color to a black-and-white drawing.

Or, you can select the live trace option from the Windows menu (with a placed image selected, choose Object⇨Image Trace) to turn your drawings into vector objects, which will look more polished and will remain fully editable as your work progresses. This technique works best with stronger contrast sketches, like ones done with ink or marker. From the Image Trace dialog box, you can control the *tolerance,* which sets how tightly the trace will follow the lines of your drawing. More precise tolerance will result in more anchor points. "Expand" will break the tracing into editable vector shapes, which allows you to see your art in greater detail.

You can also click the Image Trace button in the Control panel, or select a preset from the Tracing Presets button.

10

Designing Infographics
in Photoshop

*A*dobe Photoshop gives ordinary folks the power to edit photos to appear extraordinary by smoothing away blemishes, adding features, and altering composition. Photoshop, which has added features over the years, has become a standard tool for graphic designers. Photoshop is a key part of the Adobe Creative Suite, and as of 2013, is available through Adobe's Creative Cloud (CC) subscription service.

If you're working in the Creative Cloud (CC) versions of Adobe's Creative Suite software, you'll likely notice similarities between your workspace in Photoshop and Illustrator. Adobe has designed a common user interface between related programs, making it easier to apply what you know about one program when you're learning another. The workspaces look very similar and have similar commands, panels, and tools. Read more about all this in Chapter 11.

Photoshop is a *raster graphics* editor, which means that users can create or edit drawings or photographic images by manipulating pixels. Compare that with *vector image editors* — like Illustrator — which allow users to manipulate lines and shapes. (Read all about using Illustrator in Chapter 9.)

Different tasks may call for different programs; we'll talk about some of the benefits and drawbacks of both kinds of programs. Nowadays, an infographic designer should have a good working knowledge of both. We'll use the same infographic we use in Chapter 9 to show you how designers typically use Photoshop in their infographic projects. Here's how to get started with Photoshop.

Getting Started with Photoshop

Has a parent or coach ever told you, "You have to walk before you can run"? Photoshop is a bit like that. Mastering the basics and getting a handle on how to organize your work will help you build a good foundation for the trickier features that can really make your work stand out. In this section, we talk about some of Photoshop's essential functions and give you some tips for keeping your work organized so that you don't lose track of your hard work.

Labeling layers

Photoshop allows you to work with different layers, applying features to them individually or in groups. Using layers allows you to create great depth and visual interest in your projects. Also, a layered structure allows you a high degree of control. For example, it's pretty easy to fine-tune your design by altering color, shadows, and special techniques.

Here's how to get started with layers.

1. **Open or create a new Photoshop document.**

2. **Open the Layers palette by choosing Window⇨Layers.**

   When you create a new Photoshop document, it will start with one layer by default. That layer is called `Background` and is locked. That layer can be unlocked, used, or deleted. See Figure 10-1.

Think of layers as a stack of individual images on your canvas. The image you see in your workspace depends on the opacity, order, and position of each layer. Layers can be sorted, grouped, or locked; and the visibility of that layer can be turned on or off. In Figure 10-2, you can see that each main element of the Uncle Sam graphic has its own layer.

Using layers allows you to edit or apply effects to particular parts of your image without affecting the rest. You can try out changes and effects to your image, and then simply turn that layer off or delete it if you change your mind, leaving the rest of your work intact.

Here are a few other layer basics:

✏ **To create a new layer**

   a. *Click the icon at the top right of the Layers palette.*

   b. *From the fly-out menu that appears, choose New Layer.*

   c. *In the New Layer dialog box that appears, you can name that layer and also select a highlight color.*

Figure 10-1: Getting started with Photoshop's layers palette.

Name the layer something descriptive to help you easily identify layers as you work. For example, if you have a picture of an apple and want to try adding a highlight, name the image layer `apple` and the highlight layer above it `apple_highlight`.

✔ To rename an existing layer

a. *With the ⌘/Ctrl key pressed, click the layer.*

b. *Select layer then go to Layer/Rename layer from the dropdown menu along the top. The name field of your layer will become active, allowing you to type in the new name.*

Even easier, just double-click the name itself within the Layers palette. The name becomes editable, and you can start typing a new and better name.

Using folders and groups

The Layers palette can get difficult to navigate pretty quickly as your document gets more complex. In addition to naming your layers, we recommend grouping your layers.

Figure 10-2: Give each major element of your infographic a name.

Grouping of layers is done with several layers that will reside in a separate folder within the layers palette. "The group" and "folder of layers" are synonymous.

The advantages to grouping layers are

- **Layers within a group or a folder can be moved together.** They behave as a single object. Layer groups can be moved around the document canvas, and moved up or down in your layer order.

- **Groups can have effects applied to all layers within the group at once.** For example, the transparency of a group can be changed from the Opacity field at the top of the Layers palette. The default blend mode for a group you create is Pass Through, which means that the individual modes for each layer will remain intact. Changing the folder's blend mode will apply that change to all layers.

- **Your Layers palette and your document will be more organized.** Putting layers within groups or nesting groups within other groups keeps the parts of your image in order.

To create a folder, click the Create New Group icon at the bottom of the Layers palette. This makes an empty folder into which you can drag individual layers.

A more efficient way, however, is to select the layers you want to group and then create a group.

A group can help the user more quickly locate things within the Layers palette. A group can also make it much easier to move several objects at once within the design. For example, a drawing of a person would have several distinct parts: a head, arms, legs, clothing, and so on. If you want to move that person when you're assembling your infographic, it's much easier to select those body parts as a group rather than one by one. Also, using groups reduces clutter and allows for greater organization in the Layers panel.

1. **Hold Shift (keyboard) as you select layers.**

   To select contiguous layers, click the top layer and then Shift-click the last or bottom-most layer you want to include. All the layers in between become selected as well. To select noncontiguous layers, press ⌘/Ctrl and select the desired layers.

   Groups work best with layers that are ordered immediately above and below one another.

2. **With the layers selected, click the Menu icon at the top right of the Layers palette.**

3. **Choose New Group from Layers.**

   A dialog box appears where you can name the new group, and all your layers will be inside.

To open the folder, click the triangle to the left of the group name. The folder will open, displaying all the layers inside. See Figure 10-3. Those layers can still be selected and manipulated individually. New layers can be dragged into that group at any point. Click the triangle again to collapse (close) the folder.

Folders can be renamed at any point by double-clicking the folder name to edit it.

Figure 10-3: Use folders to keep work organized.

Learning the Basic Photoshop Tools

Conveniently, Photoshop and Illustrator share many similar functions. At times, you'll have to decide which program to use, but there's really not a wrong answer. Many infographic designers use Photoshop and Illustrator (see Chapter 9), sometimes alone and sometimes together. Here's a look at some of the most common Photoshop functions.

If you're working in the Creative Cloud (CC) versions of Adobe's Creative Suite software, you likely noticed the similarities between your workspace in Photoshop and Illustrator. Adobe has designed a common user interface between related programs, making it easier to apply what you know about one program when you're learning another. The workspaces look very similar and have similar commands, panels, and tools. There's no definitive answer about which program is better, but here's a look at some of the similarities and differences you'll notice in some commonly used tools.

Selection tools

Use selection tools to isolate a particular part of your infographic to move or change it in some way.

- ✔ The **Selection** tool and **Direct Selection** tools in Illustrator are similar to the Move tool and Path Selection tool in Photoshop.
- ✔ The familiar **Hand** tool allows the user to move the visible area in both programs.
- ✔ The **Magic Wand** tool selects related areas of tone or color, and it can be found in Illustrator as well as Photoshop.
- ✔ The **Lasso** tools are the same. In Illustrator, the Lasso selects vector shapes, lines, and anchor points. In Photoshop, the Lasso tool selects pixels within the defined area.
- ✔ The **Eyedropper** tool behaves the same way in both programs, picking up colors from selected points in an image.

Drawing tools

Drawing tools are those tools within Photoshop that behave, virtually, like actual drawing tools. They allow you to create, color, or affect pixels in a way that simulates the use of a pencil or a brush.

- ✔ The **Pen** tools are virtually the same. Getting used to drawing with anchor points and handles may be tricky when you're starting out, but at least you won't have to learn it twice.

- The **Pencil** tool is available in both programs, but it still provides much less control than the **Bezier Pen** tool, so we recommend that you don't bother with it.

- Both programs have **Rectangle** and **Ellipse** tools that draw editable paths.

- **Brushes** are controlled similarly in the two programs. The main difference is that brush strokes in Illustrator are more editable, both when they are being used as a line, and even after they have been expanded to create a vector shape. Brushes in Photoshop behave more like actual paintbrushes. They are intuitive, especially if you're using a tablet and stylus instead of a mouse, but they create areas of colored pixels that are edited by adding or erasing pixels.

- **Gradients** have become remarkably similar. The fact that the color choice and distances are governed by the same system of color stops in both programs makes gradients much easier to understand. Linear and radial fills are created the same way and look the same. The difference in Photoshop is the flexibility to use them as a layer effect to modify the pixels on other layers.

Gradients are a color fill rather than an actual tool. Gradients are used when a fade in color is needed or if the illustration needs one more level of realistic detail — for example, light-to-dark shadows on an illustration. As a tool that applies color and tone (albeit in a very sophisticated way), gradients count as a drawing tool.

- The **Eraser** tool also behaves similarly in both programs.

In Photoshop — as in real life — an eraser is indeed a drawing tool. For instance, if you're drawing on a dark background, you can use the Eraser tool to subtract darks by drawing with it on the dark surface. Essentially, the Eraser tool acts just like a pencil eraser: It takes away detail rather than create it.

✓ The color option is similar on both toolbars but reflects the differences in the basic uses between Illustrator and Photoshop. In Illustrator, the toolbar options are **Fill** and **Stroke;** in Photoshop, the options at the bottom of the toolbar are **Foreground** and **Background.** Toggling between the two colors as well as color selection are quite similar.

Transformation tools

Tools used to scale, rotate, skew, warp, and create perspective are found on the Tools palette in Illustrator, but Photoshop has traditionally put those functions via Edit⇨Transform. Users of both programs will still find what they need in the same places, but Illustrator has a **Free Transform** tool on the Tools palette that will appeal to Photoshop users.

Type tools

Photoshop has moved forward in leaps and bounds in the **Type** tools. The familiar **T** is available on both toolbars and now behaves even more similarly between the two programs. The regular character and paragraph parameters (Font, Color, Leading, Alignment, and so on) are controlled in windows and tabs that are laid out the same way between programs. Photoshop also now allows you to click and drag to define a text box, like in Illustrator, which makes it easier to handle a text block (sometimes called "area type") the same way with both programs.

Photographic tools

Regardless of how close the two programs get, if you're editing photos, you will most likely be editing them in Photoshop. Tools like **Burn, Dodge, Sponge, Blur, Sharpen,** and **Smudge** are key tools in the Photoshop Tools palette, whereas Illustrator keeps tools for handling vector-based elements front and center.

Changing Fonts with Character Styles

Setting up styles for your text is a great way to save time and to ensure that your text is consistent. And, the best place to start the process is to adjust your workspace.

The character window, character style window, and paragraph styles windows can all be accessed individually from the Window menu at the top. We find it much easier to use the drop-down Essentials menu, at the upper right of Photoshop's interface, which will instantly set up your workspace with all the typography windows.

Like everything in Photoshop, there are several ways to accomplish your tasks. You can make character and paragraph styles by

- ✔ **Changing all parameters of the type first:** Then, with your type selected, choose New Paragraph Style or New Character Style from the fly-out menu at the upper right of the relevant tab. The new style will have the characteristics of the text that you have made.

- ✔ **Creating the new styles first:** Then apply them to text that you add to your document later.

Whichever route you take, be sure to name your layers with names that will make sense to you later, like `Headline text` or `Body copy`. All styles can be imported from document to document, so having clear naming conventions will come in handy.

We find the most efficient way to use styles is to set up as much of your text formats in the paragraph styles first because character styles override paragraph styles information.

Follow along to create a new paragraph style.

1. **Double-click the style's name to bring up its options.**

   You can change a host of basic and advanced aspects of the type within the Paragraph Style Options dialog box, as shown in Figure 10-4.

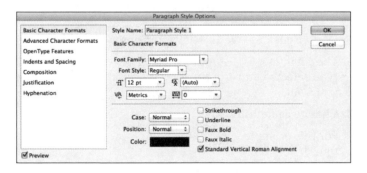

Figure 10-4: Choose text styles here.

2. **Pick a font, alignment, size, and more.**

3. **When you're satisfied with what you set up, apply it to your text by clicking the name of the style in the Character Styles (or Paragraph Styles) palette.**

Notice that the changes are applied to whatever text is selected. If nothing is selected, the changes are applied to everything. If nothing happens, perhaps an override has applied manually to the type. To fix it, choose Clear Override from the Styles palette fly-out menu.

Here's how to create a new type style:

1. **Double-click a style to see its options.**

   The Character Style Options dialog box appears. If you don't have any type selected, most of the format options should be blank, which is what you want.

2. **Change something.**

   For this example, change the color — at the bottom of the dialog box — to red.

3. **Name the style.**

   `Red` would be a grand name.

   Now you can change the color of text throughout your document without also getting a surprise change to the font or size.

You don't have to change styles exactly this way, but whatever way you choose, try to make your system methodical.

Another great thing about styles is that you can import them from other documents. So, perhaps you wrote the copy for your Uncle Sam infographic in Word, or perhaps you had been working in Illustrator and now want to bring your text into your Photoshop document. From the fly-out menu options for both styles, choose Load Character/Paragraph Styles. See Figure 10-5. Navigate to the file with the style you want to load and click Open, and the style will be loaded into the appropriate tab.

Figure 10-5: Carry over styles from different documents.

Creating Boundaries with Layer Masks and Clipping Paths

A *mask* allows you to hide or reveal parts of your image. Separate masks can be applied individually to different layers within your Photoshop document, allowing you the ability to affect the properties and visibility of those layers.

Say you have a photo with a background you'd like to get rid of. A natural impulse would be to use the Eraser tool and literally start erasing what you don't want. However, using the Eraser or the Crop tool permanently gets rid of those pixels. You should keep those pixels — just hide them. That way, you preserve your ability to change your mind and to make precise edits.

That's called *nondestructive editing*, which we can't recommend highly enough. It could save your sanity some day when you're deep into a complicated project. If you save your document as a layered PSF or TIFF file, those masks (and pixels) will still be there next time you open your document.

Photoshop offers you two main types of masks: layer masks and clipping paths.

Layer masks are bitmap images that are edited with the painting or selection tools. If you want the image or project to appear masked when it's opened in Photoshop, you can use a layer mask.

Clipping paths can be made by the Pen tool, the Shape tool, or even with text. A clipping path is a masking option that can leave your original photo looking the same but also enable a mask to be used when the image or project is saved for use in Adobe Illustrator. For instance, if you want the photo or project to seem untouched when opened in Photoshop, but also want it to be masked when observed in Illustrator, you can create a path with the Pen tool and then save it by choosing Window⇨Path⇨Clipping Path.

Layer masks and clipping paths both really do the same things, but a clipping path allows for import into Illustrator as a masked object.

Building a layer mask by cropping

Here how to create a mask with the Crop tool:

1. **Activate the Crop tool.**

   The Crop tool is the fifth tool down on the Tools palette. It looks like an overlapping set of squares (a traditional drafting tool).

2. **Click and drag to create a rectangle over the part of the picture that you want to keep.**

3. **Double-click or press Return/Enter or click the check mark at the top of your workspace**

   The crop is made. The Crop tool deletes the area outside the cropped area.

Go ahead and try it. You can always undo the edit by pressing ⌘+Z/Ctrl+Z.

Like we said, cropping works, but it's *destructive editing*. Those pixels are gone. Not good. Information that could be used is lost if a crop is made and the project is saved. That is why we warn against using this liberally.

To have a happier ending, look at the top of your workspace for the Delete Cropped Pixels check box and make sure that it's not selected. Now if you draw the crop boundary and double-click, you get a layer mask.

You can change the size and proportions of that crop box by dragging the handles at the sides and corners of the selected area.

When you choose the Move tool (the first one on the Tools palette) before clicking the to-be-edited photo, you'll find you can change what you see. The masked area (your *canvas*) acts like a window through which you can see a part of your image. Move the image around or even scale it, and different parts of your photo are shown.

Using layer masks to hide or reveal selected parts of an image

Here's how to use a layer mask to hide or reveal selected parts of an image:

1. **Define an area using the Quick Selection tool (fourth from the top of the Tools palette).**

2. **Click a part of your image with that tool.**

   It begins to select pixels that are similar in color.

3. **Select the part that you would like to hide: the background, for example.**

4. **On the Select tab, choose Select Inverse.**

   Select is located on the main menu at the top of the program. Choose Select⇨Inverse to reverse the selection originally made if you want to mask out everything inside your selection. Choose Select⇨Inverse again, and the opposite will be selected to mask.

   You want to opt for this because whatever is selected when you make the mask is the part that will be revealed by that mask.

5. **Click the Refine Edge button (at the top).**

   The dialog box that appears gives you precise control over the edge of your selection. You can experiment with it for a bit.

6. **For the Output To choice, use Layer Mask.**

7. **Click OK.**

Now take a look at your Layers pane. The resulting mask is visible as a thumbnail on that image layer. The black part is what is hidden, or 0% visible. The white part is 100% visible.

Double-click the thumbnail of that mask to see and control the properties of the mask. See Figure 10-6. Clicking the Invert button, for example, automatically flips which parts are shown and which parts are hidden.

The boxing glove in our Uncle Sam graphic uses a layer mask, and by manipulating the properties of the boxing glove, the artist could achieve many different looks.

The same principle can be employed with adjustment layers as with an image layer. An *adjustment layer* is a layer (go figure) that when added, allows you to edit the layers below it with color balance, editing curves, contrast, and so on. A layer mask can be added to this layer, to mask the area needed for the adjustment.

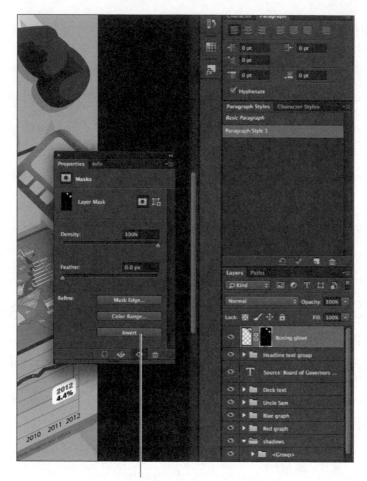

Invert button

Figure 10-6: Working with a layer mask.

Click Create New Adjustment Layer at the bottom of the Layers palette. Choose Black and White for grins to see really obvious effects. Your image now looks black and white, and the adjustment layer you made has a white layer mask thumbnail image.

Select that layer mask and use a Brush tool to paint black areas into the mask. The adjustment layer is hidden, and the colored image below is revealed, wherever you paint.

Creating a clipping path

Clipping paths are a similar concept, but are created a little differently. A clipping path is a masking option that can leave your original photo looking the same but also enables a mask to be used when the image or project is saved for use in Adobe Illustrator. For instance, if you want the photo or project to seem untouched when opened in Photoshop, but also want it to be masked when observed in Adobe Illustrator, you can create a path with the Pen tool and then save it by choosing Window➪Path➪Clipping Path. If you want the image or project to appear masked when it is opened in Photoshop, use a layer mask. They both really do the same things, but a clipping path allows for import into other programs, including Illustrator as a masked object.

Here's how to make one:

1. **Create a new layer.**

2. **On that layer, draw any shape.**

   It could be a rectangle, a complex shape done with the Pen tool, or even some text. Try text first because it's fun.

3. **Type a word, make it nice and big, and then drag it below the layer you want to mask.**

4. **Select the layer you want to mask (your image).**

   Choose Layer➪Create Clipping Mask, or choose Create Clipping Mask from the fly-out menu.

Voilà! You're left with only the word.

In Figure 10-7, an image of a brick is placed above a type layer with a word (BRICK) on it. When you select the image layer — above the type layer — and apply the clipping path, the word below that image layer becomes the clipping path/mask for the image.

Figure 10-7: Use a clipping path to mask a layer.

Making Your Graphics Pop

After you master the basics of Photoshop, graduate to some of the more advanced moves to add professional polish to your work. Again, many of these techniques have a similar version in Illustrator (see Chapter 9).

Creating depth with blend modes

Blend modes are available at the top left of the Layers palette. The default setting is Normal, but a wealth of options are hidden in that drop-down menu. These options can be used to correct an image's exposure, create contrast, and give a professional finish to your image. Or, you can use them simply for fun special effects.

The blend modes allow layers to intersect with each other. You see both layers, but one changes the look of the other. Different modes combine the layers in different ways. Working with blend modes is a very visual process. Expect surprises and be prepared to experiment until you get the effect you're looking for.

Think of it this way. You have a base layer with an image, with a blend layer on top of it. The blend layer can also have an image, a pattern, or a solid color on it, but it's the layer to which the blend mode is applied. Pixels on the blend layer combine with pixels on the base layer to create the visual result.

The types of blending effects (see Figure 10-8) are grouped by the type of result they create.

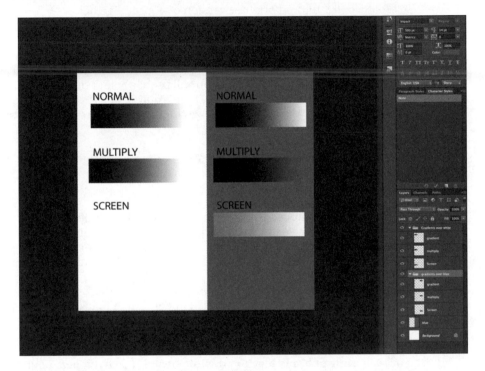

Figure 10-8: Using blending effects in Photoshop.

The options in the first set tend to darken the layer they're affecting. We find that Multiply is the handiest of that group, and explaining how it works will help you understand what's going on with the rest.

The colors on the Multiply blend layer show up if they are as dark or darker than the pixels on the layer below. So, for example, if your Multiply layer has a graduated fill from white to black, anything lighter than the pixel below it would just not show up. And, the darker areas would be compounded, making the overall image appear darker.

If you have an image that's too light, you could duplicate that layer, set the mode to Multiply, and instantly get a much darker, stronger version of your image.

The next set of blend modes tend to lighten as they're combined. Screen is essentially the opposite of Multiply. Wherever the pixels on Screen mode are lighter than the pixel below, the lighter pixels shows up. Wherever the blended image is darker than the one below it, the image disappears. This creates a lighter and brighter version of your image below.

The next group of options are light-based, and the names describe their effects pretty accurately. The effects mix colors with varying degrees of harshness or contrast. Most of these blends affect the darker and lighter pixels, leaving the midtones relatively untouched. You will probably find that the most useful of that set is Soft Light. The effects in that group get increasingly dramatic cumulating with Hard Mix, which has no gradients. Colors are either On or Off, and the effect is like posterization.

Posterization gives your image a harsh hard mix of bright and dark colors. It's almost the same effect as a high-contrast copy on a copy machine but with multiple colors.

The next set of modes are specialty modes that exclude, invert, or cancel out parts of your image. And, at the bottom of the menu, are the component blend modes that affect a single aspect of the blended color. Perhaps the most useful of that set is the Color mode in which you can add a solid color across your whole image, or you can paint spot colors. A good way to test-drive Color mode is to colorize a black-and-white image. See Figure 10-9 for a simple example of using just a touch of color on a black-and-white image.

Before you start

✔ **If your photo is black and white,** make sure to change your document mode to a color mode.

✔ **If your photo is color,** you can just put a black-and-white adjustment layer on top of your image layer. On the Layers tab, choose Layer➪New Adjustment Layer➪Black and White.

Turn the visibility of the adjustment layer off and on if you want reassurance that the colors are still there. Adjustment layers are covered earlier in this chapter.

Figure 10-9: Blend modes allow you to experiment with color, and with light and dark.

To use Color mode

1. **Make a new layer above your other layers.**

   When you create a new layer, Photoshop places the layer immediately above the layer you're working in. If you create a layer where you don't want it to be, just select it and drag it up or down your layer list.

2. **Call the Color mode layer** `Color Layer` **or something similar.**

3. **With that color layer selected, go to the drop-down menu and choose Color from the available blend modes.**

   You won't see anything yet.

4. **Select a brush and a nice, bright color, and then start painting on that layer.**

   You'll see the addition of color to the black-and-white layer, but in a transparent way. You still see all the information in your black-and-white photo, but now some parts will look colorized. See Figure 10-10.

Figure 10-10: Add color to your work.

Blend mode layers are like all the other layers. You can always control the opacity. Turn the layer up to 100% for the full effect, or turn it down for an increasingly subtle result.

Changing colors with a color overlay

There are two quick and easy ways to change colors in your Photoshop document using color overlays.

Find the first one, available in Photoshop CC, by choosing Layer➪Layer Style➪Color Overlay. With this method, color can be applied as an effect to specific Photoshop layers. If the layer you want to affect is a full image, choose Layers➪Layers Style when that particular layer is active. The Layers Style dialog box is self-explanatory, offering the ability to change color, blend mode, and opacity. Make your selections and click OK.

In the Layers palette, you can then see the effect listed below the layer's name. Any time you want, double-click Color Overlay for that layer, and change the color to something else. The view is updated dynamically, so you can keep changing the color until it's just right.

This approach can be used to make changes to isolated areas in your image as well. A type layer that's rasterized (choose Type⇨Rasterize Type Layer) or any layer with a colored shape can have the color overlay effect applied the same way, allowing you to change the color throughout your document with ease.

It's fun to experiment with the blending modes in the Color Overlay dialog box to see which suits your needs. Some add strong surface colors, and others are more subtle.

The second way to change colors in your Photoshop document using color overlays can also be used in older versions of Photoshop, and behaves similarly.

Click the Create New Adjustment Layer button (at the bottom center of the Layers palette) and select the Solid Color option. The dialog box that appears gives you the chance to select the right color. Click OK, and you have a layer that is filled with your color of choice.

The blending mode and opacity options at the top of the Layers palette can be used in the same manner. The color is added in whatever style or level of transparency you choose. Double-click the color box that shows up to change the color quickly and easily.

To do the same thing to individual parts of your image, create a selection. Draw a path or a square, or use the Magic Wand tool (under the Quick Selection tool) to select the parts that you want to affect.

With the selection active, click Create New Adjustment Layer. The solid color is created with a mask, so only that part will show up with the color you choose. Edit the opacity and blending as you see fit. See Figure 10-11.

Giving graphics depth: gradients, bevels, and satin

Photoshop provides a variety of effects, such as drop shadows or glows, that you can apply to your layers. The advantages to using layer effects are speed and sophistication of design. Also, the effects are nondestructive. As we discuss earlier, effects change the look of your layer but can be turned off or edited at any time.

You can also modify the content of a layer, and the effects are instantly applied to the modified content.

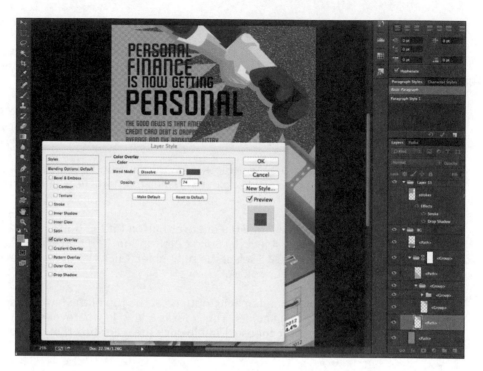

Figure 10-11: Working with a color overlay.

Working with gradients

The gradient effect is a good place to start. Gradients applied to a shape can create a feeling of depth. For example, as in Illustrator, applying a radial fill can make a circle look like a 3D ball. The popular Glossy Button effect, which makes a circle look like a 3D object made of glass, is achieved this way, using a linear gradient effect.

Here's another example, using our Uncle Sam infographic. Uncle Sam is wearing a boxing glove to show that he's ready to fight back against rising debt. Using a plain red boxing glove would look fine. But by adding a gradient effect, as shown in Figure 10-12, the art looks more three-dimensional, is more eye-catching, and gives the impression of movement. Here's how to do that.

With the glove layer selected (active), choose Layer⇨Layer Style from the menu bar. In the Layer Style dialog box that appears, select the Gradient Overlay check box on the left.

Reverse check box

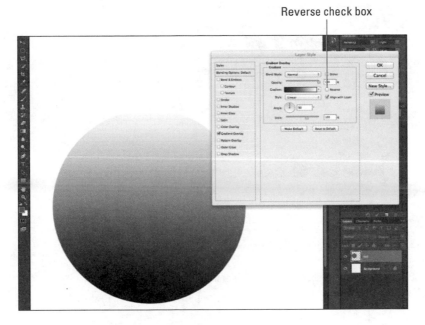

Figure 10-12: Adding depth with the gradient effect.

You will most likely see a white-to-black, linear default gradient. In the Layer Style dialog box, set the colors and features that define the boxing glove. Move the Opacity slider toward 0 to see your initial color increasingly show through.

If your radial fill is putting the black at the center, select the Reverse check box. White should now be at the center. Move the Scale slider to see the lighter area get bigger and smaller.

Okay, your glove has depth now, regardless of how much of your initial color shows through. Now it's time to change the colors in the gradient.

Click directly on the Gradient color picker (below the Opacity slider) to open the Gradient Editor to find a selection of presets. You can even create your own gradient.

In the Gradient Editor, click any of the color stops (see the small squares in Figure 10-13) along the underside of the gradient. Then, at the bottom of the editor, open the Color menu. A color picker opens, and now you can select any color you like.

The stops along the upper side of the gradient control color opacity. If you create a gradient that goes from dark blue to light blue, and the opacity is set at 100%, you would end up with a blue ball no matter what color you initially drew for your circle.

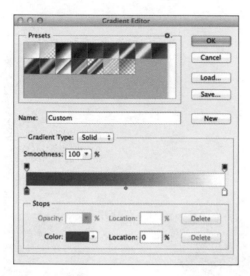

Figure 10-13: Choose colors and opacity with the Gradient Editor.

Click OK to apply the style to your layer. Or, to keep the style to use again, save it to presets by clicking the New button (upper right of the dialog box). You will be prompted to name the new style. Click OK, and your custom gradient will be saved to the Styles panel (choose Windows➪Style).

Applying style is faster than drawing and coloring a gradient-filled object. And, if you need to change the color later, you can. Nondestructive editing and sophisticated control of your effect — what could be better?

When you want to edit the gradient effect, or any layer effect, simply go to your Layers palette. Underneath the layer, look for Effects and then below that, Gradient Overlay.

Beautifying with the bevel function

Bevel & Emboss effects add various combinations of highlights and shadows to a layer to simulate depth. You can make text look like a solid 3D element or give it a raised or embossed appearance.

The effect can be applied to any object on any layer (or layer group) — as long as that layer is unlocked. To see how it looks, type any word in any color and then apply your layer effect.

For an even faster way to apply a layer style, double-click the layer itself (not on the thumbnail or the layer name) to bring up the Layer Style dialog box.

From the styles along the left of the Layer Style dialog box, select the Bevel & Emboss check box. Then click directly on the words Bevel & Emboss to advance the dialog box to the options that control the structure of the bevel. See Figure 10-14.

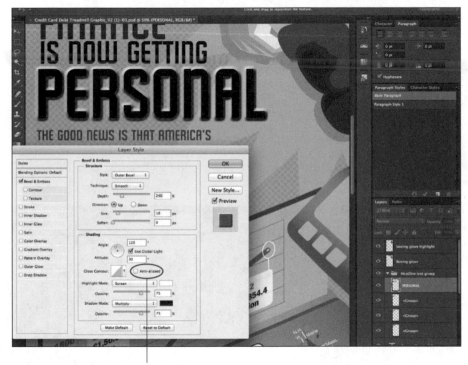

Anti-aliased check box

Figure 10-14: Exploring options for the bevel function.

From the Style drop-down menu, choose from

- **Inner Bevel:** Create a highlight at the top left and apply the effect within the area defined by the type.
- **Outer Bevel:** Create the effect outside the shape and put the highlight at bottom right.
- **Pillow Emboss:** Inset the shape, or type, into an outer bevel.

Experiment with the other options here. Selecting the Up or Down radio buttons allows you to toggle between whether the effect appears to come out of the image or appears set into it. Use the Depth slider to change the intensity of the effect. From the Technique menu, change how sharp the bevel effect appears. Select the Anti-aliased check box to smooth out any appearance of pixelation along your edges.

Adding a satin effect

The Satin effect (select the Satin check box in the Styles column, left side is the Layer Style dialog box) works like Bevel & Emboss, but it works within the defined shape, creating a rippled or satin-y surface finish.

Try out the various profiles from the Contour drop-down menu (of Satin) to see a variety of ripples that you can apply.

Striking strokes

To see how strokes can add to your design, Option-click/right-click that layer to bring up the Blending Options. There, select Stroke; see Figure 10-15. Make sure you're in the proper editing field by clicking the word Stroke itself.

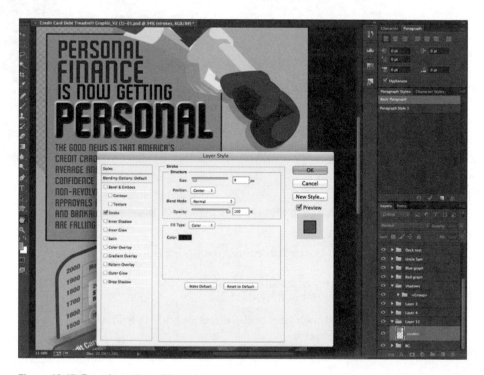

Figure 10-15: Experimenting with strokes.

✔ **Size:** The Size slider controls the width of the line. Turn it up to 10 or more pixels (px) to get a big heavy line.

✔ **Position:** From the Position drop-down menu, set where the line is drawn relative to the actual selection. If you choose Outside, the line looks curved at the corners. Choosing Inside makes the corners become sharp.

✔ **Fill Type:** From the Fill Type drop-down menu, you will see that strokes can now be gradients or patterns as well as colors.

Strokes, like any layer effect, can be applied to type, combined with other effects and applied to paths that you have drawn or imported.

Layer effects aren't the only way to create a stroke, however. Follow along to see what we mean.

1. **Create a new layer.**

2. **Select the Pen tool (press P on the keyboard) to start making a path.**

   Make sure the Auto Add and Delete check boxes (at the top of the work-space) are selected. That way, you can add and delete points without having to change the Pen type.

3. **Start drawing.**

   The Bezier Pen tool works basically the same way in Photoshop as it does in Illustrator. Clicking alone makes corner points; clicking and dragging makes curving points with editable handles. To edit one handle without affecting the other, hold down Option/Alt while you push or pull the handle.

4. **When you finish drawing the shape, open your Paths window (choose Window⇨Paths).**

   What you drew is shown in that window as `Work Path`.

   In the fly-out menu at the upper right of the Paths window, find the Stroke Path option. This gives you the ability to add a pencil or brush-like stroke to your path. Selecting the Simulate Pressure check box can give you a nice effect, too.

To see yet another way to apply a stroke, draw another path. From the Paths fly-out menu, choose Make Selection. Then choose Edit⇨Stroke to bring up a dialog box with position, width, and color options.

Apply strokes as layer effects whenever possible because they are infinitely editable. Strokes created using the other methods are bitmapped lines — colored pixels that become part of your image. Changing them later would be a pain.

Showcasing elements with shadows

Another layer effect that will come in tremendously handy is a drop shadow, which you can use underneath text, photos, or objects to give the effect that these objects are on top of the background or image below.

Start by making a series of shapes that you can apply shadows to. That will allow you to see the kind of options you have.

1. **Open a new document.**

2. **Click the Custom Shape Tool (near the bottom of the Tools palette, it looks like a squished gingerbread man).**

   A drop-down menu of available shapes shows up along the top of your workspace when the tool is selected.

3. **Choose a simple shape from the drop-down menu.**

   For this running example, start with a star.

4. **Create a series of stars (or whatever shape you want).**

   a. Create the star on the left side of the canvas.

   b. Click OK.

   c. Duplicate that layer twice.

   d. Select the topmost of your copied layers and move it to the right side of your canvas.

   e. Hold down Shift and then select the first shape and the copy layers.

   f. Choose Distribute Widths from the Align tool (at the top of your workspace).

You'll have a nice line of repeated shapes that you can start adding shadows to.

You first shadow can be a nice, soft shadow. Here's how:

1. **With the first shape layer selected, click the FX *(fx)* icon at the bottom of your Layers palette and choose Drop Shadow.**

   This is just one of several ways that Photoshop lets you select layer effects. They are also available from Layer⇨Layer Style.

   The Drop Shadow dialog box appears, revealing options much like those in other layer effects. The Opacity setting controls the strength of the shadow.

2. **Bring Opacity down to about 50%.**

   Angle and Distance controls which side the shadow falls to and how far away it is from the object. You can also select the shadow itself and move it around manually. The numbers in the dialog box change to reflect the moves you make.

3. **Click OK.**

4. **Copy the shadow directly onto the next shape.**

   a. Hold down Option/Alt and select the "Drop shadow" in your image layer.

   b. Drag it onto the next image layer.

   Both layers should now have the same shadow.

   If you hold down ⌘/Ctrl instead of Option/Alt, you can move the effects — transferring them to another layer rather than duplicating them.

For the next shadow, make it sharper-edged. (Note: Typically, shadows are sharper when the light is stronger, and the shape is closer to the surface that the shadow is to be cast on.) To edit this shadow

1. **Double-click the words** Drop shadow **in that layer.**

2. **When the dialog box opens, simply reduce the size and distance of your shadow to get the right effect.**

3. **Click OK.**

If you moved the direction or "angle" of your shadow before you click OK, you may have seen the shadow under your first shape move as well. That happens because of the Use Global Light check box. When it's selected, all shadows behave as if they are lit from the same light, which is great for unity within your design. If you don't want the shadows to behave that way, simply clear that check box.

For the third shape, try something different.

1. **With the third layer selected, click the FX button again.**

2. **Choose Inner Shadow.**

   This creates the illusion that your shape has been cut out of the background layer.

3. **Play with the parameters to change how deep the hole into your background looks.**

Managing Your Workflow

If you've followed the chapter to this point, you can see how Photoshop's features can transform your infographic into a work of art. All those bells and whistles come with some potential pitfalls, though. In this section, we discuss how to work with all those layers and also how to avoid piling on too many special effects.

Copying style effects from one layer to another

Copying effects between layers is easy. To see it in action, follow along.

1. **Open a new Photoshop document.**

2. **With the Text tool, write something in big font size and a nice, bright color.**

3. **With that layer selected, click the FX button at the bottom of your Layers panel to give your text a drop shadow. While you're in there, go nuts and give it a white stroke and a bevel as well.**

4. **Copy the layer.**

   Photoshop allows you to copy layers. You can

   - Press ⌘+J/Ctrl+J to duplicate your layer.

     or

   - Holding down Option/Alt key, click and drag over the text you typed.

5. **Move your copied type down enough so that both words are visible.**

6. **In the copy layer, double-click the T icon to begin editing your text.**

7. **Type in a completely new word.**

   Note that the effects are all still working.

8. **With your new word selected, choose Window⇨Character.**

9. **Change the color, font size, or any other attribute.**

   The layer styles you have applied remain intact.

An easier and even more flexible option is available:

1. **Create a new layer (press the New Layer icon at the bottom of your Layers pane).**

2. **Draw a colored rectangle (click and drag with the Rectangle Marquee tool).**

3. **Hold down the Option/Alt key, click the word Effects in one of your type layers, drag the styles onto your rectangle, and release.**

Clicking the word Effects brings all the styles in that group to your rectangle. Selecting a single effect — say, just a drop shadow — to click and drag to your rectangle layer means that only that effect is copied.

Using effects sparingly

It's easy to spot an infographic done by someone who has recently discovered the joys of Photoshop. Many an enthusiastic designer has piled on *all* the special effects, and unwittingly created a jumbled, distracting mess.

It takes a lot of trial and error to find out which Photoshop effects work best for each project. The good news is that no matter what tool you try, it's easy to undo your work and start again. The better news is that it's all pretty fun.

11

Expanding Your Tools and Techniques

....

....

*I*f you've been through the preceding two chapters, you have a good beginner's start on Adobe's powerful design programs, Illustrator and Photoshop. Sometimes you'll have to choose which program you're going to use for a project, and other times, you'll use both in conjunction.

In this chapter, we take a look at how to integrate Illustrator and Photoshop into your design arsenal. Once you get the hang of them, you can use them for many phases of your infographic design. We also explore the big question of how to choose between the two, depending on the requirements of your infographic project. You'll discover some ways of using the best that each program has to offer. And we show you a few additional tools for increasing the level of polish and sophistication in your infographics.

Starting Your Project with Illustrator

There is rarely just one way to create an infographic. However, Illustrator is arguably the best place to start your project. For one thing, Illustrator's vector shapes are very easy to scale, which makes this program a good choice for things such as creating logos, which may need to be reused at many different sizes.

Also, Illustrator handles type really nicely. If you start your graphic in Illustrator, the process can be easier at the outset and also more flexible throughout.

The Symbols function is also something to bear in mind at the beginning of your process. If you have navigation buttons in your interactive graphic, simple numbered bullets in your flat graphic, or even an arrow style that may need to be changed at the end of the process, using Illustrator symbols makes the changes a simple matter.

Starting an Illustrator wireframe can vary a little depending on whether your graphic is for print, web, or other, but the process is basically as follows:

1. **Create a new document, and set your artboard size to reflect the final use size.**

   If your graphic is going to be for web use, set the document profile as Web.

2. **Set all units to pixels.**

   Everything is easier if your measurements match between all your design programs.

3. **Turn on pixel-grid alignment for objects.**

   The corners of your vector shapes will be *anti-aliased* — smoothed out rather than pixelated — but lines stay crisp.

4. **Set up your guides.**

   This could involve margins, columns, headline locations, or some other measurement important to your project.

5. **Set up your layers.**

   You'll want

   - A guide layer

   - A background layer

   - Layers for elements that are "fixed"

     A *fixed element* could be an icon that appears on every page or layer of your information graphic.

   - Layers for any content parts that you want to affect separately

6. **Start to organize the visual and narrative hierarchy of your information.**

Figure 11-1 shows the set-up process in creation.

Because Illustrator makes all these upfront nuts-and-bolts setup steps easy and fast, we recommend starting there regardless of whether your design incorporates graphic vector elements.

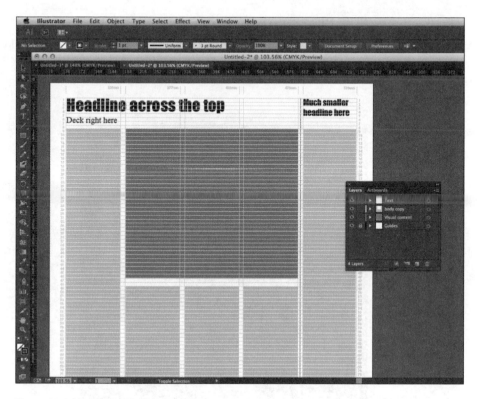

Figure 11-1: Working with Illustrator layers.

Opening Photoshop Files in Illustrator

As we discuss in this chapter, you can "place" Photoshop images in Illustrator, which is a great function that allows your photo to remain linked to the original. This means that the original image is not technically part of the file; rather, it stays in an external file. Relinking to your photo allows you to update it at any time, say to reflect changes to the image or to bring in a higher-resolution version. Illustrator also now shows a preview of the image while you're placing it and lets you place multiple images at once, which is great. Hmm. But what if you want to keep the layers of your PSD file intact?

The answer is pretty simple. In Illustrator

1. **Choose File⇨Open.**
2. **Navigate to and open your Photoshop document.**

3. **Click OK.**

4. **In the Photoshop Import Options dialog box that opens, make sure that the Convert Layer to Objects radio button is enabled and then click OK. See Figure 11-2.**

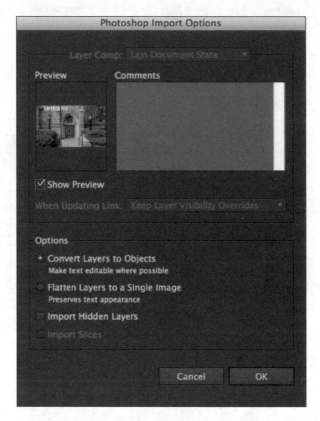

Figure 11-2: Importing Photoshop images into Illustrator.

The document comes in with the layers intact. The layers are separate rasterized images that can be moved, scaled, and affected the same way as any photo can be in Illustrator.

Like other photos, though, they can't be scaled up larger than their original Photoshop size without looking pixelated.

Watch out for layer effects, blend modes, and adjustment layers when you import files. If you have effects (such as drop shadows) applied to one layer, Illustrator will merge all visible layers upon import. If you want to keep your layers separate, rasterize any effects layers before opening the file in Illustrator.

Using Illustrator Graphics in Photoshop

Many designers like to take their Illustrator graphics into Photoshop to take advantage of the very sophisticated filters and effects. And, exporting your graphics directly from Illustrator lets you keep all your layers intact as well as your type editable. So, after you have your elements the way you like them, export your layers to Photoshop, copy and paste them into Photoshop, or import them from within Photoshop.

To get Illustrator graphics into Photoshop, you can simply copy an image in Illustrator and then paste it into Photoshop. When you do that, Photoshop will ask whether you want to paste the work as a smart object. You do, so click OK in that confirmation dialog box. As you'll find out shortly, smart objects are tremendously useful.

To try this out, try this example. You'll start with an Illustrator file with three layers:

1. **Make the bottom layer a gradient fill that goes from blue to white (or really any color that you feel represents sky), and name that layer Sky.**

2. **Make a second layer with some nice bold type on it, and call that layer Type.**

   Sensing a pattern?

3. **Make a third layer, above the Type layer, draw a few clouds on it, and call that layer whatever you want. (We named ours Clouds.) Then change the opacity on some of the clouds and move them around so that you can see the type through at least one cloud.**

4. **Choose File⇨Export.**

5. **In the Format dialog box that appears, choose .PSD as the file type and then click Export.**

   The Photoshop Export Options dialog box appears, allowing you to choose the file resolution. See Figure 11-3.

6. **Select the Write Layers radio button and the Preserve Text Editability check box, and then click OK.**

   At this point, you can also choose the resolution you want.

7. **Open that PSD file in Photoshop.**

You'll see that all three named layers are there and that the transparencies that you set in Illustrator show up in Photoshop. The text layer can also be edited with the Photoshop Type tool.

Figure 11-3: Exporting layers from Illustrator to Photoshop.

The cloud layer, however, has become a group rather than a regular layer. If you open that group (by toggling the triangle beside the folder icon), you can see that each cloud is its own layer. You can move them individually or turn them on and off.

Each layer in this file can now have Photoshop's layer effects applied to them. For grins, apply a bevel effect to your type. Cool, right?

Scaling between Programs

If you're using Illustrator and Photoshop together, you'll likely start to find the similarities comforting. The concepts behind most actions are the same. "Scaling," however, is one area where the programs' essential differences really show up.

Photoshop is a bitmap or pixel-based software. Each pixel in these raster images can be edited individually. That's why you can easily paint out blemishes with a Paintbrush tool, and why the image looks blocky when you zoom in really close.

Illustrator, on the other hand, is a vector-based program, and editing is focused on whole objects rather than on individual pixels. Each shape or line is mathematically created by the software's code, and thus can be scaled or redrawn to any size without any concern for the pixels. Your design or drawing maintains its sharp definition at any size — and that is a key benefit in creating files like logo design.

Check out Figure 11-4 to see what a difference scaling can make in both programs.

The programs work in a complementary way, but that basic difference is something to be aware of when you are planning your project.

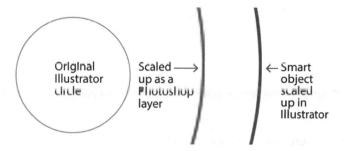

Figure 11-4: Seeing the differences between Photoshop and Illustrator.

So, if your workflow involves placing Photoshop images into Illustrator, you can rotate the images and scale them up and down, but you can't success-fully scale an image any larger than the original placed image. The photo will look increasingly blocky and blurry once you start making it larger than the original Photoshop file.

You can place a low-resolution photo image in Illustrator and then sub in a higher-resolution version of the same image afterward, but you have to plan for it. Here's how:

1. **Select a photo that you've embedded in Illustrator.**
2. **In the Links palette, open the flyout menu and choose Relink.**

   This allows you to search for and select the higher-resolution image.
3. **Click OK.**

   The image will replace the original placed file.

   If the images are not the same in every way except resolution, however, the new image won't fall in the same place.

If you're creating vector objects in Illustrator for use as smart objects in Photoshop, your scaling options are much more flexible. In Illustrator, you can scale your vector graphics as much as you like with no loss of quality.

You can do the same thing after the Illustrator image is in Photoshop — *if* you pasted it in as a smart object. To make your smart object vector layer larger, you could scale it by simply choosing Edit⇨Transform⇨Scale, but that would pixelate your image.

To scale it properly

1. **Double-click the smart object's thumbnail to edit the image.**

   It will open in Illustrator.

2. **Make your object bigger, and then save and close the Illustrator object.**

   Your changes are automatically applied within the Photoshop document.

In general, smart objects make sizing up and down a nondestructive process. If the smart object is an Illustrator vector, you can take advantage of another great Illustrator trick: *Transform Each*.

Say you're creating a map with several city dots on it. If you decide that the dots are too small in relation to the rest of the image, yeah, you *could* select each dot and scale each one up. That becomes annoying pretty quickly.

But, if the map is an Illustrator smart object (wait for it), you can select all the city dots at once and choose Object⇨Transform⇨Transform Each. (See Figure 11-5.) Then, scale all the dots at the same time, scaling each from their own center point, which keeps them all in their proper places. Sweet.

Figure 11-5: Make changes quickly with the Transform Each command.

Whatever your project, the best thing you can do for yourself is to find out the necessary production resolution at the start. Magazines, for example, need much higher resolution than will an online graphics — and you can't fake pixel resolution after the fact.

Discovering the Benefits of a Smart Object

Smart objects can be raster or vector images, but the important feature is that they can be transformed (scaled, skewed, rotated, warped, or distorted) without losing any of the original image data. Have you ever scaled down an image in Photoshop, but then changed your mind and scaled it back up only to find that the image had become low resolution? That doesn't have to happen anymore. And vector images never have to be rasterized. They can keep Illustrator's power to scale them and edit them, indefinitely.

You can make a smart object by

- ✔ Pasting the content into Photoshop and selecting Smart Object in the dialog box that appears.
- ✔ Converting one or more selected layers by choosing Convert to Smart Object from the flyout menu at the top-right corner of your Layers palette.

Smart objects behave a lot like symbols do in Illustrator. You can duplicate smart object layers, scaling and transforming each one separately. You could make a tank full of fish that way, for example.

To continue our running example, go ahead and make — then make copies of — a smart object.

Then double-click any of the smart objects or copies in your Layers palette to open and edit the image. If the image is an Illustrator vector, the smart object will open up in Illustrator. If it's a raster image, a separate Photoshop editing window will open up.

You can apply any of the regular layer effects, filters, or Illustrator changes you want. For example, you could change the color, and then save and close the editing window. The change you made to that smart object will have been made to all the related smart object copies at the same time. Figure 11-6 shows how you can apply these changes.

The fact that those changes are layers within the smart object means that the process is nondestructive as well as fast. If you don't want that filter or color applied anymore, just open an instance and turn off the effect layer.

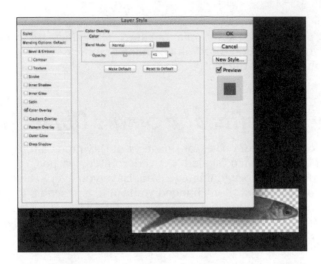

Figure 11-6: Change properties easily with smart objects.

You can also use smart objects as a tool for cleaning up your Layers palette. You never need to merge or flatten layers again. Just select several layers at once and convert them to a smart object, and they essentially become one still-editable layer.

Working with Smart Filters

If you're seeing the benefits of smart objects, you'll enjoy working with smart filters, too.

They work like layer effects. They can be turned off and on, or thrown in the trash without harming the original layer. They are a handy, nondestructive editing feature, and they can speed up workflow.

Control-click/right-click a smart object, and a context menu appears. Choose the Replace Contents function to swap out your image for an image with higher resolution. That means you can do all your edits and finessing on a lighter and faster low-resolution file, and then add the heavy image at the end.

Or you could set up a PSD (Photoshop) file with a series of smart filters applied, and then use the Replace Contents command to swap in completely different photos as often as you need to, as we demonstrate in Figure 11-7. Your publication or website could have a signature look for all its photos, used every day, but created by filters that you set up but once.

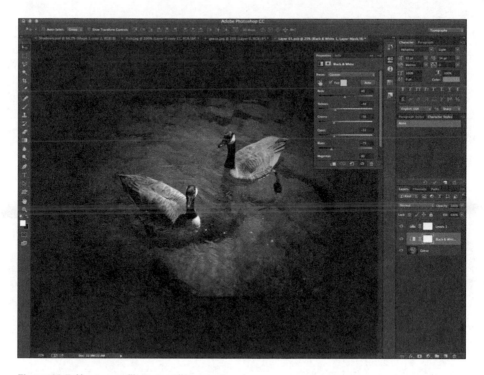

Figure 11-7: Use smart filters to edit content.

Determining which Program Works Best for Your Needs

Sometimes, one of Adobe's powerhouse programs *will* work better than the other one. Over time, you'll develop a sense of whether Illustrator or Photoshop is a better fit for various tasks. Until then, here's a primer on how each program handles various elements of graphic design work:

Graphing

Photoshop is not a graphing program. You can create graphs but not dynamically from data. The process is more like hand-drawing a chart.

Illustrator offers flexibility. Built as a graphing program, Illustrator lets you create several distinctly different types of graphs and customize them to suit your needs.

Detailed icons

Photoshop has sophisticated visual effects. Its blend modes and layer effects are first-rate and can provide a high level of polish to icons. The color overlay feature enables you to change icon colors quickly.

Illustrator offers scalability and sophisticated visual effects. Vector icons can be used small on business cards, or blown up to billboard size without any changes or loss of quality. However, Photoshop offers more robust options regarding drop shadows and opacity changes.

Patterns

Photoshop has a pattern overlay feature, which is a layer effect that can create a scalable seamless pattern to use in concert with other layer effects and blend modes. Custom shape tool has great presets that can be used to create patterns.

Illustrator offers a Pattern Creation tool that allows you to make seamless patterns you can save as swatches and apply to any shape. More precise control with drawing tools makes creating custom objects for patterns easier than in Photoshop.

Type manipulation

Photoshop

- *Area type:* Larger type blocks can be put into area type blocks instead of as regular point type, and you can control alignment and leading, as with Illustrator, but setting up columns is not as easy.

- *Type alignment:* Photoshop has vertical and horizontal type alignment tools, but no Align to Path options.

- *Type masking:* There are several ways to use live type to mask photographs, which can help you create sophisticated effects in your infographics.

- *Type styles:* These allow easy formatting and changes to type styles.

Illustrator

- *Touch Type tool:* Use this tool to work with letters as individual objects, scaling and rotating them at will, without separating them from the rest of your type. This tool is also compatible with touch-screen or direct-touch devices, making the letter manipulation even more organic and intuitive.

- *Type alignment:* In addition to left, right, and center, type can be aligned vertically or aligned to a path. (For fun, align some type to a spiral line to see what happens.)

- *Type masking:* Create by choosing Object⇨Clipping Mask⇨Make.

- *Type styles:* These allow easy formatting and changes to type styles.

Working with Other Design Tools

Here at Infographic World, we've known for some time that infographics are an increasingly popular form of sharing information. The mechanics of crafting an infographic have historically been a bit complex, requiring that you need certain software and design skills. Lately, though, some "new kids on the block" offer some interesting and simplified ways of making and sharing infographics. Working with these tools can be a good way to practice some of your developing skills as an infographic designer.

Online, you can find a few free sites to help you create nice-looking graphics without buying and navigating graphics software — and without too big of a time commitment. And in this section, we'll show you some "new kids" to meet and become friends with.

What makes a graphic good is the *content* — not the decoration. You can use the best icon, font, and color choice these websites can offer, but if you don't have good content as a base, your graphic runs the risk of becoming just another piece of visual static.

Microsoft programs

If you're truly just starting out, or if you want to create a simple graphic without buying a new software package, you can make basic infographics with two Microsoft programs, which you may already have on your computer:

- **PowerPoint:** Think about it: PowerPoint presentations are often filled with statistics, facts, and dense data, so using PowerPoint to create an infographic is a natural match.

  Various sources have published free templates for making infographics in PowerPoint, so check out these options to add visual interest to your PowerPoint session.

  - *Hubspot:* `http://offers.hubspot.com/how-to-easily-create-five-fabulous-infographics-in-powerpoint`

  - *B2B Infographics:* `http://infographicb2b.com/downloads/category/powerpoint-templates`

- **Publisher:** This desktop publishing program is pretty easy and intuitive, and you find templates for that, too.

  - *Microsoft:* `http://office.microsoft.com/en-us/templates/results.aspx?qu=Charts#pg:2|`

  - *Stock Layouts:* `http://www.stocklayouts.com/Templates/Free-Templates/Free-Sample-Microsoft-Publisher-Template-Design.aspx`

Infogr.am

Infogr.am (`http://infogr.am`), which touts itself as "the world's simplest application for making infographics," is an online graphics creation and sharing site. You can share the graphics by sending them directly to Facebook and Twitter, or copy the embed code to paste the graphic into your website. The graphics are clean and legible, the colors are editable, and there are several design themes to choose from.

After you register and log onto the site, you'll find the interface extremely easy to navigate. All you need to do is select the Infographic tab or the Charts tab, pick your design theme, and get started.

The instructions are really straightforward. For example, following such simple directions as `Double-click to edit chart` leads you to placeholder text fields for your headline and description text, so just start filling in the fields. (See Figure 11-8.) You can customize by adding or deleting elements to suit your needs.

In the Infographic design area, you'll see a few icons on the right that allow you to add pictures, text, maps, charts, and even video.

The Charts section features 14 main chart types, most of which come with subtypes or variations. Click Add Chart and you get the same editing features as are found in the Infographic field.

Although we like a lot of things about Infogr.am, keep in mind the fact that your content is public. Anything you upload is visible and shareable by anyone. Upgrading to the subscription Pro level for $18 per month allows you to share graphics privately, which you probably want if you're creating proprietary graphics for a client. The Pro level also allows you to download your graphics in editable formats, such as PDF.

Easel.ly

Easel.ly (`www.easel.ly`) is another free graphics-creation site. The site is still in beta, but it works pretty well. Easel.ly has an upload function that lets you load images from your desktop, so you could work in another program and upload a static chart to your layout if you needed a chart.

To get started, you first need to register. Then simply log in and get to work.

The interface is straightforward. All the elements you need to work are along the top. The Vhemes (Easel.ly's contraction of the term "Visual Themes") tab gives you some templates to work with. Choose your elements, including background color, some useful shapes, and text from the menus along the top. Adding them to your graphics is as easy as dragging them onto your canvas. The size of the canvas is determined under the same menu as background color.

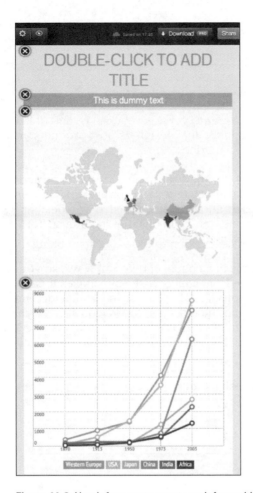

Figure 11-8: Use Infogr.am to create an infographic.

Many fonts are available as well as a variety of objects that you can drag into your composition. Objects, grouped into broad general categories such as People and Transportation, are pre-made drawings and icons. You can drag the images into your graphic and then edit the color and opacity to suit your design.

The Upload feature lets you upload your own JPG and SVG formats. For uploaded SVG files, you can edit the colors and opacity the same way as you can edit Easel.ly's content.

Edit the text, save your graphic, and then click Share to download a JPG of your graphic, view it in a browser, copy the web link, or get the embed code and post it on your own site. Unlike Infogr.am, Easel.ly lets you set the graphic settings to public or private without an extra charge.

An interesting feature of Easel.ly is that you can open, edit, save, and post other people's graphics — which is perhaps a point to consider before you set your own beautiful creation to "public."

Creative Market

Creative Market (`https://creativemarket.com`) is kind of like a version of Etsy for digital products. Individual designers post products, manage their own content, and set their own prices.

You can browse for graphics (vector illustrations, 3D, patterns, and so on) to use in your designs, or you can buy templates for everything from business cards and resumes to presentations and responsive web designs. Other products include fonts, themes, and add-ons that include custom designed Photoshop brushes, actions, and effects.

The products are searchable in a couple of different ways, so you can view by type or just pop in to see what's recent. The site makes it easy to pay by PayPal, but the process involves buying credits in various increments. For example, you may have found the most perfect $4 icon set, but the smallest increment of credits that you can buy is $20. (This probably won't be a problem for you for long, though, because there's usually a nice variety of things for sale.)

The site also maintains a design blog worth checking out (`https://creativemarket.com/blog`).

Part IV
Ready to Distribute

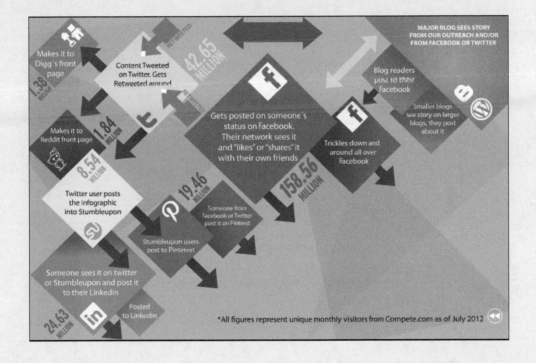

In this part . . .

- ✔ It's time to publish your work! We'll show you how to use your own website or blog as a platform for your projects.

- ✔ We'll show you how to encourage readers to share your work, setting the stage for your infographic to potentially go viral.

- ✔ We'll review the most popular social-media channels, and show you how to mine them for the people most likely to love your work.

- ✔ We'll talk about the optimal times to release your infographics.

12

Launching Your Infographic

So you just completed building your infographic. Now what? The possibilities for publishing your graphic depend mostly on the purpose you set out with as you worked on your research, your artistic elements, and your technological flourishes. The audience for infographics has changed considerably in the past decade. The bad news: Many newspapers and magazines that used to publish infographics have gone out of business or shrunk. The good news: The web opens up nearly endless possibilities in terms of space and interactivity.

By now, your graphic should have been so well thought out that you *know* your desired audience, and your goal is to make sure they see your work. Consider your intent in creating an infographic in the first place. If your work has a defined audience — say, customers or employees of a certain company — then the placement and marketing of your work will be done for you by an editor, a publications director, or some sort of project manager. Those folks will set your deadlines, make sure your works meets their technical specifications, and release your infographic according to their schedule.

But hey, this is the Internet age. If you're working for a print client, you don't really need to worry about publishing your infographic because the newspaper or magazine does the work. If you're working for yourself, the responsibility is all yours, and you need to be prepared to capitalize on the traffic patterns of the web. The possibilities for publishing your infographic to the web are pretty much endless. And after you turn your work loose to the web, it may very well go viral, attracting thousands more views, comments, links back to your personal website, and potentially more business for you as an infographic designer.

Is this what you want? Making this call is key because it will determine what your next steps are. Assuming this *is* what you want, we will spend most of this chapter talking about how to publish your high-quality graphics to your own website, in the hopes of your work going viral. The timing and technical details we discuss here can certainly be applied to any client's work, so bear these tips in mind to help your clients get great results from your work, too.

Deciding Where to Publish

The market for online infographics has truly exploded over the last few years. See Figure 12-1 for a high-level look into just how popular infographics have become. The screen shot was taken from Google Trends (www.google.com/trends), which is a great tool to see how search volume for various keywords changes over time. In this case, we used the term *infographics*. As you can see, the popularity of the keyword was pretty flat up until about 2011.

Figure 12-1: Charting a trend of rising interest in infographics.

In 2011, awareness and interest in infographics began to take off. Justin can personally speak to the validity of these numbers. He started building Infographic World in late 2009 and early 2010. At the time, if he walked into a room of 100 people, he was often the only person who knew what an infographic was.

As time went on, though, awareness of what infographics are, and the power they hold, has risen. In that same room of 100 people, probably 40 percent of the people know what infographics are. (Justin is working on the other 60 percent.)

And even though infographics have absolutely exploded in popularity, we're still only seeing the tip of the iceberg. "Infographics" are not truly household names yet. That means that as time goes on, there is still a growing opportunity as far as how big the market can grow. New blogs and websites pop up every day. And, to be honest, the human attention span isn't getting longer. The market for clear, compelling information with a powerful visual element is huge.

Major blogs and online news outlets are always looking for great content to share with their readers. This has always been the case, and will always be the case. Sites like Mashable, TechCrunch, and The Huffington Post have become as big as they are because they have great content for their readers. What happens then is a bit of a trickle-down effect. Content on these big websites gets seen by smaller blogs, who then share the same content on their site, assuming it's relevant to their readers. If a big site like The Huffington Post is featuring a piece of content, it's likely to be high-quality and something that smaller sites will want to emulate.

Publishing Infographics on the Web

We say "sneezing baby panda," and you smile at the cuteness. We ask you what the fox says, and you'll almost surely be singing that annoyingly catchy song for the next few hours.

These are simple examples of web content gone viral. The term "going viral" is probably a bit overused these days, but it's really what you want for your infographic. Essentially, you want to get enough exposure for your infographic that it begins to spread around the web in an organic manner. Someone thinks it's so cool that their 12 best friends just have to see it, and then their 12 best friends, and so on and so on. (This is obviously more cost-effective than, say, paying for ads to generate views for the infographic. It's a great strategy for you as well as any company you're designing infographics for.)

If your goal is create an infographic that will drive traffic back to your website, build valuable links through search engine optimization (more on this in a moment) and get general buzz and exposure for your brand, the only real option for housing the infographic is your website. If you want to take part in the benefits that come with creating such high-quality content, you need to make sure you are publishing it in the most advantageous way.

If your personal website doesn't yet include a blog, we recommend starting one right now. These days, blogs are very easy to set up and maintain, and after yours is up and running, it's a great platform for sharing your work. The two main blogging platforms, WordPress and Blogger, are tops in terms of name recognition, and they're both easy to use and maintain. If you don't want to set one up yourself, any website developer can add this onto your page pretty easily.

Make sure that the style of your blog fits with the rest of your website from a branding standpoint. One of the fastest growing blogging platforms is Tumblr. It's cool and highly visual — but also the territory of teenage *Twilight* fans. Depending on the image you want to present, it might not be the right platform for your work.

Publishing infographics to the web requires some work on the technical details. First, you need to look at the infographic file itself, particularly the size of the file.

Determining the right size

If you're creating an infographic for a print or web client, the client will probably specify the size. If you're publishing it yourself, you have the power to decide. Still, following some of our guidelines will help optimize the way your graphic looks and the likelihood that it will be shared on other websites.

The more complex your infographic, the larger it's likely to be from a megabyte or kilobyte standpoint. Features such as animation and high-resolution photos make for awesome graphics but can quickly drive up the size of the files. At a certain point, that creates diminishing returns: You'll drive viewers away if your graphic is so big that it doesn't load easily. You might have a stunning, entertaining, and informative graphic, but if all the bells and whistles have driven it up to 7MB, it will load so slowly you'll think you're back in the dial-up modem days. You know what happens when something loads slowly on a page? The reader leaves. Simple as that.

In a 2009 survey, Forrester Consulting discovered that 47 percent of the population expects web pages to load in two seconds or less. An earlier Google report showed that when load times increased from 0.4 seconds to 0.9 seconds, traffic and ad revenues dropped by 20 percent. Well, that was almost a decade ago, and attention spans have only shrunk since then.

These days, you have merely seconds to grab someone's attention and to keep them on your website. Too many other things compete for your reader's attention online.

Keep your graphic as close to 1MB as possible. You can get away with it being a bit larger than that, but try not to go too much larger than that.

Another option is investing in a content delivery network (CDN) to take the bandwidth burden off of your own servers. Many companies offer this service. I recommend speaking with your IT group or doing a Google search for CDN, speak with a few companies, and explain what you're trying to accomplish. This can be a smart option if you are routinely working with large files.

Creating filenames that generate traffic

What's in a name? When it comes to your infographic, choosing the right name can also help drive traffic to your work. You want anyone seeing the post to know within one to two seconds what the post is about.

Learning how to name your graphic well requires a basic understanding of search engine optimization (SEO). As you may already know, *SEO* is a process of using words and terms in such a way that Internet search engines find your material quickly, and give it a prominent place in search results. It's an important part of creating any form of content for the web. Why should you care about SEO? Well, *everyone* who contributes content to the web should care about it. When the technology is at its best, it doesn't just generate readers — it gets you exactly the audience you want. (Read about SEO in depth in *Search Engine Optimization For Dummies,* 5th Edition, by Peter Kent.)

So, how you name your infographic has a direct impact when it comes to SEO implications. Google search bots routinely crawl the web looking for more and better information. At some point, it will find your infographic on your website, and in turn decide (based on an ever-changing algorithm) where your graphic will show up in search results. The more explicitly your graphic uses relevant keywords, the greater the chances it will pop up on the first page of Google search results. Obviously, the possibilities are endless; you just need to consider what basic terms a reader might seek when they're looking for information online.

Good news: The process of SEO really isn't a mystery. Even the mighty Google wants readers to find the information they seek, and Google constantly refines the process to make that happen.

The Google algorithm is always changing. From the time of writing this book to the time you're reading it, the algorithm has undoubtedly changed several times. Stay on top of things to keep up with how Google reads and evaluates content.

A few tips on how to keep current:

- **Check out the Google Webmaster Tools page.** Google maintains a webmasters guide, which does a very good job of explaining a lot of seemingly complex things about web searches. You can read about Google's "crawling" process, how Google indexes things, and tips you definitely should keep in mind. Remember that Google wants the most relevant content possible showing up. See

  ```
  https://support.google.com/webmasters/
  ```

- **Follow Matt Cutts, who is the Head of Search at Google.** (Hopefully he will still be so by the time you're reading this. If not, search for "Google Head of Search" to find out who the new person is. Yes, we see the irony.) Matt frequently speaks and writes about best practices and updates and what to keep in mind, and how things may change in the future. Very brilliant guy. (Hey, Matt, if you're reading this by some miracle, I hear Infographic World should be #1 for every infographic keyword on the planet. Just sayin'.)

- **Check out Moz (`http://moz.com`; formerly SEOmoz).** This company was founded as an SEO consulting company and has recently broadened its focus to all manners of Internet marketing. They are SEO wizards over there, and have a great blog at `http://moz.com/blog` that's always current with what's going on in the SEO world. Aside from their paid consulting work, Moz offers amazing tips on SEO and all sorts of content marketing.

- **Set a Google Alert for the phrase "Google algorithm update".** You'll get e-mails everyday with articles relevant to that phrase.

Using appropriate keywords

After you get the general idea of how to integrate SEO terms into your work, use them wisely. What you *don't* want to do is cram your infographic so full of keywords that the search engines read it as spam. Google will see right through people trying to "over-SEO," so to speak.

What you want to do is use keywords in the name of the file that are important to you from an SEO standpoint. Imagine that you're working for Canine Cuisine, a company that sells dog food. You created a thorough, well-researched, informative infographic guide for dog diets. Now you want to embed keywords relevant to your infographic within the filename itself.

Your graphic is most likely to be picked up by Google's "crawl" if the content looks natural, real, and relevant. One way to do this is to create a filename so it reads as a natural statement, not just a collection of keywords.

So, for our dog food graphic, one effective way to name the file would be

A consumer's guide to healthy dog diets and dog food. Healthy Dog food.

Simple. Straightforward. And you didn't stuff the filename with a ton of keywords that are repetitive and blatant about their intention.

By contrast, here's an example of what not to do:

Canine Cuisine. Dog food. Bestselling dog food. Healthiest dog food.

See what we mean by spammy and obvious? Don't laugh; people really do this.

Introducing readers to the infographic

You know that quote that says, "Every problem is an opportunity in disguise"?

We think they wrote it about infographics.

Of the millions of people surfing the web every day, thousands probably don't know what an infographic is. They've certainly seen them, but they might not recognize them as their own unique form of information.

Is that a problem? Nope. With a simple naming strategy, an infographic is an opportunity to catch a reader's eye and introduce him to this unique way of presenting information. Your readers may not think they know what an infographic is, but with the visual appeal of your graphic enhancing information they're looking for anyway, they may very likely be intrigued and want to see what the content is all about.

Getting back to the wonderful dog food example, imagine that you're preparing to post that infographic to a blog. Here are a couple ways to signal to readers that the content is an infographic:

- **Put the word "infographic" in the title.** One possible title for your post can be "Keeping Your Dog Healthy. Five Ways To Ensure That Your Dog Has a Long Healthy Life (infographic)." Putting the word "infographic" in parentheses at the end signals to your website readers that this piece of content is different from the others. It's not a story, not a photo — it's an infographic!

- **Include an introductory paragraph for the infographic.** This introduction is a lead-up for your readers, to give them an idea of what they are about to read. You should get them interested and excited to read the infographic, so maybe pull an interesting fact or two from the infographic and mention it here. You don't want to give it *all* away, but give the reader just enough to want to read more.

Including an intro paragraph also helps search engines validate your blog post and qualify it as meaningful content. Google and its rival search engines are wary of blog posts that contain only images because "blog bots" are notorious for auto-publishing images without written content. Also, search engines are better at crawling the sentences in your blog post than the images, thus helping boost your SEO value.

Making the most of your space

Another thing to keep in mind with posting an infographic to your site has to do with the available space you have to put it up. Every web page has a width to it, measured in pixels. On any given page, all that matters for our purposes is the available space to put the infographic. Say your web page has 1,000 pixels of width from left to right. On this page, though, a certain amount of width (250 pixels) is taken on the left or right side of the site — say, by advertisements or links to other areas of your website. (See Figure 12-2.)

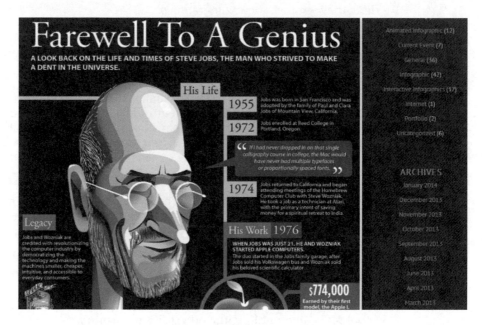

Figure 12-2: Size graphics to allow for other features on a web page.

That means you only have 750 pixels of width available for your infographic. Therefore, you want to make sure that when you build your infographic, you have your software (whether it's Photoshop or Illustrator) set to a width of 750 pixels so that when you put the infographic on the web page, it's sized properly, and everything can be read easily.

Sharing Your Work

After you decided that your infographic will be placed on the web and shared to a wider audience, you'll be able to take advantage of some easy tools that make it easy to share content. Because social media is always changing, do your best to stay on top of new developments in social media. In this section, however, we briefly discuss implementing social sharing buttons and embed codes to get you started sharing your content with the wider world.

The key element behind every sharing button and embed code is this: Content is king. Make sure to generate the highest quality content in your infographic. Use your resources and time wisely as you promote it, and you'll be in a good position to get exposure for your infographic and your brand.

Providing social share buttons on the page

When you see content on the web that you find funny, insightful, or just interesting in general, you probably want to share that content with others in your social network. Maybe it's a fascinating news story or a hilarious YouTube video. If the content has social sharing buttons, all you need to do is click the right button, and everyone in your network can see what you're seeing.

This is the mindset you need to have when posting your infographic to your website. Think about what social networks your readers are likely to use, and then have a button on the page that allows them to easily share the infographic.

The best place for these social network sharing buttons is right above the infographic image, below the title and introduction paragraph. You can also get away with putting the same buttons again right after the infographic. Some websites put the buttons to the left of the infographic, which is fine, too.

Don't overload the page with every social networking button out there. Keep things simple. Our recommendation is to consider six major buttons:

- ✔ Facebook Like/Share
- ✔ Twitter retweet
- ✔ Google+
- ✔ LinkedIn
- ✔ Pinterest
- ✔ Reddit

Ignore the other buttons. Having too many will simply overwhelm the reader and make them disinterested. You could place the sharing buttons at the top of or below your infographic. Or, consider stacking them and having them scroll with the user while reading. (See Figure 12-3.)

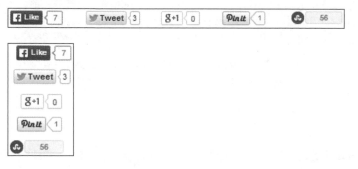

Figure 12-3: Preparing to share your graphic on social media.

Getting the buttons on the page is a snap. For example, just search online for "Facebook share button," and you'll get step-by-step instructions on how to get the button onto your page, which involves simply copy and pasting a code that Facebook provides into the back end of your website. The other platforms offer similarly simple methods.

Keep your audience in mind. For example, Pinterest is heavily used by women, so if the content of your infographic appeals mostly to women, Pinterest is a must. If the content is male-oriented, perhaps you'll skip that button.

Audience, audience, audience

In Chapter 6, we talk about how to mine your research to create an infographic for various audiences. Considering the audience is really important when deciding where to publish, too.

The topic and the tone of your infographic should match the channels where you're trying to publish it. So, a detailed explanation of political strife in Ukraine is not Pinterest material. It may be a terrific tweet, and will elicit hundreds of smart comments and thousands of retweets, so perhaps you'll spend most or all of your time getting the graphic ready to travel via Twitter.

By contrast, an infographic that shows a back-to-school checklist and tips for starting a new school year is tailor-made for Pinterest. Sending your work out to the most relevant channels isn't limiting; it's just smart.

Giving out an embed code

Embed codes have become an important part of infographics. They enable your audience to easily share your infographic on their website or blog. Embed codes can simply be copied and pasted directly into HTML or blogging platforms like WordPress.

Embed codes are an essential part of the infographic landing page. The more easily your infographic can be shared, the more links and traffic will come back to your infographic.

Creating an embed code

The easiest way to created an embed code is to use an online tool. Many embed code generators are available online, but one of the best ones is by Siege Media:

```
www.siegemedia.com/embed-code-generator
```

This embed code generator offers you enough control without being overly complicated.

Testing your embed code

Test your embed code before you use it. A simple mistake can really hurt your entire infographic marketing campaign. Use a real-time CSS and HTML editor like Scratchpad (`http://scratchpad.io`) to test your embed code before using it.

13

Promoting Your Infographic

. . . .

In This Chapter

▶ Determining who can help promote your work

▶ Sharing your infographic on social media channels

▶ Figuring out when to share your infographic

. . . .

*I*t's go time. All the hard work of building your infographic is done, and it's time to promote your infographic to the world. A lot rides on how the next phase goes. After all, no one wants to invest the resources, time, and money into building an infographic and then have it go nowhere. So, how can you make sure that you're putting your infographic in the best possible position to succeed? Bottom line: No one will know about your infographic if you don't tell them about it.

In writing this, we can't help but think about an old IBM commercial that goes something like this: Workers are sitting around in a conference room while the boss is asking questions to everyone in the room about a new website they built. He's asking about how the technology is working, the design of the site, the messaging, the servers, and so on. Everyone in the room is very proudly answering every question to the boss's satisfaction.

The boss then asks how many customers have come to the website. Every face goes blank, and someone meekly says, "Zero". It was something no one even thought about. They spent all of this time building this amazing website, but none of their efforts went toward getting people to actually come to the website.

Infographics — and Internet content in general — are not like the Field of Dreams, where if you build it, users and traffic will come. At least when you're beginning, you need to market your work. We've learned some great strategies for reaching the right readers at the times they're most likely to pay attention. We've also figured out how to use technology to help us target our work and make it look great as it travels through cyberspace. In this chapter, we'll share some of the lessons we've learned.

Collecting Influencers

The first step in any promotion is the preparation phase. In the case of promoting an infographic, this is all about collecting *influencers* — those people who already have a media presence and can help you share your content and get noticed.

One of the original influencers is Guy Kawasaki. He formerly held the title of "evangelist" at Apple, building brand loyalty and constant buzz for Apple's products. He's now with Google and is clearly a major influencer, with 1.4 million (and counting) Twitter followers. If you can get him to tweet out your infographic, you have 1.4 million potential viewers for your work. Any or all of them could potentially retweet the infographic to their respective networks, jumpstarting the viral process.

An influencer like Guy Kawasaki or a blogger at Mashable would be interested in your content because these influencers are in a constant quest for fresh content. Today's media brokers thrive on aggregating content — pulling together interesting stories, quotes, GIFs, photos — and yes, infographics — from a wide variety of sources. Your hope is that your piece of content falls in line with something they might be interested in sharing.

So how do you know what key influencers may be interested in sharing? Check out what they've shared before. Say you admire a certain blogger at The Huffington Post. It's very easy to see his content by simply going to the website, searching for his name, and clicking it. In doing so, you can see all the articles he has written and content he has shared. Look for certain topics he tends to be interested in. If your work overlaps, you may want to consider this person as a potential influencer. The same concept applies for Twitter influencers. Just look at the links they've shared. ***Hint:*** This exercise will be more time consuming because a major Twitter user is going to post a lot more content than a web blogger.

Getting prepared to go viral

In the end, your goal is to get your content to "go viral." That phrase is most certainly overused at this point, and people have different definitions for it. Our definition of "going viral" is simply giving something enough of a push out the door where it then begins to spread around the web on its own.

Creating viral content is very difficult. We often recommend that clients create a series of infographics or plan for ongoing content creation. That way, all your eggs are not in one basket, with everything relying on the success of just one infographic.

In most cases, having something go viral is not an accident. A lot of hard work and planning — and most importantly, execution— lies behind a piece of content becoming that successful. In Figure 13-1, you'll see some of the steps you should take to set the stage for your graphic to go viral.

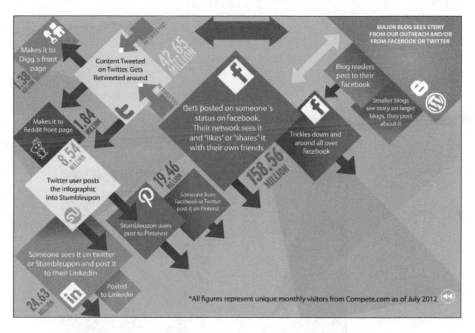

Figure 13-1: Preparing your work to go viral.

Building a list of influencers

It's time to make a list and check it twice. Actually, check it more than twice. Identifying the right influencers is one of the most important things you can do in the entire process. You need to find the *right* people to reach out to as you encourage them to become ambassadors of your content. This list can make or break your promotion.

A common mistake people make here is that they think that *every* website would love nothing more than to feature their infographic. They end up pitching their work to every major website and setting themselves up for failure. The reality is that only a small percentage of infographics created are going to get featured on major websites like The Huffington Post, Mashable, or Buzzfeed. Having said that, keep reaching out to reporters and bloggers on those sites.

Timing is everything

When Steve Jobs passed away in 2011, the Infographic World team embarked on a wild 24-hour period of building a great infographic looking back on his life while simultaneously preparing our plan to market the infographic. Our homework paid off: We were able to get the infographic featured on Mashable, and it became the number one story on that site for a few weeks. That led to it getting picked up and featured on thousands of other websites, with hundreds of thousands of social shares and millions of page views. This was the living,

breathing definition of something going viral. At one point, I got an angry call from our website developer, wondering why I hadn't warned him about all the traffic that was coming to the website. We were getting so many hits that our server was close to crashing!

This is the kind of phone call you want to get. You want your work to generate so much interest that your website servers are holding on for dear life. The servers will survive. You'll thrive.

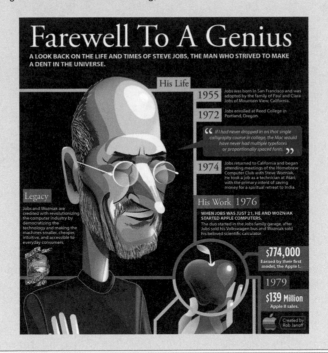

 TIP

A better tactic, however, is to first home in on the media outlets that are most likely to be interested in your content. You find the right media outlets by knowing your audience. If your infographic is about dogs, for example, a website that is very tech-focused like Mashable may not be the right site for you. Instead, in this instance, you should be researching the top dog blogs and then make those sites your first targets.

In this section, we show you which tools — Google, Technorati, Twitter, and Pinterest, to name a few — to use to help you target the right outlet and audience for your infographic. You can read about using Facebook in the upcoming section, "Using social media."

Google

A straightforward and easy way to start identifying the right websites and blogs to target is to search Google for the topic in mind. Say you created an infographic on dogs, which you've titled "The History of Dog Breeding in the World."

Type something like **dog breeding history** into Google. (Read more about searching online in Chapter 5.) You'll get a mix of results, as shown in Figure 13-2, including Wikipedia pages, news stories related to dog breeding, and websites about dog breeding. You'll want to dig through the search results and locate the ones that come from blogs dedicated to dogs and dog breeding.

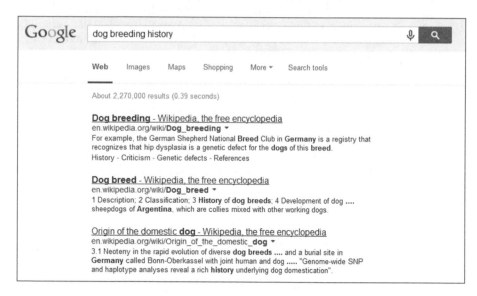

Figure 13-2: Using Google searches to find an audience for your work.

Now, this actually is a measurable science. By copying and pasting the URL of the site into sites like Compete (www.compete.com) and Alexa Internet (www.alexa.com), you can see how much traffic the websites receive. Sites like these measure traffic on a daily (or weekly, monthly, yearly, and so on) basis — and such information is important because you want your infographic featured on the platforms that get plenty of traffic.

After you target some good potential websites and blogs, take a look at the posts that have been published. See how many social shares the posts tend to get. Take a look at how many readers tend to comment. You want to find websites that have active and engaged readers. With an engaged readership, many posts make their way to Twitter, Facebook, and the other main social sites.

In the digital media landscape, posts that receive a lot of comments and a lot of shares are the gold standard. The nature of comments matters, too because those websites and blogs that provoke smart, engaged conversation are the ones you want to target. Even a small or medium-sized site may be worth targeting if its comments are relevant and its audience seems excited. Naturally, it won't have the metrics like The Huffington Post, but it may be the right audience for you right now.

Technorati

The Technorati Top 100 can help you search for the right websites and blogs to add to your list. In the middle of the Technorati page (http://technorati.com), you can find its overall Top 100 list, which contains the usual suspects of largest blogs in the world: The Huffington Post, Buzzfeed, Business Insider, and others.

The really valuable element of Technorati is its directory (http://technorati.com/blogs/directory), shown in Figure 13-3. In this directory, you can search for the largest blogs on the web by category. So if you created an infographic on dogs, you can just click the Pets section to be taken to that directory and ranking of largest pet-related blogs on the web. Thanks to its focused rankings, you could really just rely on Technorati as the main tool to build your list of websites to reach out to during your promotion and be just fine.

Topsy.com

Topsy.com is an amazing social analytics tool that will also allow you to identify influencers on various topics. Here's how to get started with Topsy:

1. **Go to www.topsy.com.**

2. **In the search bar, type in a keyword related to your infographic.**

   You'll get a long list of content related to your keyword. On the left side of the screen, you can change the period of time. Use this function to see, for example, how recently someone tweeted about your subject.

   Note (on the left side) the Influencers icon. This is who Topsy believes are the best influencers on the topic you typed into the search bar. They are the most likely to tweet about your infographic topic.

3. **Broaden this function by clicking Everything to see all people who have shared similar content, not just the top influencers.**

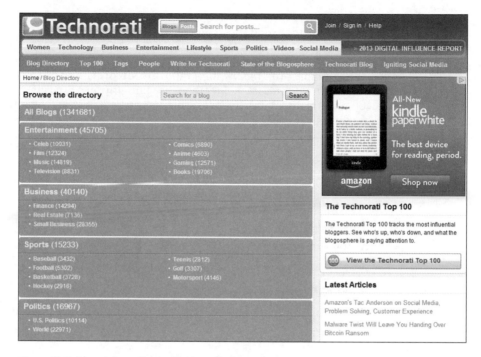

Figure 13-3: Search for relevant blogs on Technorati.

Here's another way to use Topsy: Do a Google search for content similar to your infographic topic. Find a big story that did very well virally (perhaps it got picked up on Mashable or The Huffington Post). Copy and paste that story's URL into the Links section of Topsy to see which influencers shared it. You can then add these people to your list of influencers to reach out to.

Klout

Klout (`http://klout.com`), which is a website and mobile app, can help you determine the best influencers. Klout uses an algorithm to measure the influence a given person has. Type your infographic topic into Klout, and you'll get a list of all the influencers on those high-level topics. This is a great way to locate more influencers, figure out who they are, and be able to reach out to them.

Infographic directories

As far as outreach is concerned, one obvious but sometimes overlooked approach is reaching out to infographic directories and aggregators. Sites like this do nothing but feature infographics, so they naturally have potential. However, there are some downsides to this approach.

Most infographic directories are general in focus. They feature infographics that they like, rather than those dedicated to any specific topic — and that won't help you get your content to people definitely interested in your topic.

Also, there simply aren't many infographic directories that have enough traffic to be worth your effort. Remember that infographics are relatively new to the web, hitting the mainstream Internet media in 2008/2009. As a result, infographic directories really haven't had much time to build up their followings and user base.

Those caveats aside, infographic directories are still a viable and logical option as you promote your infographics. Here are a few to consider adding to your list (as of the writing of this book).

- **Daily Infographic:** http://dailyinfographic.com
- **Alltop Infographics:** http://infographics.alltop.com
- **Infographic List:** http://infographiclist.com
- **Infographics Archive:** www.infographicsarchive.com
- **Best Infographics:** www.best-infographics.com
- **Great Infographics:** http://greatinfographics.com
- **Chart Porn:** http://chartporn.org

You may want to consider searching Google for "infographic blog" and "infographic directories" to look for any new ones.

Twitter

We want to revisit Twitter for a second because it's a very valuable website when it comes to the promotion of infographics. Twitter never turns off, and there's always a desire for fresh content. Heavy-duty tweeters want to be the ones to share great, relevant content with their followers. Through offering them your content, you may develop a symbiotic relationship: You're helping the influencer share great content with their followers while also naturally helping yourself.

In determining the right Twitter users to go after, the easiest approach is to go onto Twitter and simply type the topic of your infographic into the search bar. This launches a search for people using a hash tag that relates to your content. Folks who are active on a hash tag are looking for things to tweet, so giving them something educational, newsworthy, or something their audience will value will make sense for them to tweet out.

Using Followerwonk to find Twitter influencers

A powerful tool for determining Twitter influencers is Followerwonk (`http://followerwonk.com`). This site searches Twitter bios for whatever keywords you want, which will allow you to identify people who would be ideal targets to reach out to. On the Followerwonk site, click Search Twitter Bios and then type the keyword or keywords that are related to your infographic or industry. The search results that come up will show the following items:

- **Tweets:** How many tweets the Twitter user has sent out, which will show how active the user is

- **Following:** How many people the Twitter user is following

- **Followers:** How big of a following the person has, which is a factor in determining how much of an influencer the person or company is

- **Days Old:** How long the Twitter user has been active

- **Social Authority:** A score created by Followerwonk that measures the social influence of the user

The free version of Followerwonk lets you do everything but download, so it's a really nice tool for finding influencers.

Getting back to our History of Dog Breeding in the World infographic example from earlier in the chapter, go to Twitter and search (in the search bar) for hash tags like #dogbreeding or #historyofdogbreeding. From here, go through tweets made using this hash tag and look to see who the users are.

Go person by person to see how active they are, how many followers they have, and how often they tweet about this topic. If they're active, have a good following, and use the hash tag fairly frequently, you just identified an influencer that you should add to your list.

Pinterest

Pinterest (`www.pinterest.com`) has grown at a tremendous pace and could be another good place for you to pitch your infographics. The first step is finding out which Pinterest boards are named by your topic/infographic topic. Here's a cool trick you can use in Google:

1. **Type in the following:** site:pinterest.com inurl:dogs.

   Note the space between `site:pinterest.com` and `inurl:dogs`.

   See a sample of results in Figure 13-4.

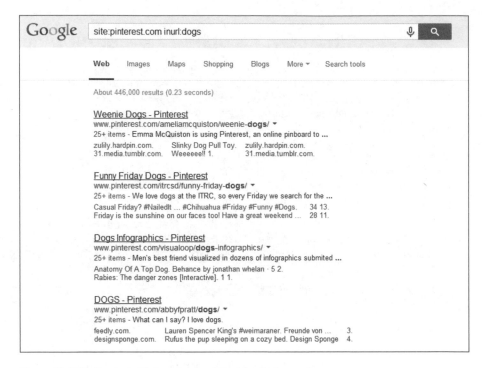

Figure 13-4: Finding potential contacts with a targeted search.

2. **Next, try this one:** site:pinterest.com inurl:infographics.

   Each time, you simply just sub in the topic you want to search for after `inurl:`. By doing this, you can see who is making boards about your topic.

3. **Reach out to those people who run the board and see whether they'll post your infographic.**

StumbleUpon

Similar to Pinterest, StumbleUpon (`www.stumbleupon.com`) is an aggregator of things that people think are cool. At StumbleUpon, you can search by topic, find users and groups that are talking about your topic, and then reach out to them individually. Or, you can use the site command approach as we explain in the preceding section. Simply put in this: **site:stumbleupon. com inurl:dogs** (again, using a space between `site:stumbleupon.com` and `inurl:dogs`).

LinkedIn

Business networking site LinkedIn (`www.linkedin.com`) can also be valuable for promoting an infographic. Keep it in mind if your infographic is about business, professional, or industry topics.

To find a potential home for your infographic on LinkedIn, search LinkedIn for groups that are related to your infographic topic. Then you can create a new discussion and share the infographic there. Personally, we don't love tactics like this. Most users are pretty savvy, and they recognize that you are plainly trying to promote content for your own benefit. That said, it's not very time consuming, and may be worth a shot because LinkedIn is full of key influencers.

Google+

Pay attention to Google+ (`https://plus.google.com`) as well. Go into Google+ and search by the topic of your infographic. Then look for a search result that has a lot of + signs and activity. From there, click the drop-down arrow on the top right and then click View Ripples. You can see how your search result has been shared and who was sharing it. You can list the people who shared it and then reach out to them.

There is also a big community element to Google+. You can join a community relevant to your infographic and then share the infographic there within the community. On top, next to Everything, click More to see Communities to find which are the big communities on the topic and also how many posts there have been.

Don't spam your new contacts. Just be honest and say you created an info-graphic that's relevant to their community, and you wanted to share it with them. If your infographic is really relevant and of interest to those people, they just might send it out for you.

Organizing your list of influencers

After you find some influencers and outlets to target, keep them organized as you plan your pitch. One simple approach is to create an Excel spreadsheet, as shown in Figure 13-5.

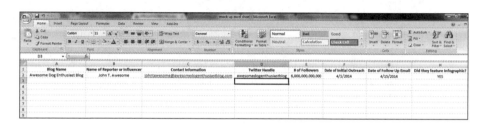

Figure 13-5: Keeping your contacts organized in a spreadsheet.

You can build a spreadsheet that lists very simple things, such as

- Blog name
- Name of the reporter, blogger, or Twitter influencer
- Contact information of blogger
- Twitter handle (and perhaps the number of followers they have)
- Date of initial outreach to blogger

- Date of follow-up e-mail to blogger

    If they don't respond after two tries, it might be time to move on.

- Featured infographic

On a spreadsheet like this, use several tabs to keep things organized. For example, use a different tab for every industry you're targeting. So, back to our dog infographic. When planning a pitch for that infographic, we would set up the following tabs:

- Dog enthusiast blogs
- Pet blogs
- General animal enthusiast blogs
- General-interest websites that have been known to feature infographics (like The Huffington Post or Buzzfeed)
- Infographic websites and directories

Within each tab, list the relevant information for every website and influencer you want to reach out to for your promotion.

Putting Your Plan in Place

After you make your list of key influencers to go after, with the hope that some of these websites and people will be interested enough in your infographic that they will want to share it with their followers, now comes the time to implement your plan. You'll need to take the time to reach out to these potential influencers individually and find a way to interest them in featuring your content.

Building relationships

In an ideal world, if you're responsible for creating content and marketing it within a particular niche, you may already have relationships with your potential markets. If you don't, now is the time to start building a relationship with these people. This will likely not be the last infographic you ever create within this space. Even if it is, you'll still be creating other kinds of content that will also need an audience. You need to have contacts and relationships that you can tap into to get exposure for your website or content.

Here are a few overarching tips as you get started:

- ✔ **Reach out individually.** No one wants to receive an e-mail pitch that was blatantly blasted out to hundreds or thousands of people. You want to make it personal, especially when you contact someone for the first time.

- ✔ **Keep it simple.** Tell them who you are and why the content is relevant to them and their readers. Perhaps hook them with a few interesting facts from the infographic.

- ✔ **Clarify how the relationship benefits them.** Give a suggestion or two on how they can tailor the infographic for their audience. If you're reaching out to a Twitter influencer, it might make sense to even include a few suggested tweets they could send out.

- ✔ **Don't be too pushy or presumptuous.** Remember that this person doesn't know you, and you're essentially asking a favor. You want to be humble here, without demanding anything or assuming that they will even be willing to help.

After you e-mail your prospects, the waiting game begins. Plenty of people will simply ignore your e-mail or may never even see it because it ends up in their spam folder.

Wait several days after sending out your initial e-mail before reaching out again. If you still don't hear back several days after that, it might be time to move on.

Here's why that Excel spreadsheet (which we discuss creating in "Organizing your list of influencers") will continue to be valuable. Use this tool to help you remain organized: If you're lucky, you may have to juggle a lot of conversations at once. For instance, you might get some nibbles from folks who are interested but have follow-up questions and requests. Other potential influencers might ask whether you can send them things like an embed code (if one exists; see Chapter 12 for more about embed codes). You could also be asked to send a piece of the infographic that they can put up on their site and then link back to your site.

Offering exclusives

If there is some lead time between when the infographic is complete and when it needs to go live, offer some of the major websites an exclusive of the infographic. At Infographic World, we've done this with great success. Here's how it works:

1. **Identify a top tier of websites that you would love to see publish your infographic.**

2. **Pin down your list to just a few prime candidates.**

3. **Offer them the chance to be the first website to feature the infographic — even before you put it up on your own website.**

   This exclusivity can be very enticing to websites because they all want to be the first to feature something great. Dangling this carrot could be a way to get a big site interested in featuring your infographic.

4. **If you get an exclusive, negotiate with the editor or other person-in-charge the day and time of publication.**

5. **After they post your infographic, you can then put your infographic live on your own website, perhaps linking back to the site that first published it.**

We've developed a lot of great relationships with major bloggers through the use of exclusives. If your work gets them a great response with lots of social sharing and traffic, the blogger may begin to consider you a reliable source for great content. And guess what? You just opened the door to future projects.

Using social media

Reaching out to potential influencers and pitching your work is all external effort. You'll need to plan an internal phase of publication, too. This involves placing the infographic on all your social channels.

Sizing your work for Facebook

Start with Facebook (`www.facebook.com`). From an infographics perspective, your most important duty is sizing your infographic to fit properly on there. Facebook does allow for easy sharing, but there are some potential pitfalls. Online infographics tend to be pretty big files, and very rarely will the full infographic be readable on Facebook.

One approach is simply to take a thumbnail of the infographic and upload that within your post. Another is to pull from the infographic the most interesting section, or perhaps just the top portion that shows the title and a small portion of the top of the infographic. Save this small image. Then create a Facebook post, upload that image to the post, and include a link to your website, where readers can find the full-sized infographic.

Using meta tags

Another approach is to use Open Graph (`https://developers.facebook.com/docs/opengraph`) meta tags. Open Graph is a programming interface that affects how Facebook displays and promotes your material. Any time you go to share content from your website on Facebook, Facebook automatically searches through the page to find a visual to add to your post. Sometimes, Facebook seems to pick an image at random to be the visual that accompanies the post. In other instances, it pulls a bunch of images that you can choose from to be the visual that accompanies the post. What you want to do here is work with Facebook and make it easy to find the images that best represent the infographic.

Open Graph allows you to make sure that Facebook is pulling the right images to showcase your work. For example, an infographic on your website that's 1,000 pixels wide is way too big to fit within the Facebook dimensions. So, try creating a second image on the blog post page that's not visible, but is rather just in the meta tag itself.

When Facebook comes along, the meta tag lets Facebook know that this version (the smaller hidden one) is made just for it. Now, thanks to the meta tag, when someone shares your infographic on Facebook, it will only show the image you want them to. For more information on using this technology, check out

```
http://wordpress.org/plugins/facebook-featured-image-and-open-graph-meta-tags/
```

Looking for Facebook groups

You'll also want to consider looking for groups and pages on Facebook that relate to your infographic topic. These can be very valuable for reaching out. After you identify these communities, you can reach out to the people running the groups to see whether they have any interest in the infographic you created.

Using hash tags on Twitter and Pinterest

To take advantage of Twitter, you'll need to build up some skill with hash tags. It's very important in the tweet you send out about your infographic that you're including the right kinds of hashtags. A powerful tool to consider is Hashtags.org (`www.hashtags.org`), which is a search engine of hash tags. There, you can find how many people are using the hash tag you have in mind. You'll naturally want to use hash tags that people commonly search for, thus increasing the chance of your tweet and infographic getting exposure.

You can also search for your infographic subject on Twitter to see what hash tags people are commonly using when they talk about it. When you write your tweet, use only one or two hash tags in your headline. We've all seen the endless chains of hash tags that some people attach to their tweets. These look like spam, gibberish, or both, and they turn people off and make them less likely to retweet your tweet. Say you're publishing an infographic on ski jumping, timed to the Olympics. You could add #olympics and #skijumping and call it a day.

Also, when sharing on Twitter, always add an image. There is a button that makes this easy. Adding a visual element to your tweet gives your infographic a better chance of being seen and shared.

For Pinterest, post the infographic to one or two of your own boards, making sure to use relevant hash tags. If you do an infographic on the revived popularity of knitting, you could simply add the hash tags #knitting or #crafts. As with all social sites, make sure that your hash tags dovetail with those heavily used on the site.

Determining When to Pitch

Timing is everything. A cliché, true — but this cliché has serious implications when it comes to promoting your infographic. Choosing the wrong time can make or break your promotion.

Targeting influencers at the best time

When it comes to launching your infographic at just the right time, we have a few tips to offer you:

- **Never launch your infographic promotion on a Friday.** If you start reaching out to people on a Friday, you're running head first into the weekend, when people aren't checking their e-mails, and Internet traffic drops dramatically. If you launch on a Friday and get lucky enough to have a major website feature your infographic that same day, that's great news! However, you're not giving the infographic a chance to gain momentum and get shared and picked up by other websites. Instead, you'll get a decent amount of exposure on Friday, which will likely dwindle over the weekend and be forgotten by the time Monday rolls around.

- **Launch and promote your infographic on Mondays and Tuesdays whenever possible.** This gives you the entire week for people to see your infographic on your site and for bloggers and influencers to see your e-mail outreach to them and consider featuring your content.

- **Noon Eastern Standard Time is often the best time to launch.** At that time, everyone on the East Coast is deep into their day, while those on the West Coast are starting their days. Traffic levels tend to be strongest for many sites in the 12 p.m.–1 p.m. EST range. This is not the case for all websites, but it provides a good starting point.

In general, you want to time your promotion to when people are most likely to be in front of their computers. For many people, that is during work hours. Yes, you are taking away from their productivity, but hey — some sacrifices have to be made.

Timing your social media shares

Timing is also of the essence when it comes to sharing your work on social media. When using Twitter, people often tweet out their infographic once, then just hope for the best. Twitter allows you to post many times in a week, however, and you should take advantage of this.

The inherent nature of Twitter means that people's feeds move very quickly and become very crowded. Therefore, promoting your work in several tweets reduces the chances that your work will be overlooked. A much more effective approach is to follow these steps:

1. **Queue up three or four key facts from your infographic.**

2. **Tweet them out over the course of a week, each time linking to the infographic.**

3. **Send a follow-up tweet a week or so later.**

With Facebook, share your work in one post on Monday, and then another post on Friday. For each one, use a different visual image to catch readers' eyes. Facebook is very different from Twitter when it comes to this, and you should not do too many posts. Make your posts high-quality; then let them stand on their own.

Part V
The Part of Tens

the
part of
tens

Check out www.dummies.com/extras/infographics for an additional Part of Tens chapter on ways to generate great infographic ideas.

In this part . . .

✔ We'll take a look at the best, smartest ways that people are using infographics right now, and we'll show you how to take advantage of those trends in your own work.

✔ We'll look to the future, and consider how infographics will be used in the weeks, months and years to come.

14

Ten Infographics Trends to Follow

Part of the beauty of design is that it's always changing. Artists and designers weave in elements of fashion, pop culture, color theory, and even psychology as they create work that's beautiful, interesting, and appealing to an audience.

Because design is always in flux, it can fall prey to trends. An infographic recently published in *The New York Times* will look vastly different from one published in 1985. Font size, font style, colors, and simplicity versus complexity are just a few infographic design elements that have been influenced by trends over the years.

Trends can be a loaded term. The desire to capitalize on a trend has opened the door to some notorious failures (Milli Vanilli and powder-blue blazers). But with a judicious eye and a careful hand, you can use trends to keep your infographics current, beautiful, and intriguing to your audience.

This chapter shows you ten emerging trends in infographic design. Have a look at how to incorporate the best of the trends without creating a graphic as dated as your grandpa's plaid pants. You'll want to embrace at least some of these in your upcoming projects.

Adding Interactive Features to Your Graphics

Without a doubt, interactivity is the hottest trend in infographics. The rise of online sources of news and entertainment content has made us all curators. We choose the websites we want to visit, the links we want to click, and the information we want to share.

So, it's only natural that when we're given the chance to play around with our information, to dive into a sea of data and make it work for our own purposes, we love it. You don't need to be a programmer to add interactive features; a working knowledge of Adobe Flash Player is enough to get you started.

But you can't rest there. Even as we go to print, web-design languages like HTML and CSS are threatening to overtake Flash in the field of interactive graphic design. If you want to make sure your graphics read well on mobile devices, start working on adding HTML5, CSS3, and JavaScript to your programming language toolbox.

Interactive graphics promise a depth that an ordinary print graphic could never convey. The possibilities are endless and often fascinating to readers. Here we briefly describe two ways how infographics designers are making their work more interactive.

Placing information on different pages

When print media was the most common platform for infographics, the entire graphic had to be viewed as a unit. Whether the graphic took up a single column in a newspaper or a two-page spread in a magazine, design rules called for the entire graphic to be self-contained.

No more. In an online platform, you can present a simple block of information in an opening page. To move on to your next block of information, you could create a vertical design, allowing your reader to scroll down the page to move on to the new information.

Or, you could place your second block of information on an entirely new page, with a link encouraging the reader to click for more information. Add another graphic element, place it on a third page, again with a call-to-action link.

This approach may be tremendously appealing for clients who use page views to determine advertising rates and overall popularity. The downside of a click-through graphic: Your reader may not stick with you through the whole thing.

Letting the reader choose

Say you created an infographic to show the percentage of the population in each U.S. state that holds a college degree. Simple, right? You probably made a map of the United States, with a percentage figure in tiny type in each state.

Interactivity allows you to take many other approaches. You could skip the numbers entirely. For example, start by color-coding your states. Perhaps states with less than 50 percent of the population having a college degree are light green; 50 to 65 percent is medium green; and 65 percent or more is a forest green.

You can then embed your data, using HTML5, so that a reader could hover the computer mouse over a single state, and see the exact percentage. You can add plenty of data this way. Perhaps you'll break out the percentages of men and women who hold college degrees, or you could use a slider bar to change the data according to decade.

Using Video or Animation in Graphics

If interactivity is the hottest trend in infographic creations, video and animation is in second place, surging toward the lead. In general, video is used more and more to present information, and with that is a serious rise in the creation of video and animation infographics.

Two particular video approaches that are becoming especially popular are whiteboard animations and explainer videos. Most people know what a whiteboard animation is because of the UPS commercials featuring a man drawing on a whiteboard. Many companies are beginning to embrace the idea of telling a story through the use of whiteboard animation, whether it's about their company, their product, or something industry-related. Explainer videos are becoming a go-to approach for telling the story about products and initiatives. Both of these approaches, along with animated infographics in general, are becoming more and more popular as people want to watch more videos while online.

Initially, Flash technology drove most animated infographics. However, Flash is falling out of favor because it doesn't always work when readers view infographics on mobile devices. Now, the Adobe After Effects software is a popular way to add animated features.

Designing for Tablets

With the astronomical rise in tablet use, it's only natural that there has been a rise in the creation of content designed specifically for them. Infographics World has created a good amount of work that has been used exclusively on tablets, and we foresee this trend becoming more of a go-to approach. From the designer's perspective, tablets are a great medium because scrolling downward through a graphic allows readers to take in much more information than they could in a fixed-size graphic.

Using Data to Drive Your Project

Data is big. Really big. In fact, the term "big data" has become a popular buzzword. In today's world, we have so much information, about so many topics, from so many sources, that it can all be a bit overwhelming.

This is great news for infographics. After all, infographics designers have been mining statistics and presenting them clearly and artistically for decades. If the torrent of data threatens to overwhelm readers, corporate executives, media types, marketing gurus . . . well, that's where you come in as an infographics designer. Your clear, concise graphic can help the reader distill the information they want and need from a sea of numbers.

An increasing emphasis on data has given rise to some new names for infographic designers. You may justifiably call yourself a data journalist, a data visualization expert, or a data-driven journalist. The terms don't really change the work you do.

Prospects appear bright for this sort of infographic work. In fact, in November 2013, *The New York Times* announced the creation of a new website emphasizing data-driven journalism. We anticipate that this publication will use graphics to enhance its work.

Developing Graphics for Market Research

Lately, we've had a lot of clients ask us to help them communicate their market research in a more visual and appealing manner. We would even go so far as to say that about 25 percent of our work these days is taking market research that clients have done and turning it into infographics. It's really a perfect fit: Market research consists of tons of statistics and data points about various items within your industry. When you go to communicate these findings, which would you rather do — put a bunch of stats in a PDF document, or have an infographic created that shows the same points but in a visually compelling manner? Pretty simple decision if you ask us.

Using Graphics to Bridge Cultures

According to the U.S. Census Bureau, 382 languages are spoken in American households. You probably aren't surprised to learn that English and Spanish are the most common, accounting for a strong majority of household languages. But that leaves 380 languages that may not always have a ready translator.

That's where infographics come in.

Every time you buy an appliance, you've probably noticed that the directions come in multiple languages. And there's no possible way to translate information into some less common tongues. Clear, graphical representations of information can be an important way to reach people across cultural and language barriers. The furniture company IKEA is famous for its reliance on visual cues rather than words. Figure 14-1 shows the universal symbol for elevator; one of dozens of established symbols that cut across language barriers.

Figure 14-1: The international symbol for elevator.

Not only instruction manuals will be important as the world becomes more intertwined. Say, for example, you work for a nonprofit group focused on breast health. A clear, simple diagram of how to examine one's breasts could provide life-saving information to a woman who may not understand written text or even a doctor's verbal advice.

The DIY Graphics Movement

Here are some words that may strike fear into the hearts of professional infographic designers: _Anyone can make an infographic._

You're probably thinking that if anyone can make an infographic, who would ever hire you to create one?

It's a valid question, but look at it this way: The quantity of published infographics has risen astronomically. Along the way, the quality has improved, too. With the help of this book, you can learn the importance of great research, a well-designed plan, and awesome technical skills to create graphics that beautifully bridge the worlds of data and design.

Attention spans keep getting shorter! The global marketplace has an insatiable need to present information that works across language and cultural lines. You should be able to find plenty of work.

And there's plenty of room for people who are not designers to play around with the form. Some cool things we've seen:

- **Tableau Public (a division of Tableau Software www.tableausoftware. com) allows a user to submit raw data, which Tableau's programming language turns into "data visualizations."** The finished products are shared to the general public, and can also be uploaded to the user's website, blog, or other platform. Some major media outlets are using Tableau, but it's free to anyone.

- **IBM runs a program called Many Eyes (http://www-958.ibm.com/software/analytics/manyeyes/) that allows users to create free infographics based on data sets.** The program lets users try out more than a dozen different treatments of their information, from pie chart to bar graph to flow chart. Finished products are publicly available and ready for review by other Many Eyes users.

- **In 2012, Stanford professor and social-media maven Drake Martinet's proposal to girlfriend Stacy Green took the form of an infographic.** Martinet used statistics and female icons to prove that Stacy was the one perfect woman for him. This is a classic case of knowing your audience: Green is the chief marketing officer for online news site Mashable.

✔ **Some intrepid job seekers are creating infographic résumé.** This is a bit of a gamble. Getting a job is serious business; especially in traditional industries, you don't want to appear too whimsical. In creative fields, though, a résumé in the form of an infographic might just help you stand out and show your prospective boss just how creatively you can think. Perhaps your career history is shown on a subtly illustrated timeline. You could place your most relevant skills in bubbles, perhaps overlapping with key terms from the job description. Former employers could be shown, not listed, with small icons based on their corporate logos. An infographic résumé would also provide an easy way to link to your previous work. Figure 14-2 shows how one young job seeker put his résumé in graphic form.

Figure 14-2: An infographic can serve as a résumé.

Infographics for Presentations

These days, if you're conducting a presentation for work or school and would like to put your viewers to sleep, we would recommend going with the standard PowerPoint presentation.

Perhaps we're exaggerating, but we're not far off. Many an audience has glazed over while presenters click through text-heavy PowerPoint slides. By turning some of your information into attractive charts, graphs, and illustrations, you can keep your audience engaged. Keep your information clear, your text light, and your style consistent with the company or project you're representing.

Make a List, Check It Twice

Social media is chock full of lists these days: anything from "25 things people from upstate New York love" to "The 9 types of people who show up for Thanksgiving dinner" to "23 reasons why trying to be cute on the Internet is a terrible idea." There's even a brand-new buzzword to describe these stories: "listicles."

We highly doubt that this type of story is around for the long haul. But they're fun, easy to share, and tailor-made for reading on devices, such as smartphones and tablets. They also lend themselves very well to graphic treatment; many already use GIFs (graphics interchange format; a type of graphic file) to add visual appeal.

A list-oriented infographic also allows you to ask the reader to click through multiple pages, which is good news for clients looking to increase their number of page views. Check out Buzzfeed (www.buzzfeed.com) and Mashable (http://mashable.com) for some good examples of listicles as well as some inspiration for turning your list into an infographic.

Keeping It Small

Throughout this book, we talk about every cool feature, program, and design trend there is. We show you how to make complex, multisection graphics for print or online publications.

Well, don't forget the small stuff. Once in a while, try bucking the trend toward big graphics with all the bells and whistles. In the age of interactivity and the wide-open spaces of the Internet, adding more and more features and details to your infographic can be tempting. Sometimes a simple, clear chart or map is all that's needed. Do your research, make your plan, and keep your basic design skills up to speed. Sometimes, the small ones are sweeter.

15

Ten Future Infographic Uses to Try Today

The world of infographics is changing so quickly that it's imperative to stay on top of new developments in the content, use, design, and technology that drives them. Whether you're creating infographics for one client or many, for profit or an altruistic cause, you always want to stay true to the infographic's ultimate aim: Make a complex idea simple and use attractive design to present a clear message.

We at Infographic World, along with some leading figures in the infographics industry, are always looking ahead to see how we can be prepared to create the next wave of infographics. Here are ten ways we think infographics will be used in the future.

Education

Today's students are wired from birth, and by the time they reach school age, they're accustomed to colorful, graphic, entertaining presentations. Enter the infographic. We foresee several ways that infographics will play a stronger role in education in the next decade and beyond:

- **To explain complicated concepts:** We've all struggled through something in school. Whether it's the circulatory system of a frog or the causes of Middle East tension, an infinite number of topics can just be tough to understand.

  Infographics could be the answer. Maybe you can improve upon the frog diagrams in a biology book with an interactive graphic that more clearly explains the topic. Maybe the social studies book publisher will pick up your timeline of major events in the Middle East.

- **To fill in gaps left by cash-strapped school districts:** Say a teacher is saddled with a textbook from 1985. By creating an up-to-date infographic on her topic or finding one online, a teacher can bring her students the most relevant information. And even if schools are still using textbooks, expect more and more schools to switch over to online course materials. Those, too, will certainly become a forum for infographic presentation.

✔ **To help teach technology skills:** From kindergarten through college, students are using technology more frequently. Even very young students are sharing iPads and working on *smart boards,* interactive boards that allow teachers to show video, access the Internet, and entice students to participate. These are a great match for infographics. Teachers could show the very latest infographics, perhaps even interacting with the material with the push of a button or the click of a mouse.

✔ **To encourage student creativity:** Students may also be asked to create their own infographics. The younger generation is swamped by data, and learning how to carefully mine it and synthesize it into a coherent message is a valuable life skill. Do-it-yourself websites like those discussed elsewhere in the book make it easy for teachers to assign infographic projects to their students.

✔ **To aid in online learning:** Online learning is likely to become even hotter, with cyber charter schools and "massive open online courses" continuing to gain popularity. When students are learning online, they are primed to take advantage of the visual appeal and quick impact of a good infographic.

Digital Interactivity

There's no limit in sight for the possibilities of interactive graphics. Recently, academic research has begun to confirm what some infographic designers already believed: If a static infographic is good, an interactive one should be even better.

In 2012, researchers from Stanford University and the University of Maryland wrote, "A single image . . . typically provides answers to, at best, a handful of questions. . . . Meaningful analysis consists of repeated explorations as users develop insights about significant relationships, domain-specific contextual influences, and causal patterns."

Repeated explorations: Those two words encapsulate the power of interactive infographics. You want to make your interactives so compelling that the reader will explore them at great length. By offering multiple ways to explore your infographic, you encourage readers to find the patterns and relationships relevant to their lives.

Interactive infographics give the reader choices. So when planning your project, make choices obvious and interesting as well as easy to navigate (by clicking, dragging an icon, or hovering the mouse). Some companies are bringing interactive technology to print documents; this could be very interesting territory for infographic designers. Also make sure the graphic makes sense whether the reader peruses every word of it or just a small portion.

Sound Medium

Infographics are, of course, a visual medium, but adding sound can add a whole new dimension to your infographic project. In coming years, we believe sound will become a more common feature, increasing the interactive appeal of some graphics.

Sound in infographics can be as simple as a background audio file of instrumental music.

Do not simply upload any old song into your infographic! You don't want to violate any copyright laws. Seek out stock audio services, akin to stock photo services, that supply safely usable files. If you plan on releasing your sound infographic to the public, buy yourself a copyright-free audio file. Here are a few sites to check out:

www.istockphoto.com/audio

www.productiontrax.com

www.stockmusicsite.com

Adding sound also opens the door to some really creative treatments. For example, you could have a highlight feature that highlights text as the voice reads it. You could also tailor the sound specifically to the information you're showcasing. For example, say you're creating a graphic on the ten countries with the highest bread consumption. You could record, "Pass the bread, please" in ten languages. When readers hover a mouse over say, Italy, they would hear that phrase in Italian.

Sound does create a few potential complications. Remember that some people might be reading your infographic in a public place and won't want to run the sound file. Adding features also requires you to be extra careful about technological compatibility.

Multicultural Uses

Some of the world's most pressing concerns could benefit from an infographic treatment. Take, for example, the availability of potable water. The United Nations estimates that by 2025, two-thirds of the world's population won't have sufficient access to clean water. The shortage is expected to be most severe in impoverished countries.

CNN recently did a great infographic that showed the percentages of urban residents with access to safe drinking water. In the United States, 97 percent of residents have it. In Kenya, the number drops to 47 percent; in Haiti, 21 percent, and in Uganda, just 11 percent. CNN showed these and several other percentages in an elegant bar graph designed to look like water flowing from a tap. The message is abundantly clear to speakers of any language.

One fundamental role of an infographic is to incite a "call to action." Going forward, we anticipate that more organizations will turn to infographics to present their message in ways that cut across cultural and language barriers. This is a potentially life-changing way to call people to action.

Viral Topics

Earlier in the book, we talk about the exciting possibilities for graphics to go viral. To date, many of the graphics that have swept the web originated from a newspaper, an online news site, or a blog.

Well, what if you jumped right around the middle man? The days of artists and writers relying on a certain publication or periodical to present content are done. And that's not necessarily a bad thing. With an established publication, the goal is mass distribution of content that appeals to a general audience. Working on your own, you can target your work however you like — which can potentially free you up to jump on topics that you know will intrigue readers. In the most recent Winter Olympics, slopestyle skiing emerged as the hottest new sport, with various tricks to challenge the athletes and amaze the audience. An infographic breaking down the tricks would have undoubtedly gone viral during the Olympic season. You should be prepared to seize on topics like this. It's probably a more practical way to get published these days than waiting for an editor to say "yes." It just takes one reader, sparked by your information, to forward your infographic and light a blaze of interest.

Demographics

Never in history has information been so readily available. For many readers, it's just too much. Information is much more effective when each member of your audience feels that you're speaking to him personally rather than the general masses as a whole.

You need to tap into this as an infographic designer. Earlier in this chapter, we use the example of quantifying potable water worldwide. This time, instead of putting out your message to the whole world, think about ways to tailor that message to various demographic groups. Table 15-1 shows a sampling of ways that you could create clean water-related infographics targeted to various audiences with a desire or need to know certain facts about that potable water. These ideas are really just the tip of the iceberg.

Table 15-1	How One Topic Appeals to Many Audiences
Infographic Focused on This	*Speaks to This Demographic*
Ways to use rivers recreationally without contributing to pollution	Residents of a river town
Exploring plant and animal life in rivers	Students
The processes of making unsafe water safe to drink	Chemistry
Water usage of various household appliances	Homeowners
How various fish have been deemed safe and unsafe as pollution has fluctuated in various bodies of water	Fishermen and others who enjoy outdoor activities

Always consider various target audiences before you start designing your infographics. And with more data available virtually every day, it's not hard to do.

Social Media

In Chapter 13, we talk about the importance of making your infographics easy to share on social media. Going forward, social media could be your main calling card as an infographic designer.

Consider Facebook, with its wide and deep top banner. That banner could be a magnificent stage for an infographic. We've seen infographics in use as wedding information pages and résumé. With a bit of research and a little art, you could create a platform for you, your cause, or your business and then use that Facebook banner to share it with all your contacts. Of course, Facebook also makes sharing content easy, so if one of your readers likes your stuff, he can pass it along with a click of the mouse.

Immersive Interactive Graphics

Virtual-reality graphics and educational tools have been around for a while. Technology is improving all the time, allowing readers to feel truly immersed in their experience.

Video games have been the first frontier of virtual-reality graphics. Going forward, some of the technology that has brought virtual-reality video games tantalizingly close to consumers will undoubtedly bring infographics to new dimensions. Researchers have been working on integrating all five senses into virtual reality. Can you imagine reading an infographic on the rainforest while feeling dewy humidity on your skin and smelling the intoxicating perfume of orchids?

Whether the graphics are meant for education or entertainment, the possibilities are exciting.

Naturally, this type of technology will come with a steep learning curve, and will probably be cost-prohibitive for many designers — but there was a time people said that about personal computers. Stay tuned.

Print Media

Print isn't dead, but it's certainly troubled. Going forward, the best way for any media entity to survive will be to strengthen the ties between print, online, and even augmented-reality content.

Think about one potential scenario. Imagine that you've won an assignment from a national news magazine to depict current Army training strategies. You design a stunning, well-researched piece that takes up a full page in the magazine. Nicely done.

But that's not enough for the new media landscape. You will probably be asked to create a web version of the graphic, too. Perhaps that version will add a few interactive features, like a scroll bar that lets the reader travel back in time to read about military training in the past. Maybe there's embedded data that provides information about the military experience in nations around the world. Again, nice work.

Using augmented reality, though, you could potentially put the reader in the place of a young soldier learning the latest military maneuvers. It's an experience that most people won't ever have, but you could bring it to them in the form of an infographic. The media company benefits by linking its content in one form to all the other forms, enhancing readers' experience and enticing them to come back for more. Pretty exciting stuff.

Presentation Tools

Have you ever sat through a year-end sales report from an executive who droned on and on without a single break, churning out number after number without a single visual cue?

We've all been there, but infographics can — and should — play an increasing role in making presentations like that a relic.

First of all, even the driest oral presentation can usually benefit from graphic aids. For example, a bar graph showing a company's sales figures for the past five years is way more effective than a mere recitation of numbers.

Secondly, it's not too hard to actually put graphics to work in your presentation. Say you're using presentation software (PowerPoint or Keynote) to illustrate those sales figures. As you're standing in front of your audience presenting your report, why not show the bars of that graph one at a time, with a new year's information in each slide? Each portion of the presentation is a piece of the overall infographic.

Using basic office presentation software is never effective if it's used simply as a text-driven recitation of fact. Integrating infographics is an effective way to capture your audience's attention, and the applications are endless in business, technology, education, and more.

Index

● S ●

About the Author

Justin Beegel, MBA is the founder and president of Infographic World, a New York City based infographic and visual communications agency. He started the company in 2009 at the age of 23, and plans to be a serial entrepreneur the rest of his life. Before starting Infographic World, Justin was the social media marketing manager for Hachette Filipacchi Media, working with *Elle, Car and Driver, Road & Track,* and *Woman's Day.*

Justin is a part of several startups, one of which is launching in 2014. Alongside his father Robert as co-founder, SocialProtection.com will help parents protect their children on social networking sites like Facebook, Twitter, and Instagram.

Dedication

To my amazing fiancé, Danitte, my other half who keeps me going and keeps me strong. To my loving parents, Robert & Rhonda, who have always been there for me, and my brother Ryan, a constant source of humor and entertainment.

Author's Acknowledgments

The phrase "team effort" can often be overused. In this instance, however, there is truly no other phrase I can think of to describe this book being put together. I want to thank the people at John Wiley & Sons, Inc. — Nicole Sholly, Brian Walls, Teresa Artman, Amy Fandrei and Steve Hayes. You made the process for a first-time author as easy and pain-free as possible. Thank you to A.J. Ghergich, the SEO wiz and founder of Ghergich & Co., and Jay Willingham, the brilliant owner of Daily Infographic. Thanks to Eileen Glanton Loftus who steered the ship and helped everything come together. Marc Bain got us going with the foundation of the book. And Tonia Cowan, thank you for your amazing insight and the awesome illustrations throughout various sections of the book.

Publisher's Acknowledgments

Acquisitions Editor: Amy Fandrei

Project Editor: Nicole Sholly

Copy Editor: Teresa Artman

Technical Editor: Claudia Snell

Special Help: Brian Walls

Editorial Assistant: Anne Sullivan

Sr. Editorial Assistant: Cherie Case

Project Coordinator: Patrick Redmond

Cover Image: ©iStockphoto.com/serkorkin

Apple & Mac

iPad For Dummies,
6th Edition
978-1-118-72306-7

iPhone For Dummies,
7th Edition
978-1-118-69083-3

Macs All-in-One
For Dummies, 4th Edition
978-1-118-82210-4

OS X Mavericks
For Dummies
978-1-118-69188-5

Blogging & Social Media

Facebook For Dummies,
5th Edition
978-1-118-63312-0

Social Media Engagement
For Dummies
978-1-118-53019-1

WordPress For Dummies,
6th Edition
978-1-118-79161-5

Business

Stock Investing
For Dummies, 4th Edition
978-1-118-37678-2

Investing For Dummies,
6th Edition
978-0-470-90545-6

Personal Finance
For Dummies, 7th Edition
978-1-118-11785-9

QuickBooks 2014
For Dummies
978-1-118-72005-9

Small Business Marketing
Kit For Dummies,
3rd Edition
978-1-118-31183-7

Careers

Job Interviews
For Dummies, 4th Edition
978-1-118-11290-8

Job Searching with Social
Media For Dummies,
2nd Edition
978-1-118-67856-5

Personal Branding
For Dummies
978-1-118-11792-7

Resumes For Dummies,
6th Edition
978-0-470-87361-8

Starting an Etsy Business
For Dummies, 2nd Edition
978-1-118-59024-9

Diet & Nutrition

Belly Fat Diet For Dummies
978-1-118-34585-6

Mediterranean Diet
For Dummies
978-1-118-71525-3

Nutrition For Dummies,
5th Edition
978-0-470-93231-5

Digital Photography

Digital SLR Photography
All-in-One For Dummies,
2nd Edition
978-1-118-59082-9

Digital SLR Video &
Filmmaking For Dummies
978-1-118-36598-4

Photoshop Elements 12
For Dummies
978-1-118-72714-0

Gardening

Herb Gardening
For Dummies, 2nd Edition
978-0-470-61778-6

Gardening with Free-Range
Chickens For Dummies
978-1-118-54754-0

Health

Boosting Your Immunity
For Dummies
978-1-118-40200-9

Diabetes For Dummies,
4th Edition
978-1-118-29447-5

Living Paleo For Dummies
978-1-118-29405-5

Big Data

Big Data For Dummies
978-1-118-50422-2

Data Visualization
For Dummies
978-1-118-50289-1

Hadoop For Dummies
978-1-118-60755-8

Language & Foreign Language

500 Spanish Verbs
For Dummies
978-1-118-02382-2

English Grammar
For Dummies, 2nd Edition
978-0-470-54664-2

French All-in-One
For Dummies
978-1-118-22815-9

German Essentials
For Dummies
978-1-118-18422-6

Italian For Dummies,
2nd Edition
978-1-118-00465-4

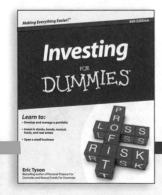
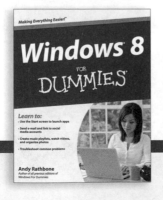

Available in print and e-book formats.

Available wherever books are sold. **For more information or to order direct visit www.dummies.com**

Math & Science

Algebra I For Dummies,
2nd Edition
978-0-470-55964-2

Anatomy and Physiology
For Dummies, 2nd Edition
978-0-470-92326-9

Astronomy For Dummies,
3rd Edition
978-1-118-37697-3

Biology For Dummies,
2nd Edition
978-0-470-59875-7

Chemistry For Dummies,
2nd Edition
978-1-118-00730-3

1001 Algebra II Practice
Problems For Dummies
978-1-118-44662-1

Microsoft Office

Excel 2013 For Dummies
978-1-118-51012-4

Office 2013 All-in-One
For Dummies
978-1-118-51636-2

PowerPoint 2013
For Dummies
978-1-118-50253-2

Word 2013 For Dummies
978-1-118-49123-2

Music

Blues Harmonica
For Dummies
978-1-118-25269-7

Guitar For Dummies,
3rd Edition
978-1-118-11554-1

iPod & iTunes
For Dummies, 10th Edition
978-1-118-50864-0

Programming

Beginning Programming
with C For Dummies
978-1-118-73763-7

Excel VBA Programming
For Dummies, 3rd Edition
978-1-118-49037-2

Java For Dummies,
6th Edition
978-1-118-40780-6

Religion & Inspiration

The Bible For Dummies
978-0-7645-5296-0

Buddhism For Dummies,
2nd Edition
978-1-118-02379-2

Catholicism For Dummies,
2nd Edition
978-1-118-07778-8

Self-Help & Relationships

Beating Sugar Addiction
For Dummies
978-1-118-54645-1

Meditation For Dummies,
3rd Edition
978-1-118-29144-3

Seniors

Laptops For Seniors
For Dummies, 3rd Edition
978-1-118-71105-7

Computers For Seniors
For Dummies, 3rd Edition
978-1-118-11553-4

iPad For Seniors
For Dummies, 6th Edition
978-1-118-72826-0

Social Security
For Dummies
978-1-118-20573-0

Smartphones & Tablets

Android Phones
For Dummies, 2nd Edition
978-1-118-72030-1

Nexus Tablets
For Dummies
978-1-118-77243-0

Samsung Galaxy S 4
For Dummies
978-1-118-64222-1

Samsung Galaxy Tabs
For Dummies
978-1-118-77294-2

Test Prep

ACT For Dummies,
5th Edition
978-1-118-01259-8

ASVAB For Dummies,
3rd Edition
978-0-470-63760-9

GRE For Dummies,
7th Edition
978-0-470-88921-3

Officer Candidate Tests
For Dummies
978-0-470-59876-4

Physician's Assistant Exam
For Dummies
978-1-118-11556-5

Series 7 Exam For Dummies
978-0-470-09932-2

Windows 8

Windows 8.1 All-in-One
For Dummies
978-1-118-82087-2

Windows 8.1 For Dummies
978-1-118-82121-3

Windows 8.1 For Dummies,
Book + DVD Bundle
978-1-118-82107-7

ℯ Available in print and e-book formats.

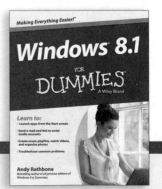

Available wherever books are sold. **For more information or to order direct visit www.dummies.com**